DATE DUE

MR 16 '99			
NO 26 '03			
AG 5 04			
FE 1 06			

CORAZON AQUINO

AND THE

BRUSHFIRE REVOLUTION

CORAZON AQUINO
AND THE
BRUSHFIRE REVOLUTION

ROBERT H. REID

AND

EILEEN GUERRERO

Louisiana State University Press
Baton Rouge and London

3 2 1

Brothers, Inc.

Printer and binder: Thomson-Shore, Inc.

Library of Congress Cataloging-in-Publication Data

Reid, Robert H.
    Corazon Aquino and the brushfire revolution / Robert H. Reid and
Eileen Guerrero.
        p.   cm.
    Includes bibliographical references and index.
    ISBN 0-8071-1980-6 (cl. : alk. paper)
        1. Philippines—Politics and government—1986—   2. Aquino, Corazon
Cojuangco. I. Guerrero, Eileen. II. Title.
DS686.614.R44   1995
959.904'7—dc20   95-30684
                                                                                    CIP

The paper in this book meets the guidelines for permanence and durability of the
Committee on Production Guidelines for Book Longevity of the Council on Library
Resources. ∞

TO THE PEOPLE OF THE PHILIPPINES

CONTENTS

ILLUSTRATIONS

Bridge destroyed by Mount Pinatubo eruption, 1991

Statue buried by volcanic ash, 1991

Imelda Marcos partying after return from exile, January, 1992

Imelda Marcos campaigning for presidency, May, 1992

Vice-Admiral Robert Kelly, the "last man" to leave Subic Bay naval base, November 24, 1992

President Aquino appearing before a civic group in Manila

Maps

PREFACE

IN FEBRUARY, 1986, millions of people around the world watched the spectacular televised pictures from Manila showing many thousands of Filipinos rising up against an authoritarian government. Their standard-bearer was a middle-aged widow whose credentials for leadership were moral authority and the adulation of her people. As the crowds chanted "Cory, Cory," it appeared that the entire Filipino nation was behind her. The promise of democracy and popular reform won admirers for her throughout the world. Within months, however, Corazon Aquino was fighting for her political life. The promise of a new era in Philippine politics was lost in the din of coup attempts, assassinations, and political intrigue.

Foreigners are often baffled by events in the Philippines. Much of this confusion is caused by the contradictory nature of the society. The Philippine cultural fabric is a rich weave of varied social traditions, some Western, others profoundly Asian, that manifest themselves in seemingly incongruous behavior. Never were these paradoxes so apparent as during the presidency of Corazon Aquino. How can a leader be so revered today and so reviled tomorrow? Why are causes so passionately espoused forgotten as quickly as last night's dream? How could a nation so enamored of the United States expel American military bases from its soil?

The persona of Corazon Aquino was equally mystifying. A woman who seemed so untuned to the rough-and-tumble of politics found herself the leader of a factious, turbulent nation. She seemed a welter of contradiction—sometimes naive, at other times shrewd and cunning. Seemingly devoid of ambition, she held on to power under the most trying of circumstances and outlasted most of those who sought to destroy her.

What made Corazon Aquino and her country so difficult for foreigners to understand was the gap between image and reality. Americans often viewed Aquino and the Philippines generally through the prism of their own cultural heritage, which is vastly different from that of the Philippines. Terms such as *democracy* and *representative government* may be common to both peoples but are applied quite differently in each political culture. Likewise, the Corazon Aquino of the media was profoundly different from the woman who ruled her country.

This book attempts to summarize and explain the Aquino presidency and its role in Philippine history. It was an era (1986–1992) when many of the conflicts that had long raged in Philippine society boiled to a climax. As journalists, the authors witnessed most of the events depicted in this book and are acquainted, personally and professionally, with many of the key figures of this era. Much of the material comes from our first-hand observations, as well as countless interviews and conversations with leading figures over a period of eight years. It is hoped that our observations can help explain why the Aquino administration unfolded as it did and will give historians information that can be valuable in judging its place in history. We also hope that the story of the Aquino presidency will provide insights into problems faced by other nations in transforming from authoritarianism to democracy.

Each of us brought our own perspective. An American, Robert Reid has been a foreign correspondent since 1977. As a Filipino, Eileen Guerrero offered insights into the character of the Philippine social and political culture that no foreigner could match. She conceived the phrase *The Brushfire Revolution*, which comes from a Tagalog idiom, *ningas cogon*, roughly translated as "brushfire." Cogon grass, a dry weed, often catches fire but burns out hot and fast. The idiomatic expression refers to a Filipino tendency to lose interest quickly in projects that begin with the greatest of fervor.

A word about the languages spoken in the Philippines is in order. The 1987 constitution made English and Filipino, which is actually Tagalog, the official languages, although there are some eighty-seven languages and dialects recognized in the country. Spanish is no longer official or even a required course. In keeping with common usage in the media and publishing, we have not used most of the diacritical marks usually associated with the Spanish language and have retained current spellings of names even though they may be inconsistent at times.

In preparing the book, we are deeply grateful to many Filipinos and foreigners; their numbers are too great to cite each one separately. Apart from those credited in the text and footnotes, we would like to thank Tita Valderama, who covered the presidency for the *Journal* newspaper, for her observations based on daily contact with Mrs. Aquino, as well as Professor Alex Magno, a political scientist, and Professor Renato Constantino, a historian, who shared their expertise in numerous conversations over the years. From Bernabe Buscayno, a former Communist leader and later friend of Mrs. Aquino, we gained insights into her character as an individual.

We would also like to thank Louis D. Boccardi, president of the Associated Press, for approving this project and to acknowledge the invaluable assistance of Dr. Benjamin F. Martin of Louisiana State University for his assistance in referring us to LSU Press. We are also grateful to copyeditor Sarah Whalen for her incisive editing and suggestions that helped focus the manuscript and brightened the prose. And finally, special thanks must go to Margaret Dalrymple, editor-in-chief of Louisiana State University Press, for her encouragement and guidance in the preparation of the manuscript.

CORAZON AQUINO
AND THE
BRUSHFIRE REVOLUTION

I CORY GOES TO COURT

THE CROWD MADE way for the smiling, confident Corazon Aquino as she marched into a steamy courtroom of the Manila City Hall. It was February 11, 1991, two weeks short of the fifth anniversary of her storybook rise to power and two weeks past her fifty-eighth birthday. Maria Corazon Cojuangco Aquino was no longer the self-effacing wife who captivated the nation when she returned from the United States more than seven years earlier to bury her husband, Benigno, murdered as he came home to challenge his archrival, President Ferdinand Marcos. After Benigno's brutal assassination on the tarmac of Manila's airport, Cory Aquino assumed her husband's mantle and became the symbol of the Filipino struggle for freedom.

Behind her standard, Filipinos rediscovered their courage. Despite Communist and Muslim uprisings, the vast majority of Filipinos had lived subserviently under the Marcos rule for two decades. Inspired by Cory Aquino's example, the Filipino people confronted Marcos's tanks and brought down his twenty-year authoritarian regime in a bloodless, three-day revolution in February, 1986, that astounded the world. Aquino, modest, religious mother of five, became the seventh president of the Republic of the Philippines and an international symbol of democracy. *Time* magazine honored her as Woman of the Year, and she was received throughout the world by statesmen who had shunned Marcos.

Cory Aquino had given the world a lesson in moral courage. She was the forerunner of the wave of democracy that swept Eastern Europe three years later. The Philippines, the United States' only overseas colony, had been a laboratory for American-style democracy in the developing world, and the success of the Philippine democratic experiment could serve as a model for other Third World nations struggling to build democratic institutions amid massive economic and social problems. Doubts about Aquino's abilities emerged, however, even before she assumed office. Politically inexperienced, she seemed too naive, too pious, to govern a factious country confronting poverty, social injustice, and armed insurgency.

When her term ended six years later, Cory Aquino left behind a mixed legacy. The forms of democracy remained in place, and those who had challenged her rule—Communist rebels and military dissidents—had been neutralized. But she had made little headway in improving the quality of life of her people. The democratic institutions she struggled to rebuild remained flawed and weak. Corruption prevailed, and Filipinos were increasingly cynical about the state of their nation. And yet, many of the problems that dogged Aquino throughout her presidency were of her own making.

Aquino's strengths and weaknesses as a leader were graphically displayed that morning in 1991 when she went to court, seeking legal redress and to punish a tormentor. Two years before, a prominent newspaper columnist, Luis Beltran, had written that Cory Aquino "hid under her bed" during a coup attempt in August, 1987. Beltran claimed the image was hyperbole, but the words deeply offended a president sensitive about her image. She summoned reporters, marched them to the presidential bedroom, lifted the sheets of her bed, and showed there was no room to hide. Afterward, she proceeded to the office of the city prosecutor and personally filed criminal libel charges against Beltran and executives of his newspaper, the *Philippine Star*.

It seemed strange that a president would go to such lengths. Fewer than 10 percent of the sixty million Filipinos read newspapers regularly, and by 1991, fewer still doubted Cory Aquino's physical courage. But she was a stubborn, headstrong woman. Beltran had assailed her image.

Aquino's concern for image was an extension of the Filipino concept of *hiya*, or "face." Concern for one's face, or public image, is among the strongest social values in Philippine society. How one is perceived by outsiders is of paramount importance. For Cory Aquino, image was her prime credential for national leadership. It was her image 'of political purity that had led to being chosen as opposition standard-bearer against Marcos in the February, 1986, election. When the electoral system denied her victory, image propelled her to office as tens of thousands of Filipinos took to the streets and brought down the Marcos administration. Image protected her when rivals, in turn, sought to bring her down.

The real Cory Aquino was a far more complex figure. Educated in the conservative, cloistered world of convent schools, she had little use for compromise. She could be obstinate, even arrogant, when dealing with adversaries. In her 1989 State of the Nation address, she defended her strengths and dismissed her opponents thus: "Added to that faith was the will to stand for no more nonsense from military adventurers who thought that failure to shave qualified them for national leadership [Honasan wore a moustache]. Some people don't like the way I dress. Well, I don't like the way they look. I am in power and they are not."[1] Earlier, in 1987, when Senator Joseph Estrada offered to mediate between her and the legal center-right opposition, she snapped: "Why should I talk to these people when they are the ones agitating for my downfall?"[2]

She was courageous but also stubborn and vindictive. Her mother's maiden name, Sumulong, also means "to go forward" in the Tagalog language, and she often told advisers, "I am a Sumulong. I never retreat." She loathed the very idea of defeat, even when conceding a point to her opponents could have served her long-term interests. These qualities baffled even those who knew her best. "She's an enigma," said her brother-in-law, Agapito "Butz" Aquino. "Nobody can track her moods. There are no logical conclusions."[3]

1. Corazon Aquino, State of the Nation address, National Assembly Building, Quezon City, July 24, 1989, Philippine Information Agency, Manila. All of President Aquino's speeches, announcements, and other public communications were widely reported by the news media, and texts are available through the government's Philippine Information Agency (PIA), the office of the president's press secretary (OPS), newspaper archives, and the National Library. The authors' notes covering the events leading to and during Aquino's presidency, as well as transcripts of their interviews with key players, are in their personal files and those of the Associated Press, Manila.

2. Estrada, the current vice-president of the Philippines, was elected to the senate in May, 1987, on the opposition ticket and later switched parties. His attempt to reconcile Aquino and the opposition, especially Enrile, in the summer of 1987, was rebuffed and widely reported in all Manila newspapers.

3. Agapito Aquino, oral communication to Eileen Guerrero, Manila, September 13, 1991.

Despite her image of political novice, Cory Aquino was instinctively political; her skills, however, were those of a tactician and not a strategist. She brought no detailed, grand vision to the presidency. She left behind no great body of political writings, and her speeches were for the most part drab and banal. She spoke of "people power" but offered no clear definition of the limits of popular rule within a framework of republican government. Without a philosophic compass, her government appeared to wander aimlessly, first to the political left, then to the right, and then back to the center, depending on the demands of the times and the views of her advisers. "Cory is no great intellect," confided one longtime aide. "She has no sense of history, no ideology. She is only driven by politics. She is addicted to politics."[4]

Her gentle public demeanor and well-honed image presented the picture of a political saint. In fact, she could be shrewd and ruthless with her adversaries. "The worst things you can say about a politician you can say about her," the aide added.[5]

Occasionally, however, circumstances would force the "real" Cory Aquino to appear. One such occasion was her appearance in court on that February morning in 1991. Her adversary, Luis "Louie" Beltran, was an avuncular, teddy bear of a man who seemed an unlikely candidate for the presidential wrath. Beltran's newspaper was among the most proadministration of the capital's more than twenty English-language dailies. In addition, his credentials as a victim of the Marcos government were impeccable. He was among thousands arrested in 1972, when Marcos imposed eight years of martial law. Beltran was released after a short time and went on to become dean of students at the University of the Philippines before returning to journalism.

In April, 1986, two months after the "people power revolution," Beltran had hosted Aquino during a television interview in which he was so fawning and deferential that he seemed to be interviewing his own mother. "What you are about to see is probably one of the most difficult interviews I have done in my entire life," Beltran told the audience. "To begin with, the subject of the interview is so liked by everybody." His first question

4. Horacio Parades, President Aquino's press secretary, oral communication to Eileen Guerrero, April 5, 1991, Manila. An aide at the time, Paredes remains an Aquino admirer.
5. *Ibid.*

to the new president was how she would cope with the public perception of "political saint." [6]

Aquino's personal lawyer, Dakila Castro, and her legal affairs adviser, Adolfo Azcuna, had both tried to talk her out of pursuing the case. [7] Scores of libel cases are filed annually in the Philippines, but few ever end in conviction. Most are either dropped on legal technicalities or are settled by a face-saving formula such as a public apology negotiated out of court.

The case might set messy legal precedents. The Philippine government is organized along U.S. lines, following the principle of separation of powers. In pursuing the case, Aquino, the president, was submitting herself to the judicial branch, setting a precedent that might have far-reaching implications for future presidents. Furthermore, taking legal action against a prominent journalist raised questions about the government's commitment to freedom of the press. The judge who would hear and rule on the case was an Aquino appointee. Regardless of how scrupulously he followed the rules of evidence, there would always be suspicion of a vendetta if Beltran were convicted.

But these considerations did not outweigh Aquino's desire to humiliate Beltran. After seven coup attempts, political assassinations, natural disasters, and other storms of the Aquino years, would anyone remember, let alone care, what Louie Beltran wrote in a single column so many years ago? "She really had no case because by the time of the trial, no one questioned her courage and no one would have been convinced otherwise by Beltran's column," said Senator Rene Saguisag, a former human rights lawyer and Aquino adviser. [8] Dakila Castro died a few weeks before the trial, and Aquino instructed her new lawyers to continue the case.

The presidential staff had arranged for the proceedings to be televised live nationwide, so confident were they that Aquino would make short work of Beltran. As the broadcast began, she mounted the witness stand and took her oath as an ordinary citizen. "I am president of the Republic

6. Interview with Corazon Aquino by Luis Beltran, People's Television, Manila, April 21, 1986 (aired April 23). People's Television is the government-owned network. The authors monitored all television and radio broadcasts for the Associated Press; notes are on file with the AP, Manila.

7. Rene Saguisag, oral communication to Robert Reid, Pasay City, April 4, 1991.

8. *Ibid.*

of the Philippines," Aquino told the clerk of court. "I live on Arlegui Street. I am sorry, there is no street number."[9]

Years of deferential treatment by military aides, fawning staff, and respectful Filipino reporters, who usually addressed her as "ma'am," had not prepared Cory Aquino for what would follow. Even when she was president, Aquino's most loyal aides and advisers had taken pains to avoid situations where she would have to speak extemporaneously about complicated issues. But if she and her supporters expected special treatment by the court, they were soon disappointed. Judge Ramon Makasiar set the tone early in the testimony by instructing the president of the republic to address her lawyer and other officers of the court as "sir."

Under the gentle questioning of her lawyer, Cristino Carreon, President Aquino outlined the events that led to the charges. She had read Beltran's column in 1987 and had become infuriated at his inference that she had cringed in fear during the coup attempt. As a presidential candidate, Cory Aquino had played on the image of the vulnerable widow to gain sympathy from a public that loves the underdog and whose Catholic heritage accords mystical respect to a suffering, pious woman. But now she was the female leader of a "macho" society that reveres physical courage.

"Since I am commander-in-chief of the Armed Forces of the Philippines, I did not want any officer or any enlisted man or woman reading this or to be hearing it from any other sources. . . . My credibility as the commander-in-chief of the Armed Forces of the Philippines certainly will greatly suffer because of this lie," Aquino said sternly. She demanded $150,000 in damages, which she would donate to the poor. "Your witness," Carreon told the defense.

Representing Beltran was Antonio Coronel, called the "Dean" by his peers, who acknowledged him as one of the country's most skillful trial lawyers, a master of cross-examination. Coronel also specialized in defending celebrated enemies of the Aquino administration. His clients included Marcos's widow, Imelda, as well as defendants accused of killing Aquino's own husband.

9. The quotations from Aquino's examination are from the official text of the court proceedings, which Guerrero personally attended and Reid monitored on the live telecast. A full transcript of the proceedings was published in Antonio Coronel's *Libel and the Journalist* (Quezon City, 1991). Transcripts also available from the archives of the Manila Regional Trial Court.

Coronel, whose hawklike face and scraggly goatee gave him the appearance of an aging werewolf, was also a colorful advocate with a flair for the dramatic. Once he became so excited while arguing on behalf of a client charged with rebellion that he spit out his dentures. The false teeth flew into Coronel's right hand, which was raised and opened wide in a gesture to emphasize a point. Coronel glanced momentarily at his teeth smiling at him from his palm, then slapped them back into his mouth and continued his argument over giggles from the spectators.

As he began his cross-examination, Coronel leaned forward, rested his elbows on the defense table, and stared at the president. Had the president read Beltran's columns regularly, he asked?

"You could say that I was a regular reader of the columns of Mr. Luis Beltran," the president replied. Judge Makasiar reminded the president to address the lawyers as "sir."

"It's all right with me, your honor," Coronel said. "She isn't used to saying 'sir.'" Aquino's body stiffened, her back arched like an angry cat. Her steely eyes fixed on Coronel. It was a gaze her advisers knew well: the president was angry. This time, she was not facing an aide or cabinet member who owed his position to her. This time, she was on the foreign turf of a coequal branch of government.

"Would you like me to say 'sir' to every question?" she snapped at the judge. "That's correct," came the crisp reply. Sensing the witness was rattled, Coronel led her through a maze of rambling, seemingly unconnected questions designed to keep her from maintaining her train of thought. Did she read Beltran's columns every day? Did she read them in entirety? Did Beltran call her a coward? Is a soldier who takes cover during an attack a coward—or simply prudent?

In feigned deference, Coronel addressed the president as "madame," knowing that she despised that title because it was favored by Imelda Marcos. Aquino's answers popped from her pursed lips like the sound of a dry twig cracking. At the end of every sentence, she paused before spitting out the word "sir." "My main issue here is truth," she fired back. "And I believe that all of us here have a responsibility to seek truth and make known the truth—sir."

Her quest for truth began to look more and more like a personal vendetta. Coronel read passages from other Beltran columns in which he had praised Aquino's courage and tenacity during the 1987 coup attempt. Did those words sound like they were written by someone who thinks his president is a coward, Coronel asked. "When you did look back at the August 29 column . . . did you not change your mind at all about your opinion of Mr. Beltran having imputed cowardice to you in this October 12 column?" Coronel asked.

Aquino bristled and answered firmly: "If I may be allowed by this honorable court, I would liken it to a husband who tells his wife from Sunday to Friday that he loves her very much, and then maybe on Saturday he does something which does not show his love. So whatever he does on Saturday would probably negate whatever he did from Sunday, Monday, Tuesday, Wednesday, Thursday, Friday—sir." Marital fidelity was important to Aquino. She once fired a cabinet member who refused to end a liaison with a beauty half his age. [10] Nearly a year after the court appearance, she would weigh fidelity as a consideration in endorsing a candidate to succeed her as president.

For Cory Aquino, loyalty was an absolute, and criticism was unappreciated, whatever the motive. The affairs of state and political judgments were often couched in the simple, austere, and unbending terms of the faith in which she was born and reared. "Well, I appreciate the fact that Mr. Beltran never called me a coward. But again, may I just say that Mr. Beltran did not say I did not hide under the bed—sir." At one point, Judge Makasiar asked if she would be willing to drop the case if Beltran apologized and admitted she never hid under her bed. No, she replied, matters had gone too far to stop now. To her, truth was absolute, and personal slights were not easily forgotten.

Coronel reminded Aquino of her administration's public commitment to freedom of the press. It seemed like a soft lob for a president who loved to remind her people that she had restored democracy. Of course, the Aquino administration supports press freedom, she replied. Then, Coronel asked, why had she singled out Beltran for punishment? "I believe, as you, that we have to uphold the freedom of the press," she replied. "But I hold also that along with the freedom comes a very serious responsibility and obligation—sir." Her stalwarts in the courtroom burst

10. This refers to a sexual liaison involving her secretary of tourism, Antonio Gonzalez, which was widely reported at the time he was dismissed on April 15, 1989. Gonzalez made no secret of the affair.

into applause. "This is not a political rally," Judge Makasiar reminded the audience.

Coronel probed deeper. Did her administration accept the principle, enshrined in American libel law, that a public official must learn to "suffer under a hostile and unjust accusation" in the greater interest of maintaining freedom of expression? Most democratic leaders come into power after long political careers in which they learn to cope with criticism, fair or not. "The Aquino administration adheres to that principle—sir," she replied. Her answer raised doubts as to why she had then bothered to file the charges. But Aquino was often inconsistent, presenting one face in public statements and another in her actions.

The case languished in the Philippines' complicated legal system until after Aquino's term ended in the summer of 1992. On October 23 that year, Makasiar found Beltran and another newspaper executive guilty. They were sentenced to two years' imprisonment and ordered to pay $80,000 each in punitive damages. Although Beltran died in 1994, because other defendants are still alive, the case is considered active in the Court of Appeals.

In the days that followed Aquino's testimony, Philippine newspapers reflected on her performance. Some praised her courage, others questioned her wisdom in pursuing the case. In one telling commentary, the *Philippine Daily Globe* wrote: "One could only wish she were as stubborn and clear in the defense of the national interest. . . . How the country longs for that leader who . . . once inspired a whole nation to rise above itself." [11]

11. *Philippine Daily Globe,* February 12, 1991. This was a Manila daily that is no longer in business. Copies of it, as well as various papers cited here—the *Philippine Daily Inquirer, Malaya,* the *Philippine Star,* and the Manila *Chronicle,* among others—can be found in the archives of the Manila Press Club.

2   CORY'S ROOTS

WHEN CORAZON AQUINO took office in 1986, she was widely portrayed in the international media as the champion of the impoverished masses. But her roots were deep in the Philippine elite, a privileged class that jealously guarded its position and power. The Foreign Area Studies Division of the American University found in a 1972 study that political life in the Philippines was controlled by about four hundred families who dominated industry, agriculture, banking, and politics. "Institutionally, important constitutional powers were vested in the presidency and Congress, but the real roots of power were not in those bodies but in the geographically dispersed political and economic fiefdoms of powerful families."[1]

Wealth, often derived from large land-holdings or tariff-sheltered industries, enabled the elite to control the political process in a country where the middle class is small and institutions of government weak. Control of politics has enabled the Philippine elite to ensure that successive governments took no measures that would undermine their position. The elite moved effortlessly in and out of government, serving in elective office or financing campaigns for their surrogates. As a class, they had survived by cooperating with Spanish, Japanese, and American colonial rulers, who used them to help control the nation. The elite maintained their

1. Nena Vreeland *et al., Area Handbook for the Philippines,* 2nd ed. (Washington, D.C., 1976), 216–17.

preeminent position after the Philippines gained independence from the United States in 1946.

It was into such a family that Cory Aquino was born on January 25, 1933. She was the sixth of eight children born to Jose "Don Pepe" Cojuangco and Demetria Sumulong. Don Pepe served variously in both the Philippine senate and house of representatives. Cory's maternal grandfather, Juan Sumulong, was a senator and political czar of Rizal province, which borders metropolitan Manila.

Like many influential families, the Cojuangcos traced their roots to China, specifically, the village of Hong Jian in the southern coastal province of Fukien, from where Aquino's great-grandfather emigrated around 1861. He was baptized "Jose" and Hispanicized his Chinese name to "Cojuangco," fusing its three elements, Xu Yu Huan.

The Cojuangcos established a thriving freight business, but a historical accident promoted them to the ranks of the superrich. According to legend in central Luzon, Cory's great-aunt Ysidra became the mistress of General Antonio Luna, a hero of the Philippine uprising against Spain and later against the United States. Luna fell out with his supreme commander, General Emilio Aguinaldo, and on June 5, 1899, was slain by Aguinaldo's guards. Before his death, Luna entrusted Ysidra with gold and land titles he had amassed to pay his troops. After his death, Ysidra kept the wealth, and the Cojuangco fortune was born. [2]

Jose's descendants, however, were to fall out in a family feud; their story shows how such families influence the country's political system. During an election in 1963, members of the family approached a Tarlac politician, Eliong Castro, and urged him to run for mayor of the town of Paniqui. After two weeks of deliberation, Castro told Eduardo "Danding" Cojuangco, Cory's first cousin and later political rival, that he was willing to run.

But the choice did not sit well with Aquino's mother, Demetria. Leader of the Catholic Women's League of Tarlac, "Doña Metring" had never forgiven Castro for having opened a nightclub in the neighborhood. Doña Metring convinced her children to support another candidate, but Danding, recalling the incident a generation later, said he refused to go along. "How could I tell him to step aside? After all, I'm the one who convinced

2. Lucy Komisar, *Corazon Aquino: The Story of a Revolution* (New York, 1987), 12.

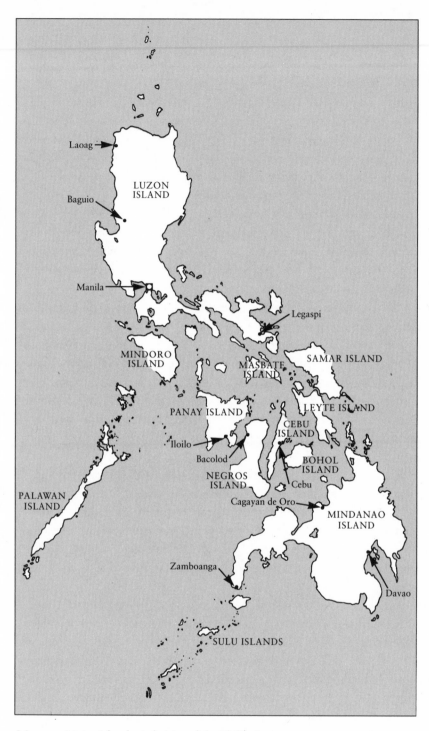

Map 1. Major islands and cities of the Philippines.

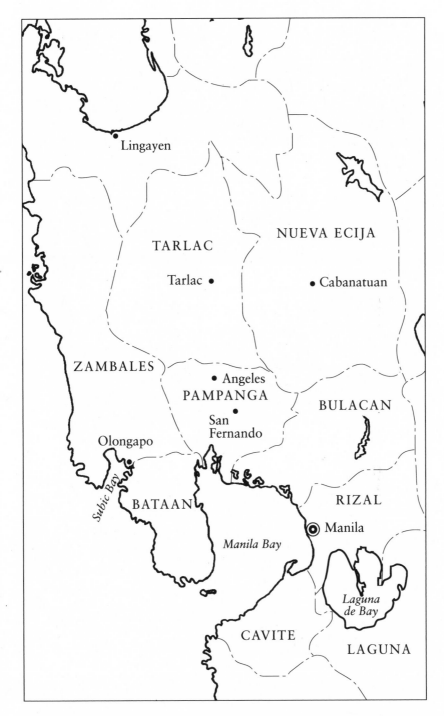

Map 2.   Central Luzon, the political stronghold of the Aquino and Cojuangco clans.

him to run in the first place," Danding told the author in 1990.[3] Castro eventually was elected, and the battle lines within the Cojuangco clan were drawn.

Years later, Danding Cojuangco had accumulated a huge fortune in business, farming, and banking, and he sided with Marcos against his cousin. Nearly thirty years after the initial break, rival wings of the Cojuangco family fought one another in the 1992 election to choose her successor as president. A family feud that began over a provincial beer joint had assumed national significance.

Family values and the Roman Catholic faith were the strongest factors molding the young Cory Cojuangco. She spent her first years in conservative Roman Catholic convent schools in Manila but went with her family to the United States in 1946, after World War II left the Philippines in ruin. She was enrolled in Raven Hill Academy in Philadelphia but later transferred to Notre Dame Convent School in New York. After graduation, she enrolled in the College of Mount St. Vincent, a sheltered, conservative enclave in the Riverview section of the Bronx. She graduated with a degree in French and mathematics.

After graduation, Cory returned to the Philippines in 1953 and enrolled as a law student at the Far Eastern University, a private institution owned by the Cojuangcos and three other families. She began dating an old acquaintance, Benigno "Ninoy" Aquino, Jr., scion of another powerful Tarlac clan. Ninoy's father, Benigno Aquino, Sr., served as speaker of the National Assembly in the collaborationist government during the Japanese occupation. That government was headed by Jose Laurel, whose son Salvador would later become Aquino's vice-president and political rival. She dropped out of law school and married Ninoy on October 11, 1954, at Our Lady of Sorrows Church in the Manila suburb of Pasay City.

It seemed an unlikely union. Ninoy Aquino was a garrulous, gregarious extrovert, driven by consuming political ambition. His wife appeared to be very reserved and ill at ease in the company of strangers.

Much has been said and written about Cory Aquino's presumed shyness. Part of her mystique lay in the riddle of how such a retiring figure could persevere against coup attempts, political intrigues, and the machinations of skilled and powerful rivals. The "shy Cory" image developed

3. Eduardo Cojuangco to a group of foreign correspondents, Quezon City, February, 1990.

from her hardly visible role during her husband's years in politics. "At dinners, Cory would make sure everyone was served and got dessert but Ninoy did all the talking," recalls Senator Ernesto Maceda.[4]

Her seeming reticence was actually a well-bred quality of aloofness, which is found not only in the British nobility but in the superrich, landed gentry of the Philippines as well. "I've known Cory for over thirty years and I've never heard her raise her voice," recalls her brother-in-law, Agapito Aquino. "When she doesn't like something, she just gets up and leaves."[5]

Ninoy was determined to build a political career, and within two years of his marriage, he was elected mayor of Concepcion, a dusty market town about sixty miles north of Manila. For a young wife fresh from college in New York City, the adjustment to provincial life was difficult. Concepcion had no electricity except between sunset and sunrise. There were few diversions.

In the countryside, the activities of a mayor and his wife are grist for gossip by the townsfolk. Tales of what Cory and Ninoy ate for breakfast, what they were wearing, and whether they quarreled that day were spread throughout the town by hundreds of flapping tongues. "It was such a small town that everyone minded each other's business," Cory told the Manila magazine Mr. and Ms. in 1983. "Everyone knew what we had for lunch."[6]

The only entertainment was listening to soap operas on her transistor radio. "If I hadn't had my religion and made my vows to stick with this man for better or worse, maybe I would have had second thoughts," Cory told Time magazine in 1987.[7] She took every opportunity to visit Manila, which was about three hours away by car.

Life in Concepcion, however, was the beginning of Aquino's political education. She learned to deliver speeches and shake the calloused hands of peasant voters, although Ninoy cautioned her never to let people see her wash her hands afterward for fear they would take offense. The role

4. Interview with Ernesto Maceda by Robert Reid, Manila, May 15, 1991.
5. Interview with Agapito Aquino by Robert Reid, Manila, May 8, 1991.
6. Interview with Corazon Aquino by Neni Sta. Romana Cruz, Mr. and Ms., September 20, 1983, p. 17. Although the magazine folded in the 1980s, copies are available in the archives of the Press Foundation of the Philippines, Manila.
7. "Woman of the Year," interview with Corazon Aquino, Time, January 5, 1987, p. 17.

of mayor's wife also meant using the family car for late-night trips transporting the sick to Manila and attending the obligatory rounds of baptisms, weddings, and funerals.

Six years later, Ninoy was elected governor of Tarlac province, a post that brought him into contact with the remnants of the pro-Soviet Huk Communists who had waged guerrilla war against the pro-American Philippine government after World War II. The Huks had been routed by the mid-1950s but still operated in central Luzon.

One of Ninoy's Huk contacts was Faustino del Mundo. Known as Commander Sumulong, del Mundo was an occasional guest in the Aquino home. Commander Sumulong's aide at the time was a young peasant named Bernabe Buscayno, who would later break away from the Huks to form the Maoist New People's Army (NPA). Buscayno recalled that during his first meeting with Ninoy, a woman walked silently through the room. Ninoy did not bother with formal introductions but simply motioned toward her. "That's Cory," he said, and continued his monologue.[8] Years later, President Cory Aquino would set Buscayno free from ten years in prison, and the two would play important roles in one another's lives.

By the early 1960s, Ninoy Aquino's political star was fading. Ninoy supported President Carlos Garcia, standard-bearer of the Nacionalista Party, for reelection in 1961. But Garcia's government was marred by corruption and inefficiency, and he was soundly beaten by Diosdado Macapagal, Garcia's own vice-president although a member of the rival Liberal Party. Macapagal promptly shut off the pork barrel tap to Ninoy's province, and the patronage he desperately needed for support dried up. There was only one option to remain politically viable: switch parties. Ninoy joined the Liberals.

About the same time, another ambitious politician, Ferdinand Marcos, also switched parties, jumping instead from the Liberals to the Nacionalistas that Ninoy had abandoned. Marcos won the Nacionalistas' presidential nomination from Emmanuel Pelaez, who would later serve as Aquino's ambassador to Washington. Marcos went on to defeat Macapagal in the November, 1965, presidential election.

8.   Interview with Bernabe Buscayno by Eileen Guerrero, Tarlac province, April 11, 1991, AP files, Manila. The interview was conducted mostly in Tagalog and translated into English by Guerrero.

As a Liberal Party member, Ninoy was elected to the senate in 1967, where he built a national reputation as a critic of the Marcos administration. Their rivalry escalated after one of the most traumatic events in modern Philippine political history, the Plaza Miranda bombing. On August 21, 1971, candidates of the Liberal Party planned to launch their campaign for the November elections with a rally in Plaza Miranda in Manila's Quiapo district. About ten thousand people were gathered there for the rally, which was to begin at 9:15 P.M. All the major Liberal Party figures would attend: Jovito Salonga, John Osmeña, Ramon Mitra, and, of course, Benigno Aquino.

Five minutes before the rally was to begin, two fragmentation grenades exploded on the podium, killing nine people and injuring more than one hundred, including several candidates, but Ninoy was late for the rally and escaped unharmed. The Liberals blamed Marcos for the brutal attack. Although Marcos accused the Communists and implied that Aquino may have had a hand in it, responsibility for Plaza Miranda has never been fully established. Three months after the attack, however, the Liberals captured six of the eight senate seats in the November elections; this outcome was widely seen as public repudiation of the Marcos government.

The country was sliding inexorably into chaos. In the south, violence between Muslims and Christians had claimed one thousand lives by 1972, eventually exploding into a full-scale Islamic secessionist war.

In Manila, student activism was sweeping the campuses, fanned in large part by Marxist groups affiliated with the reinvigorated Communist Party of the Philippines.

On September 18, 1972, Ninoy Aquino appeared as a guest on a television talk show and claimed Marcos was planning to declare martial law. His allegation was widely dismissed as histrionics. Four days later, however, Marcos ordered troops from the barracks. They seized power plants and television stations, and rounded up thousands of political opponents, among them Benigno Aquino.

Marcos claimed he imposed military rule to restore public order, confront the fledgling Communist insurgency, and break the power of the oligarchs by building his *Kilusang Bagong Lipunan,* or "New Society Movement." Promised reforms stumbled as Marcos simply replaced many of the old economic elite with a new set loyal to him. But his promise of a New Society soon placed him in conflict with members of the Old Guard elite, as well as leftists and moderates opposed to dictatorial practices.

Ninoy's arrest transformed him from political gadfly to an international figure and symbol of resistance to oppression. For Cory Aquino, it was one of the most trying times of her life as she struggled to hold the family together. Ninoy was moved to Fort Magsaysay in Luzon's Nueva Ecija province, where he was held for a month incommunicado. Cory begged Defense Minister Juan Ponce Enrile for word of his whereabouts. Ninoy was eventually returned to Fort Bonifacio in Manila, and she was allowed visits, including conjugal ones. But the strip searches and constant surveillance were a humiliation.

Incarceration did not silence Ninoy. He staged hunger strikes, which nearly ruined his health, to rally his followers. In August, 1973, Marcos placed Ninoy on trial before a military court on charges of murder, subversion, and illegal weapons' possession. A military lawyer who took part in the prosecution recalls that Marcos installed a closed circuit television system so he could monitor the proceedings from his office. "When Aquino was speaking, Marcos would call up the judge on a hotline and say, 'Shut him up, why are you letting him speak?'"[9]

The trial dragged on for four years. Ninoy was joined in the dock by Bernabe Buscayno, the young Communist guerrilla from his Tarlac days, and Victor Corpuz, a young lieutenant who defected to the Communists after leading a raid on the Philippine Military Academy armory. Buscayno recalled that during the trial, he began to see more and more of the quiet wife whom he had noticed fleetingly at the Aquino home years before. If Aquino were absent, she would ask him, "How's Ninoy?" Buscayno said. "Sometimes when we were in court, Ninoy would see an attractive woman and tell me, 'Hey, look at that one, she's very sexy.' But with Cory it was always, 'How's Ninoy?'"[10]

The tribunal finally sentenced the three to death by firing squad on November 25, 1977, but the sentences were never carried out. By that time, Ninoy Aquino was an international figure, and Marcos could not afford the worldwide condemnation that an execution would have brought upon his government.

9. Colonel Jose Reyes, oral communication to Eileen Guerrero, judge advocate general's office of the Armed Forces of the Philippines (AFP), Quezon City, May 21, 1991.

10. Buscayno interview by Guerrero, April 11, 1991.

The rigors of prison and trial had taken their toll, however, and in March, 1980, Ninoy suffered a heart attack. He refused surgery at the Philippine Heart Center, and in May, 1980, Marcos allowed Ninoy and his family to leave for the United States for coronary bypass surgery. Afterward, they moved to Newton, Massachusetts, a Boston suburb, where Ninoy accepted a fellowship at Harvard.

Cory Aquino describes her stay in Massachusetts as among the happiest years of her life. Without the usual servants she had had in the Philippines—a common practice there—Cory had to do the marketing, cooking, and cleaning. "That's really the first time I was actually a housewife," she told the author in 1989.[11]

Ninoy refused to take political asylum and actively planned his return to confront Marcos. By the spring of 1983, Ninoy felt the time was right. In order to improve his international image, Marcos had formally abolished martial law two years before but had retained the right to rule by decree. Ninoy began hearing rumors that Marcos was gravely ill, possibly dying, and he feared his old nemesis would name a successor, possibly his wife Imelda.

On August 13, Ninoy said goodbye to his family and left Boston for Singapore. For security reasons, he traveled under the name of Marcial Bonifacio, using as his surname the name of a military garrison where he had been imprisoned. After a stopover in Singapore, he journeyed to nearby Malaysia and then caught a plane for Taipei, Taiwan. There, he and a press contingent boarded a China Airlines jet on the morning of August 21 for the three-hour flight to Manila. As the plane approached the Philippines, Ninoy rose from his seat, walked to the bathroom, and returned wearing a bulletproof vest. The aircraft landed on schedule and taxied to the arrival ramp. As the passengers remained in their seats, three uniformed soldiers from the air force Aviation Security Command entered the aircraft and escorted Ninoy through the aircraft door leading to the stairs.

Moments after the group disappeared from view, passengers heard voices shouting, *Ako na, ako na, pusila, pusila*—"I'll do it, I'll do it, shoot, shoot"—in the Visayan language, followed by the crisp crackle of pistol

---

11. Corazon Aquino, oral communication to Robert Reid, Foreign Correspondents Association of the Philippines luncheon, Manila, October 26, 1989.

fire. Ninoy Aquino lay dead on the tarmac near the body of his alleged assassin, Rolando Galman.

Back in Massachusetts, the telephone ringing awakened the Aquino family to the news they had feared. The caller identified himself as a reporter for Japan's Kyodo News Service. There had been shooting at the Manila airport, he told them, and it was reported that Ninoy was dead. The night was warm and humid, but Cory shivered as if it were winter. [12] She gathered her children and told them their father was dead, then led them in prayer. Three days later, Cory Aquino stepped from a plane at Manila airport, home to bury her husband.

Ninoy Aquino's assassination profoundly shocked a nation long accustomed to political violence. Never before had such a prominent national politician been slain, and never in such a brazen manner. Marcos claimed the assassin was Galman, whom he described as a Communist. Somehow, Galman had slipped through the security cordon with a weapon and shot Aquino before guards killed him. A Marcos-appointed commission came to the same conclusion. More likely, Galman was set up as the fall guy and then killed to ensure his silence. [13]

Subsequent investigations revealed that Galman was a petty criminal with links to the police. His family said that days before his death, Galman left his house in the company of several police and soldiers. Public pressure for justice was strong. General Fabian Ver, Marcos's chief of staff, and twenty-five others were tried for the murder but were acquitted in December, 1985. After Cory Aquino came to power, the Philippine Supreme Court overturned the verdicts and ordered a second trial. Nearly ten years later, a civilian court convicted sixteen soldiers, including the three escorts, of murder and sentenced them to life imprisonment.

Ninoy Aquino lay in state for ten days in an open casket, his body still clad in the clothes he was wearing when he died. His mother, Doña Aurora, wanted the thousands of mourners who passed by the bier to see

12. Interview with Corazon Aquino by Maria Shriver, "Sunday Morning," NBC News, October 6, 1987, transcript from OPS, AP files.

13. The details of the Aquino assassination are public record. In addition, Marcos appointed a fact-finding board on October 14, 1983, to investigate it. The Agrava Commission was chaired by Corazon Agrava, former appeals court justice, and had four other members. In its report, completed on October 22, 1984, it recommended indictments against twenty-six members of the military, including Marcos's chief of staff, General Fabian Ver. Additional material can be found in the trial proceedings before the Sandiganbayan court, which took place in 1990 (see Chapter 15).

what was done to her son. When he was finally buried on August 31, two million people lined the streets to watch the carriage take his body to a cemetery in Manila. As the coffin was closed, a sobbing Cory bent over and kissed her husband farewell. "I told him, 'Ninoy, I promise, I will continue your struggle.'"[14] Within a few weeks, bloody riots had broken out in Manila, and demonstrations against the regime were spreading throughout the major cities.

The unrest produced a crisis of confidence in the business community, already upset over Marcos's favoritism toward his businessmen allies. New foreign investment was curtailed, loans were suspended, and wealthy Filipinos began transferring their money to safe havens abroad. The U.S. Embassy became alarmed that Marcos was losing control at a time when the Communist rebellion was spreading, not only in the hinterlands but on the campuses of the nation's most prestigious universities. That posed a threat to the six U.S. military bases in the country as well as the substantial American investment in the Philippine economy.

Although the political picture was growing ever darker, there was no clear sign that the Marcos administration was facing imminent collapse. The notion that Ninoy Aquino's assassination unleashed a ground swell of popular outrage that swept Marcos from power oversimplifies an intriguing drama involving, among others, the Catholic church, the U.S. government, the business community, the Old Guard political elite, and the armed forces—the real arbiters of power in the Philippines.

In 1984, a group of Catholic businessmen and intellectuals began meeting to formulate a political strategy and choose a candidate to oppose Marcos in national elections set for 1987. Members included Jaime Ongpin, a Harvard-educated businessman and the first Filipino president of the giant Benguet Consolidated Mines; the Reverend Joaquin Bernas, president of the Jesuit-run Ateneo University; Emanuel Soriano, president of the University of the Philippines; and Dr. Alfredo Bengzon, a prominent physician. They were associated with Jaime Cardinal Sin, the archbishop of Manila and a Marcos critic.

During the Aquino presidency, members of this group would become known popularly as the "Council of Trent," after the sixteenth-century papal commission that steered the Roman Catholic church toward reform

14.   Corazon Aquino, campaign speech, Bacolod, December 22, 1985.

to stem the tide of the Protestant Reformation. The description was appropriate. Members could be described as conservative reformers. They opposed Marcos because of his authoritarian rule and manipulation of the economy on behalf of his allies; fundamental change in the nation's social and economic system, however, was not on their agenda. They feared Marcos might die in office, and—as there was no vice-president and the law required new elections within seventy days after a presidential death—they wanted to be ready with a unified opposition candidate.

The group, later known as the "Convenors," held their first meeting in October, 1984, at the home of Cory Aquino's mother in the wealthy Dasmariñas Village subdivision in the town of Makati in metropolitan Manila.[15] The Convenors decided that three of their number would screen candidates and choose one after consultations. The three were Ongpin, Cory Aquino, and Lorenzo Tañada, venerable elder statesman of the opposition movement. Tañada was selected because of his contacts with grass-roots organizations and the left, including the Communist Party of the Philippines, which had been the most consistent opponents of Marcos throughout his presidency. Aquino was chosen as chair of the group because of her moral authority as the widow of a political martyr.

Several political figures were interested in running against Marcos: Salvador "Doy" Laurel; Ninoy's cousin, Eva Estrada Kalaw; National Assembly member Ramon Mitra; former senator and human rights champion Jose Diokno; and former senator Jovito Salonga.

Laurel was the early front-runner. Son of the wartime collaborationist government leader Jose Laurel, Doy was the leader of the United Democratic Nationalist Organization (UNIDO), a confederation of traditional political parties that formed the largest opposition bloc in the National Assembly. UNIDO was the best-organized legal opposition bloc.

The Convenors, however, had little use for the fifty-six-year-old Laurel. His family's ties to Marcos began before World War II when his father, as supreme court chief justice, dismissed murder charges against a young Ferdinand Marcos. Laurel had only recently left Marcos's New Society Movement and was considered an opportunist. In turn, Laurel sensed that the goal of the Convenors was to replace him as leader of the conservative opposition.

15. Material on the Convenors has been widely reported. See, for example, Nick Joaquin, *Jaime Ongpin: The Enigma* (Makati, 1990).

During the Convenors' deliberations, Cory Aquino began to emerge as a political force in her own right, no longer simply the widow of Ninoy. At first, her role was to lend moral authority to the Convenors, but Tañada and the others, despairing of the alternatives, began to see Aquino as the only candidate capable of uniting the opposition. They needed a candidate with a reputation for personal integrity who could appeal to conservative oppositionists, left-leaning progressives, and the broad masses. They also needed a candidate acceptable to Washington, which exerted broad influence in the Philippines, and which had long supported Marcos because of a dearth of alternatives. Aquino's seeming lack of personal ambition and deep-seated ideology made her perfect for the task.

Marcos decided to strike before the opposition could solidify its ranks. On November 3, 1985, he appeared on ABC-TV's "This Week with David Brinkley" and played his card: he announced plans for an early presidential election to reaffirm his mandate. The voting was set for February 7, 1986.

Cory Aquino was still reluctant to run. Laurel and Salonga privately offered to step aside if she wanted to run, but she assured them she would not. She claimed she changed her mind in November, 1985, after meeting with an activist priest. Aquino asked him if people in the barrios believed Marcos was responsible for their misery. He told her yes, but the people needed a candidate they could believe in, someone who would be entirely different from Marcos.

That night over dinner, Aquino told her children that she was considering running. They were not enthusiastic. She spent the next day meditating in a convent and decided she had no choice. "I'd never be able to forgive myself if I have to live with the knowledge that I could have done something, and I didn't do anything."[16]

Another factor that persuaded her to run was a signature campaign organized by Joaquin "Chino" Roces, a leader of street demonstrations who, as a newspaper publisher, had given Ninoy his first job as a reporter during the Korean War. Roces's petition drive urging Cory to run collected one million signatures. That was enough to convince her that she had a popular following.

Although Aquino reached her decision on November 10, she delayed

16.   Interview with Corazon Aquino by David Briscoe, Makati, December 3, 1985, AP files.

her formal announcement until December 3. During a speech at the Mondragon Building in Makati, she promised to lead the country "in our quest for a better nation for ourselves and our children." Aquino offered little more than her own image of piety and integrity. "Whether I liked it or not, people were waiting for me to say something," she told reporters. "I kept telling people, don't overestimate me." Reporters asked what qualifications she would bring to the presidency. She reminded them she was the wife of a veteran politician. Her interrogators asked if she had ideas of her own. "Sometimes I wonder," she replied. "I don't know, maybe I do."[17]

That such an obviously inexperienced and ill-equipped person could be taken seriously as a presidential candidate says much about Philippine society. Large segments of the electorate were so fed up with the corruption and authoritarianism of the Marcos government that anyone else seemed an improvement. Beyond that, however, is the emotional factor in Philippine politics. Among the masses, political sophistication is low. Ideology plays a small role, and personality and the appearance of sincerity are very important. Cory Aquino seemed the kind of person who could be trusted with one's children. Her image as a loving mother and religious widow struck a sympathetic chord among uneducated barrio residents and made her a potent force, regardless of her lack of preparation for the task ahead.

With Aquino officially in the race, the next problem facing her supporters was what to do with Laurel. He had already announced his candidacy, and UNIDO was busy organizing a grass-roots campaign. The task of dissuading Laurel fell to Cardinal Sin, who bluntly told Laurel that his candidacy would merely fragment the opposition and guarantee a Marcos victory.[18] Bitterly disappointed, Laurel stepped aside and ran as Aquino's vice-president.

At the urging of the United States, Marcos agreed to allow a private agency, the National Movement for Free Elections (NAMFREL) to monitor the election to ensure fairness. In fact, NAMFREL's role was to question what everyone in the Aquino camp assumed would be bogus figures showing a Marcos victory. Through a network of eighty thousand volunteers, NAMFREL was to conduct a quick count, and its findings

17. *Ibid*. After her formal announcement to run, Aquino spoke with reporters.
18. Komisar, *Corazon Aquino*, 76.

would serve as an alternative set of figures that, although unofficial, would raise doubts about the Commission on Election's numbers. Although NAMFREL was portrayed as neutral, its chairman, Jose Concepcion, had been among those Catholic businessmen closely associated with the Convenors; he was later rewarded with a cabinet post in the Aquino administration.

On election day, February 7, 1986, fraud was massive and often crude. Armed men roamed around polling stations throughout Manila, intimidating voters. Truckloads of "flying voters" drove from precinct to precinct, casting ballots at every stop. Jaime Ongpin found his own name had been stricken from the registration list at his polling place.

Cars of opposition workers were vandalized, and more than thirty campaign workers were murdered. Nonetheless, Lieutenant General Fidel V. Ramos, Marcos's second cousin and the military vice-chief of staff, told reporters the election was "the most peaceful in recent history" and that "the true winner of this election is democracy." Ironically, Ramos would become Aquino's successor in 1992.

Soon after the polls closed, Aquino broadcast a victory statement over the Roman Catholic radio station, Veritas. "The people and I have won, and we know it," she proclaimed confidently. Although early returns from Manila did show her with a slender lead, few votes had been counted from the rest of the country. That was beside the point. Weeks before the balloting, Aquino strategists had concluded that Marcos would also claim victory and produce fraudulent figures for the state-controlled media. The only way to counter such claims was to beat Marcos to the announcement and put him on the defensive.[19]

Aquino's victory statement would condition world opinion to the idea that she had been robbed, when Marcos announced his victory. That idea was reinforced when, two days after the election thirty-eight computer operators walked off their jobs at the Commission on Elections and claimed they were being pressured to falsify election figures to favor Marcos. The frightened operators took refuge in the Baclaran Church. The walkout was telecast around the world and became an important factor in undermining support for Marcos, particularly in the United States.

19. Joaquin, *Jaime Ongpin*, 249. Rene Saguisag later told Reid that the main strategy of Aquino's campaign was to draw attention to voting anomalies and to put Marcos on the defensive as quickly as possible (Saguisag to Reid, Pasay City, April 4, 1991).

Senator John Kerry, a member of the U.S. monitoring team, described the walkout as "the most damning incident yet," and Aquino's adviser, Joker Arroyo, called it the "smoking gun" that proved Marcos was trying to steal the election.

There was more to the walkout, however, than the simple outrage of the computer operators. Their leader was Linda Kapunan, wife of an air force lieutenant colonel, Eduardo "Red" Kapunan. Her husband was a member of a clique of young military officers who were secretly conspiring to overthrow Marcos. The vote manipulation was real, but the military conspirators wanted the world to know about it as justification for the action they were planning to undertake.

Evidence of massive vote fraud was mounting and was rapidly eroding Marcos's position both in the Philippines and abroad. Three days after the balloting, the chairman of the U.S. observer team, Senator Richard Lugar, told a press conference his group had received disturbing reports of massive fraud. In Washington, Senator David Boren, the ranking Democrat on the Senate Intelligence Committee, said that if the election had been fair, Marcos could not have won. And a more serious blow to Marcos later that week came when the Catholic Bishops Conference denounced the election as unparalleled in the fraudulence of its conduct.

Nonetheless, the Commission on Elections reported, as expected, that Marcos had won with a total of 10,807,197 votes to 9,291,761 for Aquino. NAMFREL stopped its count after tabulating 70 percent of the vote and declared that Aquino was slightly ahead, but NAMFREL's figures did not include totals from Marcos strongholds in northern Luzon and elsewhere. On February 16, the National Assembly dutifully certified Marcos as the winner, but Aquino denounced the decision and called for a campaign of nonviolent boycotts and demonstrations during a rally at Rizal Park in Manila.

It is pointless to speculate whether civil disobedience alone would have brought down the Marcos government. Marcos had survived grave crises, including the outrage over the Aquino assassination. He had clearly lost his popular mandate, but he retained formidable support outside Manila and in the 250,000-strong armed forces. His standing in the U.S. State Department and Congress was never lower, but he retained the confidence of President Ronald Reagan, who considered him the only Filipino leader who could stop the Communist-led insurgency.

Behind the scenes, however, Marcos's position in the armed forces was crumbling. Since martial law, the Armed Forces of the Philippines had enjoyed a privileged position in Filipino society. During military rule, senior officers served as directors of state-controlled firms, and in rural areas they wielded power like feudal lords. Marcos also tolerated rampant corruption in the ranks as a way of retaining the loyalty of the officer corps. A provincial commander could earn thousands of dollars a year, far more than his government salary, through rake-offs from gambling, smuggling, and illegal logging. In rural garrisons, it was not uncommon to find commanders' wives running the local post exchange or even selling uniforms to the soldiers. Favored generals were allowed to keep their positions long after the mandatory retirement age. That guaranteed a loyal chain of command but encouraged deep resentment among middle-grade officers, whose promotions were delayed because of the logjam at the top.

In 1984, a group of about fifteen young officers, mostly from the classes of 1971 and 1972 at the Philippine Military Academy, banded together to lobby for reforms. They called themselves the Reform the Armed Forces Movement (RAM), and their patron was the longtime defense minister, Juan Ponce Enrile.[20]

At sixty-two, "Johnny" Enrile was an unlikely figure for the role he would play. He was born Juan Furagganan in 1924, in the village of Mission on the northern coast of Luzon Island, the illegitimate son of a wealthy attorney and a fisherman's daughter. Juan Furagganan grew up poor, eking out a living as an unskilled laborer in the remote, impoverished north.

His mother told him of his father, and after World War II, he journeyed to Manila and found Don Alfonso Ponce Enrile at his prestigious law firm. Filipino culture tolerates extramarital liaisons but demands that a father take responsibility for the results. Don Alfonso, who had a wife and children, accepted Enrile into his family and paid for his education, first at the prestigious Ateneo University and the University of the Philippines and later at Harvard, where the former day laborer earned a law degree in 1955.

Enrile returned to the Philippines and became a multimillionaire, owning factories, logging concessions, and banking interests. He served var-

20.   The material about Enrile that follows was excerpted from his campaign literature for the 1987 election.

iously as Marcos's finance minister, justice minister, and later as defense minister throughout the eight years of martial law. Despite his impressive credentials, Enrile was, for millions of Filipinos, the very symbol of martial rule.

Over the years, however, Enrile's standing with the president had declined, and his relations with Imelda were rocky. His position in the defense establishment had been undermined by the chief of staff, General Fabian Ver. To protect his position, he recruited the "baron," or class leader, from graduating classes at the Philippine Military Academy for his personal staff at the Ministry of National Defense; the barons in turn recruited other promising young officers. The barons and their *bata,* or "children," formed the nucleus of Enrile's "RAM Boys."

Before Marcos called the special elections, contacts were already underway between RAM and the opposition, including Aquino's relatives and close supporters. Navy Captain Rexford Robles, a member of the clique, claims Ongpin and Jose Concepcion, later the chairman of supposedly neutral NAMFREL, even provided them money and encouraged them to move against Marcos.[21]

The RAM clique had planned a coup against Marcos by the end of 1985, but it deferred plans after he called the special election. RAM assumed Marcos could never accept defeat, and after the election results were announced, members resumed their plotting. Several plans were drafted. One called for a commando assault on the Malacañang presidential palace using rubber boats to cross the Pasig River. The leader of the assault would be Red Kapunan, husband of the woman who had led the computer operators' walkout on February 9. According to the plan, Kapunan's forces would seize Marcos, and afterward the conspirators would invite five to seven national figures to join a ruling junta, including Cory Aquino. The attack was set for the morning of February 23.

U.S. diplomats and military attachés had been in close touch with RAM contacts for months. In talks with the conspirators, the message from the Americans was that they would not sanction an unconstitutional move against Marcos nor would they tolerate violence on RAM's part. RAM conspirators came away from the meetings convinced that the U.S.

21. Captain Rex Robles, oral communication to Robert Reid, Makati, May, 1991. Robles summarized the origins of RAM in a series of conversations with Reid that month.

was playing both sides, carefully avoiding an open break with either Marcos or his enemies.[22]

Contacts were also under way between RAM and Aquino's closest supporters. On Thursday, February 20, Robles met at a restaurant in Makati with Jose Cojuangco, her younger brother, and Ramon Mitra, a former senator and later Aquino's first agriculture minister. Robles hinted to Cojuangco and Mitra that a mutiny was in the works and that Aquino would be offered a seat on the ruling junta if it succeeded. "Cojuangco kept quiet but Mitra was firm, Cory had to be the president," Robles said.[23]

General Ver was also aware of RAM's plans. He ordered land mines to be planted along the banks of the Pasig River on the south side of Malacañang Palace and drafted plans to arrest the leading conspirators. On Saturday, February 22, Enrile was having coffee at the Atrium commercial complex in Makati when he received word that security guards of Minister of Trade and Industry Roberto Ongpin, brother of Aquino's adviser Jaime Ongpin, had been arrested. Some of the minister's guards were linked to RAM, and Enrile feared their arrests indicated Ver had already begun rounding up conspirators.

Meanwhile at the Ministry of National Defense, Enrile's security chief, Lieutenant Colonel Gregorio Honasan, found out that Ver was deploying troops from rural garrisons into the Manila area, apparently as part of a planned crackdown. Fearing arrest, Enrile decided to move quickly. He telephoned General Ramos, Ver's principal rival in the armed forces, and asked for his support. A West Point graduate, Ramos knew of RAM's disaffection but had cautioned them against an open break with Marcos. He despised Fabian Ver, however, for what he had done to the armed forces and for blocking his own rise to chief of staff.

Ramos agreed to join Enrile, and the two rushed to armed forces' headquarters at Camp Aguinaldo, a sprawling garrison in suburban Quezon City that included the Ministry of National Defense and the headquarters of the armed forces general staff. The mutineers' resources were meager, perhaps three hundred men. Nonetheless, the first military coup in Philippine history was launched.[24]

22. *Ibid.*
23. *Ibid.*
24. The sequence of events after Enrile launched the coup comes from transcripts prepared at the time by AP and the Manila daily newspaper *Malaya*.

Ramos's presence at Camp Aguinaldo would prove decisive. Ramos had commanded the Philippine Constabulary for seventeen years and had built a network of personal ties within the officer corps, which mean more in the Philippines than formal chains of command. He could bring along other officers whom Enrile, a civilian, could not. Enrile was a mercurial, temperamental figure, but Ramos was steady, calm, and—although he often lingered over decisions—quick to act when he finally made up his mind.

Rumors of trouble at Camp Aguinaldo swept the city, and reporters rushed to the garrison for a hastily arranged press conference. Enrile and Ramos sat at a table, surrounded by armed troops. They announced they had mutinied against Ferdinand Marcos because he had stolen the election. Enrile declared that he could no longer acknowledge Marcos as chief executive but was evasive when asked if he considered Cory Aquino the legitimate president. "I'm not making a conclusion," Enrile replied. "Whoever is considered by the people to be representative of their will must be respected." Using words he would later regret, Enrile added: "I am morally convinced it was Mrs. Aquino who was elected. . . . I believe in my whole heart and mind that she was duly elected president of the Republic of the Philippines." With those words, talk of a junta faded, and Enrile himself linked his fate to that of Cory Aquino.

Aquino, however, was not present at the camp, nor even in the capital. She had gone ahead with a visit to Cebu, 350 miles to the south, to take part in an opposition rally. She learned what had taken place in Manila from reporters traveling with her. Aides rushed her to a convent near the city for protection, and the following day she flew back to Manila.

The decision by Aquino's followers to join the Enrile mutiny came about almost by accident. At first, the Aquino camp was uncertain how to respond to Enrile's dramatic announcement. Most of her chief advisers so deeply distrusted the military that they decided initially to let their "enemies" fight it out among themselves.

Butz Aquino heard Enrile's declaration on the radio during a birthday party for one of his colleagues in ATOM, or the August 21 Movement, an opposition group whose name was derived from the date of Ninoy's murder. Butz had spent the afternoon at a seminar on tactics of nonviolence, and one of the options discussed had been ways to exploit dissension within the military. It seemed to Butz that Enrile's revolt presented an opportunity for just that.

Butz was intrigued by the presence of Fidel Ramos, whom he trusted more than Enrile. He telephoned several key figures in the Aquino alliance but found little support for joining Enrile. Butz, however, by his own admission had taken a few drinks at the party and was "a little bit tipsy." Fired with whiskey courage, he disregarded advice to stay out of the mutiny and headed for Camp Aguinaldo. [25]

After conferring with Ramos, Butz was convinced the mutineers were serious. Ramos told him they needed all the help they could get. On his way out of the camp, Butz ran into a friend, a reporter for Radio Veritas, the Catholic station, who asked him if he wanted to broadcast a statement. Without conferring with anyone else, Butz did so, urging members of ATOM and other opposition groups to support the mutiny by coming to Epifanio de los Santos Avenue, or EDSA, a major traffic artery that runs between Camp Aguinaldo and another garrison, Camp Crame. Crowds began to converge that night all along the boulevard.

Cardinal Sin issued a similar appeal for support over Radio Veritas and the crowds swelled, first in the thousands, then to hundreds of thousands, and then, by some estimates, to more than a million. As the turnout grew, the U.S. State Department, through the embassy in Manila, delivered stern warnings to Marcos to avoid bloodshed. The conduct of the mutiny had met the U.S. conditions. By declaring support for Cory Aquino, the rightfully elected president, Enrile and Ramos were following constitutional procedures. United States law required Washington to cut off aid to any country that ousted an elected government by force, but the basis of this mutiny was supposedly to right a constitutional wrong. The mutineers were not using force to overthrow the Marcos government but were simply defending themselves from possible reprisals for backing the new president. [26]

Within hours, the crush was so large that Marcos's generals concluded it would be impossible to disperse the populace without bloodshed. Television pictures of nuns and priests praying before the gates of the camp and handing flowers to Marcos's soldiers were broadcast around the world. The pictures created the impression of a nation rising up against dictatorship.

25. Agapito Aquino interview by Reid, May 8, 1991.
26. Robles to Reid, May 10, 1991. At the time, Robles was the principal RAM liaison with the foreign press.

The rest of the story is well documented. Hundreds of thousands of Filipinos turned out along EDSA in front of the camp in what the U.S. media described as the "people power revolution." In the face of massive public support, Ramos convinced key commanders either to remain neutral or to switch sides. Before dawn on February 25, a desperate Marcos played his last card: he telephoned Senator Paul Laxalt to appeal for help from Reagan, but Laxalt told him to "cut and cut clean."

At 10:46 A.M. on February 25, 1986, Supreme Court Justice Claudio Teehankee administered the oath of office to Corazon Aquino at Club Filipino, an exclusive club in the wealthy Greenhills district. Rene Saguisag, a human rights lawyer, typed an inaugural oath, but in the confusion it was misplaced. Saguisag then scribbled a second note in longhand and gave it to Teehankee. It read: "I, Corazon Cojuangco Aquino, solemnly swear that I will faithfully and conscientiously fulfill my duties as president of the Republic of the Philippines, preserve and defend its fundamental law, execute its just laws, do justice to every man, and consecrate myself to the service of the nation, so help me God."[27]

Later, Marcos took his own oath at Malacañang Palace in a pitiful gesture to maintain his claim on the office he had held for twenty years. His vice-president, Arturo Tolentino, did not even show up. That night, as aides burned documents, a sedated and exhausted Marcos, his family, and entourage boarded U.S. military helicopters and flew to Clark Air Base, fifty miles north of the capital. Marcos was so weak that he had to be carried bodily from a limousine to the helicopter.[28]

Word of his departure swept the city. When Aquino telephoned Ambassador Stephen Bosworth for confirmation, he relayed Marcos's wish to stay the night in his home province, Ilocos Norte. Aquino was not about to accommodate the man whom she was convinced had ordered her husband's murder. "She said, 'No, he has to leave,'" recalls Aquilino Pimentel, who was with her that night.[29]

Marcos and his family were flown to exile in Hawaii, where the former president died in September, 1989. Those aboard the aircraft included Ver as well as Marcos's longtime friend and admirer, Danding Cojuangco, Cory's estranged cousin. Cory Aquino had kept her vow to Ninoy.

27. Saguisag to Reid, April 4, 1991.
28. Arturo Aruiza, *Malacañang to Makiki* (Quezon City, 1991), 157. Aruiza was Marcos's military aide at the time and one of the few persons with direct access to him.
29. Interview with Aquilino Pimentel by Robert Reid, Manila, May 8, 1991.

As word spread that Marcos was gone, Manila erupted in jubilation. Crowds of youths swarmed through the wrought-iron gates of Malacañang Palace, ransacking furnishings before police could restore order. Millions around the world celebrated what they considered a triumph of good over evil, a victory for democracy, and an affirmation of "people power." In Washington, the Reagan administration congratulated itself on a foreign policy success. The Filipino people, behind the standard of Cory Aquino, had toppled a dictator with practically no bloodshed.

In the euphoria of the moment, few wanted to consider the fine print of what became known in the Philippines as the "EDSA Revolution." There can be no doubt that Cory Aquino—not Enrile and his RAM Boys—had inspired the crowds to turn out at EDSA. [30] Enrile himself had bound his followers to Aquino's cause, but the crowds came to EDSA because Enrile, Ramos, and a clique of military officers had taken the fateful step of breaking with Marcos. That set a dangerous precedent in a country that describes itself as "Asia's first democracy."

Disparate factions from the armed forces, the United States government, the Catholic church hierarchy, traditional political parties, and social activist movements had come together to oust Marcos. Each had its own agenda. There was no consensus on how to manage the nation now that Marcos was gone. Much would depend on Corazon Aquino, who was chosen standard-bearer in the first place because of her very lack of strong, public views.

Holding that coalition together would become Aquino's greatest challenge as president. Failing to mold it into a cohesive force for social change would be her greatest failure.

---

30.   Although Aquino later claimed that she had surreptitiously visited EDSA during the upheaval, she was not seen by the crowds there and gave no speeches. It was as a symbol, not by her actual presence, that she inspired those who gathered along the boulevard.

3   CORY TAKES CHARGE

EUPHORIA OVER THE fall of Marcos quickly gave way before the grave challenges Cory Aquino faced in governing an unruly, impoverished nation devastated by political turmoil and years of misrule. Aquino had assumed leadership of a nation with a $28 billion foreign debt, massive poverty, an active Communist insurgency, three Muslim secessionist movements, telephones that did not work, roads in disrepair, schools without adequately trained teachers, an underpaid labor force, a factionalized military, and sixty million people who had been told that her leadership would bring them a better life.

Apart from the immediate crises, the new president would have to come to grips with two broad problem areas that had long plagued Philippine society, one cultural, the other economic. Philippine culture encourages individuals to build personal alliances with family and influential patrons as a source of strength. The system functions in an intricate network of mutual obligations and favors that must be repaid. Such a system of dyadic alliances, compounded by the archipelagic nature of the country, has long discouraged a sense of national cohesion. It has also contributed to a political culture where votes are cast based on advice from the landlord or some other patron, or on the candidate's family and regional origin.

Aquino would have to encourage her people to look beyond the narrow interests of their own families and regions to the greater goal of the collective national welfare. Slogans would not be enough. She would have to lead by example, even at the expense of the interests of her own clan and class.

The second broad problem area was an inequitable distribution of national wealth. Nowhere could this be seen more clearly than in metropolitan Manila. In the suburb of Makati, with its gleaming skyscrapers, smart boutiques, and glittering nightclubs, the superrich live opulent lives in so-called golden ghettos—exclusive, guarded neighborhoods that compare favorably with Beverly Hills. A few miles away, hundreds of thousands more eke out marginal existences in fetid squatter shacks perched on garbage dumps or along polluted, disease-ridden rivers.

Despite the grave situation, the months following Aquino's election to office were a time of great optimism. The Marcoses and a few of their closest associates were driven from the country. Absent, however, were the mass arrests and bloody purges that often accompany political change in the developing world. Groups that felt estranged and threatened under Marcos—among them social activists, Muslim militants, Marxists, students, labor unions, and the middle class—hoped the new, liberal political climate would enable them to achieve their aspirations. With press curbs relaxed, new newspapers appeared. Prominent exiles returned from abroad. Filipinos debated the course of their nation in countless television talk shows, seminars, rallies, and public forums.

Aquino did not have the luxury of an orderly transition. She and her followers were at the barricades one day, in power the next. Decisions had to be made quickly, often by people with few proven administrative skills and without a background in the mechanics of government. Her own lack of preparation for high office was painfully, and sometimes comically, clear. Her chief of security, Colonel Voltaire Gazmin, had to teach the new president how to salute during protocol functions. (As a young lieutenant, Gazmin had been Ninoy Aquino's jailer during his confinement at Fort Magsaysay a decade earlier.) Another time, President Aquino arrived late for an appointment at Camp Aguinaldo because no one told her that presidents do not have to stop at traffic lights.[1]

For the first two weeks, she did not even have an official office. Malacañang Palace had been ransacked on the night Marcos left, and military

1. Corazon Aquino, press conference, Manila, September 11, 1986.

teams had to clear the compound of the land mines and explosives Ver had planted to prevent attack. Unknown to the Aquino group, however, those teams also used the opportunity to plant listening devices in palace offices, so that Enrile and the RAM Boys could stay abreast of a government they helped install but did not trust.[2]

Aquino set up her offices in the Jose Cojuangco Building, headquarters of her family's business empire. "We didn't even have a typewriter," recalls Rene Saguisag, who became her first spokesman. The presidential staff was so short of supplies and secretarial help that new officials even typed their own orders of appointment.[3]

Aquino had promised that she would be "the opposite of Marcos," and her first steps were designed to make good on that pledge. In her first speech as president, delivered to a huge crowd in Rizal Park, she restored the right of habeas corpus, promising that never again would Filipinos face detention without charge. Even when she and her aides moved into the Malacañang Palace complex, Aquino set up her personal office not in the main building, where Marcos and other presidents had been, but in the palace guest house, to accentuate the difference between her and her predecessor.

Image had been the key to Aquino's rise to power, and many of her early gestures were purely cosmetic. At her first cabinet meeting, held on March 12, she waived the traditional twenty-one-gun salute that Marcos had loved. She announced that the First Family would not live in Malacañang and instead took up residence in a Spanish-style house on Arlegui Street near the presidential compound. Weekends were for family, always her first priority, and Cory announced that she would conduct no official business at home, a promise she soon found unable to keep.

Promises and public relations gestures, however, would not be enough to restore the Filipinos' faith in government. Her six predecessors had all taken office pledging progress and giving lip service to social reform. For the most part, they left behind a political wreckage that enabled their successors to make the same grandiose promises. All of their grand plans fell victim to a factious political system controlled by special interests and anchored on a foundation of patronage, parochialism, and favoritism. Filipinos often formulate grand projects, then lose interest in them quickly—

2.   Captain Rexford Robles, oral communication to Robert Reid, Manila, May, 1991.
3.   Interview with Rene Saguisag by Robert Reid, Pasay City, April 4, 1991.

the ningas cogon, or brushfire phenomenon, which has consumed many reform efforts.

In her campaign, Aquino had offered no detailed national plan beyond ridding the country of Marcos and rebuilding democratic institutions. Moreover, she lacked effective political machinery reaching from Manila to the remotest barrios, and both she and those closest to her had little practical experience in statecraft. Although her speeches were replete with slogans about democracy and people power, she had offered few specifics. For her, getting rid of Marcos—not governing the nation—had been the primary goal. She had given some clues to her plans for the country during a campaign speech delivered in the southern city of Davao on January 17, when she promised a broad social program, including self-help programs, improvements in education and health care, repeal of laws curbing strikes, peace overtures to Communist and Muslim guerrillas, and an agrarian reform program that would expand land ownership to millions of impoverished peasants.[4]

The nineteen-page speech was hardly a blueprint for social revolution. Still, that speech and others like it had raised expectations that Cory Aquino would preside over a government committed to vigorous social reform, unencumbered by the feudalistic patronage style of the past. Filipinos clamoring for reform knew what they would receive under Marcos, but Aquino offered the prospect of meaningful change. Filipinos listened to the seemingly humble, pious widow and heard what they wanted to hear.

Every promise was followed by an escape clause that placed limits on the scope of change. "My government will be one of patient consultation and personal involvement," she said during the Davao speech. "I will not ram reform down your throats." It was doubtful that meaningful and painful reforms could be implemented by consensus, however, especially in a parochial society dominated by special interests of class and region.

Aquino promised to expand agrarian reform to cover all agricultural lands, not simply the corn- and rice-producing holdings to which the Marcos land reform program was limited. Land ownership must be balanced against the need to enhance production, she said, carefully avoiding an unequivocal promise to break up large estates, including her family's

4. Corazon Aquino, campaign speech at Ateneo de Davao University, Davao, January 6, 1986.

twelve-thousand-acre sugar plantation, Hacienda Luisita. "I shall sit down with my family to explore how the twin goals of maximum productivity and dispersal of ownership and benefits can be exemplified for the rest of the nation in Hacienda Luisita," she said.[5] But who would determine whether "dispersal of ownership" outweighed the short-term benefits of keeping productive estates intact?

Another promise was to offer a cease-fire to the Communists and release political prisoners. She qualified her pledge by warning that "criminals among them" would be dealt with harshly.[6] In an armed insurgency, the line between "legitimate" rebellion and criminality is difficult to define.

The Davao campaign speech revealed that an Aquino government would be one of reform, not revolution, despite descriptions of the later events of February 22–25 as a people power revolution. Television images of thousands of Filipinos chanting her name at the barricades also obscured the fact that Corazon Aquino, a patrician promoted by conservatives within the Roman Catholic establishment, had not come to power solely through the ballot box or the crowds in the street but, more accurately, by an intricate conspiracy within an unwieldy coalition.

This became evident in Aquino's selection of her cabinet, her first act of statecraft: she followed the traditional political formula of rewarding the factions that had brought her to power. Key economic portfolios went to the Catholic business clique so instrumental in gaining her the nomination and financing her campaign. She appointed Jaime Ongpin as minister of finance and Jose Concepcion as minister of trade and industry. The appointment of Concepcion was immediately criticized in the press as a payoff for NAMFREL's apparent support of Cory Aquino during the campaign. But Concepcion was close to Cardinal Sin, and the church's influence and prestige, like that of Aquino herself, was at a high point.

At Ongpin's recommendation, she retained Jose Fernandez as chairman of the Central Bank, which controlled monetary policy. Fernandez's appointment was also criticized because he had presided over the fiscal ruin that marked the final years of the Marcos administration. But the three were widely known in business and foreign financial circles, and their appointments were designed to reassure those groups that the new

5. *Ibid.*
6. *Ibid.*

government would pursue a "responsible" fiscal policy. The post of minister of economic development went to Professor Solita Monsod, wife of the executive director of the supposedly impartial NAMFREL. Monsod's views on such issues as economic development, agrarian reform, and debt management were radically different from those of the more-conservative Ongpin and Fernandez.

Those who had been close to Ninoy were also rewarded. Many of them had been at the forefront of the street demonstrations that marked the long struggle against the Marcos regime. Ramon Mitra, a wealthy rancher and Ninoy's fellow senator from the Liberal Party, received the agriculture portfolio. Aquilino Pimentel, a former mayor who had been jailed three times by Marcos, became local governments' minister, and Ernesto Maceda, Ninoy's confidante from his Massachusetts days, was named minister of natural resources. Former senator Jovito Salonga, who had been jailed with Ninoy during martial law, was given the job of recovering the fortune Marcos had allegedly stolen during his twenty years in power. Joker Arroyo, a member of Ninoy's legal defense team and a prominent human rights lawyer, was appointed presidential executive secretary. He influenced the choices of Saguisag as official spokesman and Teodoro Locsin as presidential adviser and speechwriter.

Laurel's faction also had to be accommodated, even though Aquino's closest advisers had little use for the ambitious vice-president. Laurel himself would not be satisfied with the vice-presidency, a powerless post without a single constitutional duty except waiting for the president to die. Laurel was given the foreign ministry, a visible but also powerless job, and was named prime minister as well, a position that he assumed would give him a strong hand in appointing his own supporters to patronage jobs, thereby enhancing his own stature.

The decision to retain Ramos and Enrile as chief of staff and defense minister respectively was controversial from the start and would have far-reaching effects on Aquino's administration. One of her first actions was to sack twenty-two pro-Marcos generals who had been retained beyond mandatory retirement. But keeping Ramos and Enrile meant the armed forces remained under the control of persons identified with the previous regime.

Pimentel and others in Aquino's entourage urged her to retire Ramos and Enrile and begin a thorough reorganization of the armed forces as part of her promise of justice for victims of the Marcos regime and to remove possible threats to her power. Despite slogans about people power, however, she knew she owed no small debt to Enrile and Ramos and could ill afford to antagonize such a powerful institution as the military. Aquino was convinced that if she, the widow of a military victim, could work with the armed forces command, others in her government could too. "I am not engaged in a personality contest with Minister Enrile and General Ramos," she told reporters after announcing their appointments.

Such optimism was to be proven naive. Enrile's clique of officers believed they had toppled Marcos and that Aquino had snatched victory from them. On the day she took her oath, two of Enrile's RAM Boys, navy captains Rexford Robles and Felix Turingan, pulled aside Colonel Honesto Isleta at Camp Crame and told him, "Sir, I think we should run the government first. Then we will have an election." Isleta told them he disapproved of the idea. But the seeds of future rebellions had already been sown.[7]

The makeup of the cabinet satisfied the need to reward factions in the coalition but set the stage for intense and protracted battles over virtually every issue that would arise. Many of the appointees lacked national stature, political experience, and even expertise in the areas for which their departments were responsible. Some of those with political backgrounds, such as Mitra, represented a return to the discredited style of pre–martial law politics, hardly the sort of new, populist approach that Aquino seemed to represent. Ongpin had the credentials for the finance portfolio but lacked political experience or skill in dealing with the press, whose support would be necessary to sell unpalatable but necessary programs of fiscal reform.

People power slogans aside, the most powerful posts—defense, finance, the Central Bank, agriculture, and the armed forces—were given to establishment conservatives. Interestingly, one of the last portfolios filled was that of agrarian reform minister, despite Aquino's promise of a vigorous and expanded program in that area.

Soon after the appointments were announced, newspaper commentator Jake Macasaet observed in the daily *Malaya* ("independence" in Tagalog) that the cabinet lineup "appears to be the first negative blow to the

7. Interview with Colonel Honesto Isleta by Eileen Guerrero, Quezon City, March 27, 1990.

euphoria over the fall of the Marcos regime." The main qualifications for appointment, he wrote, seemed to be "fighting Marcos and [having] personal ties to Ninoy."[8] It was back to patronage, payoffs, and politics as usual.

Moreover, the cabinet represented such a broad spectrum that it would seem all but unmanageable without the kind of strong leadership that Cory Aquino was not prepared to give. She had promised to shift authority away from the presidential palace to the individual ministries. On some issues, however, such as release of political prisoners, Aquino accepted the views of liberal human rights advocates in her cabinet, while on others, such as fiscal policy, she favored the conservative business bloc. That approach only reinforced the picture of a government with no clear direction.

Ongpin, Concepcion, and others from the business faction were wealthy capitalists who favored programs to privatize state-controlled enterprises, dismantle monopolies, encourage foreign investment, and honor the country's overseas debt. Arroyo, Saguisag, and those in their faction supported Ongpin's desire to dismantle the commodity trading monopolies that Marcos and his associates had used to control farm exports. But Arroyo's group wanted selective repudiation of foreign debts as a means to generate capital for domestic development, despite Ongpin's fears that such a move would dry up foreign loans.

Labor Minister Augusto Sanchez was a human rights lawyer and an avowed leftist with links to the Communist underground, who saw himself as the workers' advocate in government. He quickly angered the business community by encouraging profit-sharing plans for workers and limitations on foreign investment that other cabinet members were trying to lure to the Philippines.

With such an explosive mixture, cabinet meetings became free-for-alls in which members occasionally shouted at one another and then rushed outside to regale reporters with wild stories of behind-the-scenes intrigue. Freed from the shackles of Marcos-era curbs, the press gleefully embellished accounts in the style of Hollywood gossip columnists detailing the feuds and scandals of the stars.

Pimentel describes Aquino's role in those early days as that of a referee,

8. Jake Macasaet commentary, *Malaya*, February 28, 1986, p. 6.

or a mother trying to hold together a family of quarreling, jealous siblings. When an impasse developed, she would simply tell the feuding members to "work it out" among themselves. That approach left issues unresolved and personal wounds festering.[9]

A detached style may have worked in countries with well-developed bureaucracies and institutions, but it could not work in the Philippines. Philippine culture is run by personalities rather than institutions, and the smooth functioning of public and private enterprises depends largely on the leadership of the person in charge. Issuing directives is not enough. The success of any enterprise, public or private, requires micromanagement by the supervisor, and a detached style guarantees inertia and failure.

In public, Aquino presented a picture of unflappable calm. She brushed aside charges in the press that her cabinet was unwieldy and divided. After all, differences of opinion were a sign of democracy, she would reply. "Since we promised to restore our freedoms, my cabinet members are free to express their opinions," she told *Asiaweek* magazine two months after taking office.[10]

But there was another side to Cory's personality: she was stubborn. She liked team players, and grandstanding by strong-willed subordinates did not sit well with her. In a television interview shortly after becoming president, Aquino explained, "I do have people whom I respect, whom I go to for advice." But, she added, "I hate people giving me unsolicited advice."[11] The Philippines is a country, however, where everyone has an opinion; after years of authoritarianism, everyone seemed eager to express their views. Cory Aquino was about to receive a lot of "unsolicited advice."

After putting together a cabinet, the next major problem facing the government was to consolidate its position in the provinces, which remained largely unaffected by the changes in Manila. The uprising had swept away Marcos and the central government but left intact a regional structure that included nearly sixteen hundred mayors, seventy-four governors, and thousands of village and neighborhood leaders, known as "*barangay* captains."

9.   Interview with Aquilino Pimentel by Robert Reid, Manila, May 8, 1991.
10.   Interview with Corazon Aquino, *Asiaweek*, May 11, 1986, p. 24.
11.   Interview with Corazon Aquino by Luis Beltran, People's Television, Manila, April 21, 1986.

Because they lacked a well-organized national political machinery, Aquino's advisers realized that the regional network presented a potential challenge. Traditionally, political power in the Philippines rests on an intricate web of alliances between the president and regional power brokers. The president provides pork barrel funds, and in turn the regional bosses deliver votes. As a result, many of the mayors, governors, and village chieftains retained strong loyalties to Ferdinand Marcos.

Many regional figures remained popular despite their association with Marcos. The lack of a sense of nationhood meant that regional interests were paramount. For many Filipinos, there was no inconsistency in continuing to support a mayor, governor, or village chieftain even if he had ties to Marcos.

Provincial officials had been elected in 1980 to six-year terms, which were to have expired on March 2, 1986. But the Marcos-controlled National Assembly had extended the terms until June of that year on the assumption that the national election in February would be followed by regional balloting in May.

Aquino had two options: go ahead with the May elections or demand that the officials resign and then appoint replacements. The first option was quickly ruled out. New elections so soon after the chaos of the Marcos departure would have been expensive and potentially bloody. Given the provincialism of Filipino voters, there was also no guarantee that elections would unseat the old, established feudal lords still loyal to Marcos. The government decided to demand that all local officials resign and be replaced by interim appointees pending new elections at a later date.

The task of dismantling regional administrations fell to Aquilino Pimentel as minister of local governments. Pimentel, a former mayor of Cagayan de Oro and Ninoy's ally in the PDP-Laban Party, had been among the potential presidential candidates screened by the Convenors. He had stepped aside early in the deliberations and had been among the first to call publicly on Cory Aquino to run for president. Pimentel's background, however, made him a controversial choice for such a politically sensitive task. During the Marcos administration, he had been arrested three times as an alleged Communist sympathizer. Pimentel vigorously denied the charges, but as one of the most liberal members of the cabinet, he was deeply distrusted within the armed forces because of his past.

Pimentel also represented a threat to Doy Laurel and his UNIDO stalwarts. Laurel had hoped to use his position as prime minister to appoint many of his followers to plum posts. He realized that replacing all local officials nationwide presented a unique opportunity to build a national base of support after Cory Aquino faded into history. Because she had run under the UNIDO banner, Laurel maintained that her election meant his organization had become the "ruling party." But UNIDO had simply been a flag of convenience for Aquino, and Laurel knew it. He had reason to suspect that the new administration would not object to Pimentel promoting through his appointments the interests of his PDP-Laban cronies. Although PDP-Laban had joined with Laurel's UNIDO to support Aquino, given the transient nature of Philippine politics, it was unlikely the alliance would survive her term in office. Even though Aquino did not belong to PDP-Laban, it was the party of her late husband, and she now placed the responsibility for doling out the spoils to its leader, Pimentel. The estrangement of Salvador Laurel had begun. [12]

The task of replacing so many officials would have been herculean in the best of times and with the best of intentions. For a government short on experience and still wedded to patronage politics, it nearly proved disastrous. In the rush to make changes as quickly as possible, the new government appointed many persons who were clearly unqualified or who lacked grass-roots support. Pimentel lacked the resources to screen potential appointees and relied heavily on local clerics or pro-Aquino politicians for advice. No sooner were some of the new appointees in office than they started handing out government jobs to friends and relatives, demonstrating that Filipino traditions were stronger than clichés about honest government and people power.

Aquino was forced to intervene from time to time. She overruled Pimentel and reappointed twenty-four mayors in Ilocos Sur province, a Marcos stronghold, because of their strong local following. The spectacle of patronage and bickering raised strong doubts that the rise of Cory Aquino heralded a genuine political revolution.

As the process of replacement continued, the rift between Pimentel and Laurel deepened. Pimentel named John Osmeña, scion of a once-powerful central Philippine political dynasty, to serve as acting governor of Cebu,

---

12. Pimentel to Reid, May 8, 1991. The rivalry between Pimentel and Laurel was also confirmed in several private conversations with Laurel, Maceda, and members of Laurel's staff.

a rich province that included the second most important metropolitan center after Manila. The appointment angered Laurel, who had promised the post to Osmeña's cousin, Minnie Osmeña-Stuart. Laurel's selections for governor of Pampanga province, which included the U.S.-run Clark Air Base, and for mayor of Makati, the country's financial center, were also overruled.

At the same time, some powerful local politicians were refusing to vacate their positions and began organizing private armies to defend their turf. In Lanao del Sur, a Muslim stronghold on Mindanao Island, open warfare broke out between the military and followers of the local war-lord, Ali Dimaporo, a Marcos die-hard. Bren Guiao, Pimentel's choice for governor of Pampanga province, agreed to step aside temporarily until the courts reviewed his appointment, after the local governor barricaded himself in the provincial capitol building. As tensions rose, UNIDO declared it could no longer support the "slaughter of local officials" and called instead for retaining elected officeholders until new elections. "We have been critical of ex-President Marcos for highhanded practices yet our people are doing the same thing," UNIDO's secretary-general, Rene Espina, fumed publicly. [13]

The ouster of Marcos also left unresolved the question of what to do with the Batasang Pambansa, or National Assembly. Marcos had abolished the pre–martial law senate and house of representatives and replaced it with a unicameral assembly, which he said would be more responsive politically. The former president's New Society Movement controlled two-thirds of the 190 assembly seats. Some of the movement's leading figures, including the former labor minister, Blas Ople, had publicly declared they were willing to work with the new administration. It was the assembly, however, that had certified Marcos as the winner over Cory Aquino in the February 7 presidential election. To Aquino, such a move made the assembly an accessory to a crime she could never forgive. Nevertheless, she maintained she was the rightful winner of the February election and had pledged to defend the constitution, which offered no legal basis for abolishing the assembly.

Revolutionaries, however, need not be bound by the same legal restrictions as constitutionally elected rulers, and in an effort to resolve the

13. UNIDO press statement, April 5, 1986; interview with Rene Espina, DZRH Radio, April 6, 1986.

organizational problems, the new government began a subtle reinterpretation of its mandate. Five days after Aquino took office, her justice minister, Neptali Gonzales, said publicly that the popular uprising against Marcos meant that the new administration was essentially a "revolutionary government" installed "by a direct assertion of the sovereign will."

The statement was widely overlooked in the euphoria surrounding Marcos's downfall, but it represented a subtle yet dramatic departure from the claim that the popular uprising along EDSA simply affirmed what had been decided at the polls. It meant that Cory Aquino need not be bound by constitutional and legal restrictions that were holdovers from the previous regime. Revolutionary status would allow her to disband the assembly, abolish repressive laws, and appoint whomever she wanted at any level of government.

Laurel and Enrile had proposed retaining the National Assembly until a new constitution could be drafted, on condition that the pro-Marcos members take an oath of loyalty to the new government. Leaders of the New Society Movement agreed to do so, but Aquino could not bring herself to deal with allies of her longtime enemy. They were the people who had imprisoned and killed her husband and then conspired to cheat her of the victory she considered rightfully hers.

Marcos's followers tried to dissuade Aquino through persuasion and promises from abolishing the assembly, their only hold on power at the national level. Ople announced he and his fellow New Society Movement members were severing ties with Marcos as an "act of contrition" and urged her to avoid the counsel of "Jacobinic advisers." It was no use. "We all know the Batasan of old," she said in a television interview. "They know the cheating done by Marcos. Why should I play ball with them?" [14]

On March 25, 1986, one month after assuming office, Aquino signed an interim "freedom constitution" that abolished the assembly and gave her the right to rule by decree. The document also abolished the office of prime minister, removing Laurel from his most important post.

The freedom constitution gave the president even broader powers than Marcos enjoyed under martial law. Drafted by Father Bernas from the Convenor group days, it also included guarantees of personal liberties and established a commission to draft a new constitution to be offered to

14. Aquino interview by Beltran, April 21, 1986.

voters for ratification within one year. But the right-wing opposition charged that abolishing the constitution destroyed the legal basis for Aquino's rule. Marcos's running mate, Arturo Tolentino, announced that she and Laurel should stand for election again, "to eliminate all doubts concerning legitimacy."

The decision to push ahead with the freedom constitution over objections of Enrile and Laurel showed the growing influence of the presidential staff, especially Joker Arroyo. Publicly, Aquino was committed to cabinet government and to divesting power from the staff. But it was Arroyo who controlled the flow of documents to the president and who determined whom she would see. Arroyo, who had been part of Ninoy Aquino's defense team, and his two allies, Saguisag and Locsin, saw the president every day. It was inevitable that they would wield considerable influence over a woman who trusted familiar faces and whose personal contacts had been so limited. "By force of circumstance, the government in those early days was President Cory, Joker Arroyo, Teddy Locsin, and me," Saguisag said, "in the sense that we were with her every day and access is power." [15]

Although they may have been well intentioned, Arroyo, Saguisag, and Locsin had no experience in government. Naturally, Aquino could not be expected to offer key positions to former Marcos associates, but Marcos had ruled for so long that virtually everyone with experience in the art of governing on a national level was in one way or another tainted by association with the discredited regime.

Arroyo and Saguisag had learned their politics in street demonstrations and fiery court appearances in defense of Marcos's enemies. They had spent years battling the Marcos government, and the protracted struggle had left them with strong, uncompromising views. They were courtroom lawyers, and their style was confrontational. Neither had planned to serve in government. But on the night Marcos left, both of them stood silently, shuffling their feet and staring at the floor, when Aquino asked them at the home of her sister, Josephine Reyes, to serve in her government. She reminded them that they had urged her to run. "Look, you people wanted me to run against Marcos, and you can't abandon me now," she said. [16]

They could not refuse. Arroyo and Saguisag would emerge as key fig-

---

15. Saguisag interview by Reid, April 4, 1991.
16. *Ibid.*

ures, setting the liberal tenor that marked the first months of the Aquino administration.

Joker, whose unusual first name reflected his father's fondness for card playing, jealously guarded his position as gatekeeper to the president. An elfin figure with an unruly shock of white hair, Arroyo could be witty and charming, especially with women and reporters, whom he carefully cultivated during the Marcos years. He could also be curt and abusive to those he considered his rivals, especially military officers whom he had instinctively distrusted since martial law.

Arroyo's dealings with the president also revealed the two sides of his nature. He was protective of her, shielding her from criticism or from decisions he believed she would not fully understand. But Arroyo clearly realized the limitations of Cory Aquino. Although well educated and instinctively shrewd, she was a woman of limited experience whose intellectual tastes leaned to television soap operas. Her favorite diversion was mah-jongg, the parlor game of rich, bored housewives. Cabinet members complained that Arroyo was limiting access to the president and withholding information that tended to go against his own views.

After Marcos left, the presidential staff was barraged with requests by businessmen, politicians, foreign visitors, and others, all seeking favors from the new administration.[17] Jose Alcuaz, former director of the National Telecommunications Commission under Aquino, recalls arriving one day at the Malacañang guest house for an appointment with the president. Before being ushered into the president's office, Arroyo pulled him aside. "Remember, you only have a few minutes with the president," Arroyo reminded the visitor. "Don't get involved in gossip."[18]

Arroyo proved an inept administrator. Cabinet members grumbled that position papers would sit on his desk for weeks before going to the president for a decision. In fact, Arroyo was carefully screening every recommendation so as to steer Aquino into what he considered the proper decision.

Arroyo and his faction came to power with a specific agenda different in character from others in the opposition coalition. Fiercely nationalistic, they preferred to see U.S. military bases removed from the country, although they were shrewd enough to understand the need, for the present,

17. Joker Arroyo, *Asiaweek,* September 20, 1987, p. 11.
18. Interview with Jose Alcuaz by Robert Reid, Makati, March 19, 1991.

of maintaining good relations with Washington. They were convinced that the previous government's penchant for financing development through foreign loans had benefited only Marcos and his associates, and they urged Aquino to consider selective repudiation of debts to free funds for development, a position that placed them in conflict with Ongpin and the businessmen in the cabinet.

An inexperienced staff meant that many of the early decisions proved disastrous. Aquino accepted the advice of her staff and abolished the Ministry of Energy, moving responsibility for it to the president's office. The idea was to eliminate a department that the new administration considered hopelessly corrupt, but energy policy then became a low priority.

The Ministry of Energy had fallen out of favor because of a controversial nuclear power plant that Marcos had ordered built by Westinghouse Electric Corporation on historic Bataan Peninsula, about fifty miles west of the capital. The project, which was encumbered by numerous cost overruns and safety problems, had become a cause célèbre for anti-Marcos forces. The opposition had accused Westinghouse of bribing Marcos for the contract and then running up huge cost overages. Furthermore, opposition stalwarts such as Lorenzo Tañada were philosophically opposed to nuclear power. During the campaign, Aquino had promised never to operate the plant if she were elected.

After the April, 1986, accident at Chernobyl in the Soviet Union, Aquino announced she was mothballing the Bataan plant, which had not yet begun to operate. But it was the foundation of the Marcos government's long-term energy plan for the Philippines, and removing the plant upset the entire energy strategy. With the Ministry of Energy no longer functioning, it took two years before the Aquino administration began to address its electricity requirements seriously. By then it was too late. This failure of planning eventually plunged the Philippines into a grave energy crisis in the 1990s that set back plans for economic recovery.

In the early days of the Aquino government, political stability was of paramount concern. That involved not only outflanking the residual Marcos forces but also resolving the Marxist insurgency that had mushroomed during the Marcos era. Arroyo believed that ending the insurgency was the only way Aquino could pursue her goals of protecting human rights. The problem was how to achieve reconciliation with the Communists without alienating the armed forces, some of whose members helped to install Aquino in power, but which also included many persons still loyal to Marcos.

Joker Arroyo saved his deepest contempt for the military. His legal specialty was human rights, and his clients included alleged Communist insurgents, political activists, and victims of human rights abuses committed by men in uniform. He feared that Enrile would use his position as defense minister not only to protect soldiers from having to answer for their crimes but also to build the defense establishment into a rival center of power. "They were human rights lawyers with a lot of contacts with the Communists," said Teodoro Benigno, who worked under Arroyo as press secretary. "They had an obsessive resentment, if not hatred of the military. If Cory had been paranoid, he [Arroyo] reinforced that paranoia." [19]

The contempt was mutual. Since Arroyo had defended Communists, many officers in the armed forces assumed that he himself was a Marxist. But Arroyo and Saguisag saw themselves as Kennedy liberals rather than left-wing ideologues. Arroyo's lifestyle hardly fit the image of a Marxist rebel in the hills; he was prosperous and lived in the same opulent neighborhood as Enrile. "The problem is the military started believing its own propaganda," Saguisag says of the rivalry. "Joker is certainly not a Communist. He's as bourgeois as anyone can be." [20]

The military's contempt for Arroyo was so deep that his very presence at the center of power all but guaranteed friction. "They did not forget their experience in the street," said Jose Almonte, the first colonel promoted to brigadier general under the Aquino administration. And to the military, "Joker Arroyo, his agenda, his aim, seemed to be to just destroy the armed forces." [21]

During the campaign, Aquino had granted an interview to Abe Rosenthal, the managing editor of the New York *Times,* and told him she would offer a cease-fire and dialogue with the rebels. She assured Rosenthal that the majority of them were "not really Communists." The remark sent shock waves through the Reagan administration and sent her supporters scurrying to prove she was not a naive dupe of the left.

19. Interview with Teodoro Benigno by Robert Reid, Makati, April 3, 1991.
20. Saguisag to Reid, April 4, 1991.
21. Interview with General Jose Almonte by Robert Reid, Camp Aguinaldo, Manila, April 3, 1991. Almonte at the time was director of the Economic Intelligence and Information Bureau; he is currently President Ramos's national security adviser.

Her candid remark, however, reflected the views of Arroyo, Saguisag, and others in the Aquino cadre, as well as the opposition movement at large. For years the anti-Marcos opposition had been dealing secretly with the Communists. Centrist opposition groups saw the Communists not so much as enemies of the state but rather Filipinos driven to violence by Marcos's autocratic regime. "Maybe 5 percent were ideologues," Saguisag said. "Ninety-five percent were Filipinos with a grievance who could not seek redress."[22]

Saguisag's observation was not without merit. The party had grown so fast in the 1980s that there had not been time to inculcate the depth of ideological commitment that marked revolutionary movements in China and Vietnam. In addition, the party leadership had shown great flexibility in accommodating the views of such unlikely groups as left-wing priests and nuns, who were members of the allied Christians for National Liberation.

In the euphoria of victory, Aquino's stalwarts underestimated the difficulties of reaching an agreement with the Communists and the effects of such an overture on the armed forces. The president's advisers appeared to assume that the party rank and file would embrace her as their salvation with the same enthusiasm as had the upper-class establishment. That view, however, was not entirely misplaced. The Communists' decision to boycott the presidential election had excluded them from the coalition that came to power. The decision was controversial within the rank and file, many of whose members were willing to see what the new government would offer in terms of reform.

By 1986, the rebel New People's Army was estimated to have about 16,500 fighters operating in two-thirds of the seventy-three provinces. Their numbers were still small, however, when measured against nearly 250,000 soldiers, paramilitary police, and government militias. The party's position, however, was stronger than the numbers of guerrillas implied. Its strength was based on the impressive network of cadres who had infiltrated labor unions, social activist groups, farmers' organizations, banks, university staff, the national media, and the Catholic clergy.

Organized by university lecturer Jose Maria Sison in 1968, from the ranks of the moribund Partido Kommunistang Pilipinas, the party had

22. Saguisag to Reid, April 4, 1991.

followed a Maoist ideology emphasizing a rural base. After Marcos declared martial law in September, 1972, many politically motivated Filipinos began to see the party and its National Democratic Front as the only vehicle for meaningful change. Members were recruited from the University of the Philippines, trade unions, and from among talented rural youth. The National Democratic Front (NDF), which included the party and a dozen allied underground groups, had established an office in Utrecht, the Netherlands, managed by a former priest, Luis Jalandoni. Jalandoni had taken Dutch citizenship, which allowed him to travel throughout Europe to raise funds from left-wing and charitable organizations to fight the Marcos dictatorship.

The party appeared willing to cooperate with Aquino if she had something to offer, and within days of Marcos's ouster, its executive committee urged her to "dismantle the fascist machinery" of the old regime and to pursue "genuine national reconciliation."[23] But the party refused to lay down its arms until the government had demonstrated its good faith.

One of the party's conditions for cooperation was the release of political prisoners, including Sison and Bernabe Buscayno, the founder and former commander of the New People's Army and before that, a young Huk guerrilla when Ninoy was in Tarlac. Release of political prisoners was among Aquino's campaign promises, and several obscure detainees were freed within hours of her inauguration. But Ramos and Enrile raised objections to the unconditional release of hard-core leaders, particularly Sison and Buscayno. Enrile argued that freeing those two without their renouncing the Communists' armed struggle would undermine morale in the armed forces.

Joker Arroyo and Aquino's mother-in-law, Doña Aurora, lobbied strongly to include Sison and Buscayno in any general release. In the case of Buscayno, Cory did not need much convincing. Buscayno and Ninoy had become friends in prison, and the young rebel had refused to testify against him. As noted earlier, personal loyalty was extremely important to Cory Aquino.

In a dank isolation cell at the Camp Crame stockade, Buscayno knew of the objections to his release but hoped his past association with Ninoy would be remembered. On March 4, 1986, his jailers told him he was to

23.   Statement issued to media and party cadres by the Central Committee of the NDF, March 3, 1986, authors' files.

be taken to the Cojuangco building. He suspected he would soon be released, but his first thoughts were what would happen to the chickens he was raising and the stool he had been building to pass the time in prison. [24]

Buscayno and Sison were brought separately to the building. Buscayno, known by his nom de guerre *Ka* [Comrade] *Dante,* saw a large crowd of reporters and photographers assembled outside, and their presence convinced him he would soon be freed. Aquino was waiting for them in her office. "You are now free, Dante," the president told him as the cameras recorded the meeting. "Let us help each other and do good." With that, a man who had fought authority nearly all his adult life walked free. [25]

The releases drew favorable headlines abroad and seemed to underscore Aquino's personal commitment to national reconciliation. It was among the boldest steps she would take as president. But the move deeply angered the armed forces and set the stage for a protracted struggle that would nearly drive her from office and would profoundly influence the course of her people power revolution.

24. Interview with Bernabe Buscayno by Eileen Guerrero, Tarlac province, April 11, 1991.

25. *Ibid.* In contrast, Aquino simply shook Sison's hand but said nothing to him. He is in exile in the Netherlands and not available for comment.

4 CHALLENGE FROM THE RIGHT

THE RELEASE OF Sison and Buscayno stunned not only the military leadership but the rank and file as well. Sison and Buscayno were leaders of a Communist-led insurrection that had been waged since 1969 and that was responsible for the deaths of thousands of their comrades. Soldiers shuddered at the photographs of the new president shaking hands with such men, freed unconditionally without so much as a public recantation. "We had a hard time convincing our soldiers to back up the government," recalls retired major general Ramon Montaño, who at the time was police commander of Manila.[1]

Sison presented a special problem. Years of incarceration had sapped Buscayno of much of his revolutionary zeal, and his chief priority was to return to his family in Tarlac. He had no money and spent his first night of freedom in a convent as guests of the nuns.[2] But Sison gave no sign of wavering in his commitment to armed struggle and a Maoist Philippines. He told audiences throughout the city that the insurgency would continue unless the government adopted, from his viewpoint, an "antiimperialist and antifeudal" line. Later, Sison left the country and resumed leadership

1. Interview with Ramon Montaño by Eileen Guerrero, Camp Crame, Manila, April 9, 1991. At the time, Montaño had retired from the armed forces and was undersecretary of the Department of Interior and Local Government; Montaño spoke primarily in Tagalog and Guerrero translated.
2. Interview with Bernabe Buscayno by Eileen Guerrero, Tarlac province, April 11, 1991.

of the rebel movement from abroad. He has lived in the Netherlands since 1989.

Arroyo's role in the releases fueled military resentment against him. After Enrile's RAM Boys had planted listening devices at the presidential palace, they were well informed of secret contacts between Arroyo and the guerrillas, which were undertaken to speed formal peace talks. "She is very anti-Communist," Teodoro Benigno said of Aquino. "If she released those political prisoners, it was largely the influence of Joker."[3]

A month after Sison and Buscayno were freed, Aquino declared in a commencement address at the University of the Philippines that she would soon announce an indefinite cease-fire and offer peace negotiations. After the speech, Arroyo telephoned former senator Jose Diokno, chairman of the Presidential Commission on Human Rights and Ninoy's former cellmate, and asked him to take charge of the negotiations.

Diokno, a human rights lawyer and grandson of a U.S. immigrant, seemed a logical choice. An ardent nationalist, Diokno shared some of the same goals as the rebels, especially their opposition to a continued U.S. military presence in the country. He had major differences with the Communists, especially over the tactic of armed struggle. Nevertheless, he was respected by the party's Central Committee. He was, however, distrusted by the military and the Americans because of his stand against the U.S. bases. As chairman of the human rights commission, Diokno was threatening to prosecute soldiers accused of torture, murder, and other abuses under Marcos. That alone made him an enemy in the eyes of the armed forces.

In an effort to offset Diokno and appease the United States, Aquino also named Ramon Mitra, her agriculture minister, to the panel. Mitra, a wealthy cattle rancher, had served as a diplomat in Washington and New York before entering politics and was friends with New York's Congressman Stephen Solarz, the chairman of the House Subcommittee on Asia and Pacific Affairs.

The Communists recommended as their chief negotiator Saturnino Ocampo, a forty-seven-year-old former journalist who had escaped from detention in 1985 and returned to the underground. During his detention, Ocampo's lawyer was none other than Joker Arroyo. Joining Ocampo on

---

3. Interview with Teodoro Benigno by Robert Reid, Makati, April 3, 1991.

the panel were his common-law wife, Carolina "Bobbie" Malay, and Antonio Zumel, another former journalist whose brother, Brigadier General Jose Maria Zumel, was a Marcos stalwart and former superintendent of the Philippine Military Academy.

Arroyo's past association with Ocampo was seen in the armed forces as another sign of the government's alleged left-wing, antimilitary bias. On June 4, the armed forces released an eight-page assessment of internal security; it argued that the insurgency showed no sign of abating despite Aquino's rise to power. The report claimed that the rebels were exploiting the "prevailing liberal atmosphere" to expand their control of villages throughout the islands. Moreover, the report complained that Pimentel's regional appointees were not cooperating with local commanders in curbing lawlessness.[4]

Statistics in the Philippines are notoriously unreliable, and it is difficult to judge the report's findings. Its public release, however, was a clear sign that the military was seeking to use its influence to hinder the new government's reconciliation program.

Enrile escalated the campaign a month later when he declared publicly that Communists were being appointed to important posts in the Aquino administration. He then leaked to sympathetic reporters the names of five "subversives"; none held cabinet rank but all acknowledged former ties with the underground. Most of them quickly resigned to spare Aquino embarrassment.

Meanwhile, Enrile began to suspect that the policy of reconciliation was being applied more vigorously to the political left than to holdovers from the Marcos government. Early in the Aquino administration, Enrile seemed genuinely anxious to cooperate, if for no other reason than to preserve his powerful position as minister of national defense. Although Enrile had publicly questioned the release of political prisoners, he told the president privately that he understood the necessity of that step and accepted it.[5]

Enrile also used General Almonte to relay a message to the presidential staff that spelled out his own view of his relationship with Aquino. According to Almonte, Enrile asked him to tell Arroyo that he was an ambitious politician who wanted to be president someday, but Enrile realized

4. The AFP report was distributed to news media in Manila, AP files.
5. Captain Rex Robles, oral communication to Robert Reid, Makati, May 10, 1991.

Aquino's prestige was so strong that challenging her would be political suicide. Enrile acknowledged that he needed Cory but added that if her administration tried to undermine him, "I'll fight you."[6]

But Arroyo and his allies had no use for Enrile and considered him a powerful threat. As Marcos's defense minister, Enrile had served as chief martial law administrator, something the others in government could never forgive. The fact that he had turned against Marcos only served to reinforce their suspicions that the mercurial Enrile was a fox who could not be trusted.

Rather than accommodate Enrile, the presidential staff lost no opportunity to embarrass and undermine him. In March, Aquino promoted an air force lieutenant colonel, Adelberto Yap, to full colonel after the officer's young wife Lorna, an outspoken critic of Marcos, appealed to the new president directly. Yap's career, like many others, had been stagnated because he was not a Marcos favorite. Yap was promoted over thirty-four other senior officers, and Enrile considered the move as presidential favoritism and a breach of his own authority.

Worse still, from Enrile's perspective, were remarks Aquino made on March 22 to the graduating class at the Philippine Military Academy in Baguio. She promised reforms in the ranks, including an end to favoritism, and assured the cadets that she would not hesitate to confront the Communists if they refused peace overtures. She then added that as a sign of the military's important role in her government, General Ramos, as chief of staff, would report directly to her.

Enrile, who was seated on the podium, froze at those words; the muscles of his face visibly tightened as he withheld his rage. As minister of national defense, Enrile nominally stood second in the chain of command between Aquino and Ramos. Now he was being bypassed, as he had been in the final years of the Marcos era.

The offending sentence had been added to the text by Locsin, Arroyo's ally in the palace.[7] Although the statement attracted little public attention at the time, the wily Enrile saw it for what it was: a not very subtle move by the antimilitary clique to ease him from the center of power.

6. Interview with General Jose Almonte by Robert Reid, Camp Aguinaldo, Manila, April 3, 1991.
7. Corazon Aquino, commencement speech, Baguio, March 22, 1986, AP files; the information about the addition by Locsin and Enrile's anger is from the interview with Rene Saguisag by Robert Reid, Pasay City, April 4, 1991.

Such intrigues made for a volatile and dangerous mix. At a time when the administration was preaching reconciliation, personal rivalry was widening the rifts in a government that needed cohesion and cooperation to confront its manifold crises and threats. In addition, the phenomenon of petty politics and jealousies that was tearing the coalition apart was not limited to national power struggles involving Enrile and Laurel. It had spread throughout the country. The wholesale replacement of elected officials nationwide had exported the turmoil of Manila to the provinces. Many of Pimentel's appointees proved incompetent or lacked sufficient stature to confront locally popular political leaders identified with the previous regime. The coalition that had achieved such an astonishing victory only a month earlier was destroying itself, in large measure because of political inexperience, ineptness, and pettiness at the top. It did not take long for Marcos loyalists to realize that the chaos presented an opportunity undreamed of during the dispiriting days of February.

Despite Marcos's unfavorable image in Manila and abroad, the former president still enjoyed considerable support in the provinces, especially in his native north, home of the Ilocano-speaking minority. The six million Ilocanos, a clannish, frugal people, revered Marcos as one of their own. For years after he was gone, Marcos's picture still hung in government offices throughout the Ilocano districts.

The new government promised "maximum tolerance" of public dissent, and in a public relations gesture, the Aquino administration even had the phrase emblazoned on plastic shields carried by riot police. The Marcos camp took advantage of the administration's tolerance to organize weekly rallies in Manila parks. Right-wing radio stations broadcast telephone interviews with the ousted president, who urged his followers to join the demonstrations.

On March 31, nine days after proclamation of the freedom constitution, Marcos supporters gathered at the Intercontinental Hotel in suburban Makati and called for a reconvening of the National Assembly. Two weeks later, they met again at the Asian Institute of Tourism and "reconvened" the legislature. Arturo Tolentino, who had not even bothered to show up for his own "inauguration" as vice-president, called for a civil disobedience campaign. Outside the institute, about two thousand Marcos loyalists chanted "We want our president back."

A few miles to the northwest, in Manila's San Juan suburb, about one thousand Marcos supporters barricaded the city hall to protest the government's dismissal of their mayor, Joseph Estrada, a popular film star and friend of the Marcoses. Police fired into the crowd, killing one person. Still, Arroyo and Saguisag scoffed at suggestions that the Marcos forces posed a serious threat. [8]

On May 1, during Labor Day celebrations, thousands of Marcos loyalists battled riot police. More than thirty people were arrested and nearly eighty injured. This time, the government acted. Aquino fired Manila police chief Narciso Cabrera and replaced him with Alfredo Lim, a tough Chinese-Filipino who would become one of her most trusted allies in the security forces. "Our new democracy has been criticized because it is tolerant of agitation," she said in a statement to the press. "This is regarded by certain quarters as weakness. It is not." The administration, however, was trapped by its own rhetoric. The Aquino government was swept to power in part by street demonstrations, and its leaders were veterans of protest marches. Using force to stifle dissent would have made a mockery of people power ideals and embarrassed a government supremely conscious of its image.

Restraint served only to embolden the Marcos loyalists. On June 8, nearly twenty thousand of them gathered in Rizal Park in the center of Manila and at sunset began marching to Malacañang Palace chanting *Marcos pa rin,* or "We're still for Marcos." They brushed aside the barbed-wire barricades at the Mendiola Bridge about a half mile from the palace grounds. Riot police under Lim's personal command fired tear gas and water cannons, but the protesters simply fell back, regrouped, and battled police in the side streets near the bridge. More than twenty people were hospitalized.

The government dismissed the rioters as hooligans paid by the Marcos faction. But the Marcos die-hards had fielded such a large crowd by exploiting anger at the dismissal of popular local officials such as Estrada. "Democracy is a government of the people and for the people," fumed attorney Rafael Recto, a Marcos loyalist, to reporters. "But the Philippines is the only country that has no elected officials."

The attack on Malacañang was a dress rehearsal for a loyalist putsch still to come. In February, the loyalists had seen how rapidly events had

8. Saguisag to Reid, April 4, 1991.

unfolded and how the chemistry of a small military mutiny coupled with an outpouring of people into the streets had mushroomed into a full-scale uprising. They dreamed of using the same formula to trigger their own counter-revolution and topple the new government.

Manila was an anti-Marcos stronghold. Thus, if the plan were to succeed, the loyalists would need to organize support in pro-Marcos areas north of the capital. Under a plan drafted in May by Lieutenant Colonel Rolando Abadilla, the former intelligence chief of Manila, loyalist civilians would begin marching southward toward the capital, joined along the way by soldiers disaffected with the new government's stand against the Communists. They were to converge on Manila and bring the new government to its knees.

Senior officers, including Ramos and Brigadier General Ramon Montaño, learned of the plan from informants in the ranks, but at first they believed it could not succeed. The new government, however, had been seriously weakened by factionalism, and broad sections of the military were angry over the release of leftist prisoners. The major question was, could generals loyal to Aquino muster enough support within the ranks to defend the new government?[9]

The loyalists struck on Sunday, July 6, while Aquino and Ramos were visiting Cagayan de Oro on the northern coast of Mindanao Island, about five hundred miles south of the capital. The day before, Tolentino and several of his followers had checked into the Manila Hotel, a luxurious, Spanish-style structure once used as General Douglas MacArthur's residence; of late it was the unofficial headquarters of the foreign press in the Philippines. The hotel was conveniently located near the Luneta Grandstand and Rizal Park, the favored rally venue of the loyalists. That afternoon, about ten thousand of them began gathering, as they had every Sunday for months, for the weekly rally. About 4:00 P.M., several truckloads of armed soldiers wearing bandanas of the Guardians, one of several military fraternal organizations, drove up to the hotel, barged inside, and informed the management they were taking over the hotel.

One hour later, the seventy-six-year-old Tolentino appeared in the lobby and read a letter from Marcos proclaiming him as the "legitimate head of the country until such time that I return to the Philippines." The

9. Montaño interview by Guerrero, April 9, 1991.

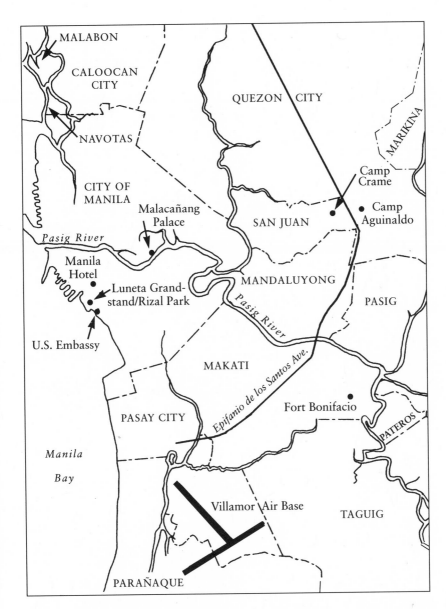

Map 3. Metro Manila. Officially the capital, Metro Manila consists of about seventeen chartered cities and incorporated municipalities, most of which are shown above. Effectively, they are all one city.

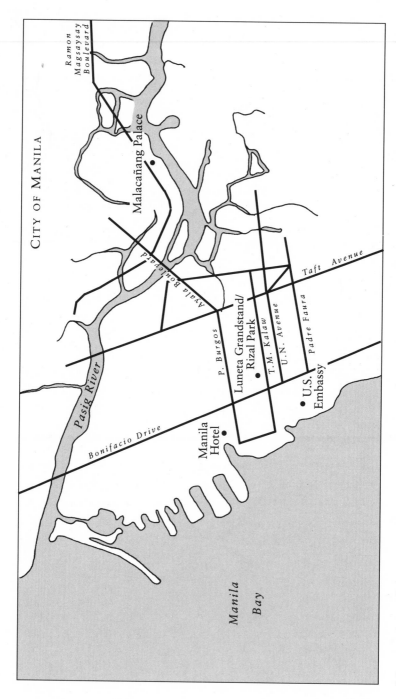

Map 4. Area of the Manila Hotel coup attempt against President Aquino in July, 1986.

proclamation also appointed Enrile as "acting prime minister" and retained Ramos as chief of staff. Tolentino and Recto then left for their rooms to telephone Marcos in Honolulu.[10]

In Cagayan de Oro, Aquino laughed off Tolentino's move and told reporters, "It's best to ignore him." To demonstrate her lack of concern, she went ahead with scheduled visits to military camps in the area. In Manila, however, military commanders realized the gravity of the situation. With Ramos in Cagayan de Oro, the vice-chief of staff, Lieutenant General Salvador Mison, ordered marines to set up checkpoints around the hotel to prevent food and water from reaching the loyalists. Montaño learned that military units were moving south from Camp Olivas, a major headquarters in the central Luzon town of San Fernando, to reinforce the mutineers.

Montaño dispatched forces to intercept them along the four-lane highway connecting Manila with San Fernando. He recalls that many of the soldiers thought they were coming to save the government from Communist rebels and to rescue Ramos and Enrile from leftists.[11] They were turned back without any major clashes. The reactions of Mison and Montaño isolated the mutineers and prevented them from receiving the help they had expected.

At the hotel, the rebellion took on a rowdy, almost carnival atmosphere, more in keeping with the Filipino spirit of frivolity than with a deadly serious challenge to the government. The crowd included former parliamentarians, military officers, and show business personalities who had been favored by Imelda Marcos. Others had been recruited from the slums of Manila and paid off with food and cash to swell the ranks. The most visible figures there were all closely associated with Marcos and the loyalist movement. They included Imelda's former bodyguard, Brigadier General Zumel; former National Assembly speaker Nicanor Yñiguez; and Lieutenant Colonel Abadilla.

The crowd acted as if they were Visigoths on a rampage through Rome. They cleaned out the kitchen's stock of expensive food and drink, drained the bar, and lounged casually around the hotel pool. The lobby was littered with empty champagne bottles, scraps of food, and other debris.

The unseen hand in the takeover, however, was Juan Ponce Enrile.

10. The Manila Hotel affair was covered by Eileen Guerrero for the Associated Press.
11. Montaño interview by Guerrero, April 9, 1991.

Enrile never acknowledged any role in the Manila Hotel incident and was careful to distance himself, but not too far, from the coup attempt. Soon after Tolentino "appointed" him as acting prime minister, Enrile joked during a television interview that although he was flattered, he was not looking for another job. But RAM's intelligence chief, Lieutenant Colonel Red Kapunan, knew of the plot in advance, as did others in the Enrile clique. According to Montaño, the unofficial leader of the RAM group, Lieutenant Colonel Gregorio Honasan, flew in a helicopter over the area and decided against joining the putsch because the loyalist force was too small. [12]

What is unclear is whether Enrile secretly helped plan the takeover or simply was aware of it. Judging from Enrile's cautious style, he probably knew most of the details of the plan but decided it would not succeed. Rather than abort the plan by notifying Aquino, he most likely decided to see how the government would react, which commanders would remain loyal, and whether the incident would frighten the palace into currying his favor.

Aquino returned to Manila on Monday, July 7, and called an emergency cabinet meeting. Major General Rodolfo Canieso, a burly, crew-cut figure with a bulldog face, offered to "level" the hotel and finish off the loyalists once and for all. [13] The idea horrified Aquino's human rights advisers. The Manila Hotel was virtually a national historical shrine; General Douglas MacArthur lived there before World War II, and the hotel had been the city's premier social gathering place for generations. It was currently filled with foreign reporters and television crews, and bloodshed there would have shattered Cory Aquino's prized international reputation as a champion of peace.

Enrile recommended that the loyalists be given a deadline to surrender without fear of criminal charges if they swore allegiance to the freedom constitution. In a gesture of accommodation, Saguisag endorsed Enrile's recommendation. To ease the tension, Saguisag joked that the loyalists be told "the last man out pays the hotel bill." [14] The cabinet gave Tolentino and his followers until 2:00 P.M. on July 8 to clear out of the hotel.

After hearing of the deadline, Tolentino summoned reporters and

12. *Ibid.*
13. Saguisag interview by Reid, April 4, 1991.
14. *Ibid.*

claimed he had "no real role" in planning the takeover. All he wanted, he said, was new local elections as soon as possible. A loyalist delegation met at the Quirino Grandstand, across the park from the hotel, with Honasan, Cory's son, Benigno "Noynoy" Aquino III, and two of Montaño's deputies to negotiate a surrender. Most of the loyalists simply drifted away, leaving behind about a half-million dollars in damage and unpaid bills. Thirty-seven hours after it began, the mutiny was over.

On Tuesday, July 8, Ramos formally accepted the surrender of the mutinous soldiers, including four generals and sixty-nine troopers, during a ceremony at the gymnasium at Fort Bonifacio, the army headquarters in Makati. Ramos was relieved the rebellion was over but confided to associates that the government had been too lenient in agreeing not to press charges. As he was fond of exercising to relieve tension, he suggested that the mutineers join him in push-ups, which they did. That gave rise to a story that the rebels had been required to do thirty push-ups as their "punishment." In fact, there was no punishment at all. [15]

Tolentino and forty others were indicted later for subversion, but the charges were quietly dropped. Political Affairs Minister Antonio Cuenco explained at a news conference that the government did not want to take the risks of divisive courts-martial or civilian trials.

The decision not to punish the loyalists widened the rift in the cabinet. Pimentel told Enrile that the mutineers should be arrested and even shot, and Locsin fumed: "The trouble is, we have a military we cannot trust." [16]

In Washington, the Reagan administration put Marcos on notice that it would not tolerate any conspiracy planned by him while he was on U.S. soil. "Mr. Marcos's political influence and effectiveness is at an end," spokesman Bernard Kalb said in a statement from the State Department.

Aquino took heart in the fact that the rebellion attracted little public attention, much less support. The rest of the city went about its business. Most military commanders had remained loyal or at least had simply sat back and waited to see how events would unfold. But the government paid a high price for its presumed victory. Allowing open rebellion to go unpunished reinforced the perception that Aquino and her ministers were weak, unskilled, and indecisive. She had vowed she would not tolerate

15. Montaño interview by Guerrero, April 9, 1991.

16. Teodoro Locsin, oral communication to Eileen Guerrero, Manila, September 15, 1991.

open rebellion but in fact had done just that. Leniency toward the Manila Hotel mutineers set off the cycle of military revolts that dramatically altered the course of the Aquino administration.

The end of the Manila Hotel episode bought time for the beleaguered Aquino government but failed to silence either its internal squabbling or protests by the Marcos followers. Aquino took trips to Singapore and the United States, where she was fawned over by U.S. politicians who had once expressed grave doubts about her leadership. At home, the administration pushed forward with drafting a new constitution, which was supposed to guarantee stability and place the government back on a firm legal footing.

Aquino also made highly publicized visits to remote areas of the country to meet with Nur Misuari, leader of the Muslim rebels, and former Roman Catholic priest Conrado Balweg, chief of a band of mountain tribesmen who had been allied with the Communists. Both agreed to work for peace. Such gestures of reconciliation, however, were not directed toward the Marcos camp, nor to Enrile's followers, still nominally part of the administration but clearly and deeply estranged.

Despite their failure at the Manila Hotel, the Marcos loyalists were soon back in the streets. Three weeks after the hotel putsch, they rallied again in Luneta Park under the guise of a singing contest. Police dispersed them, but as the crowd was leaving, members attacked and beat to death a young man who was wearing a yellow T-shirt, the color of Aquino's campaign. Several loyalists were arrested for illegal assembly but were soon freed on bail.

Aquino's problems with Enrile were getting worse. Sensing that the government was weak and that Arroyo was out to get him, Enrile struck ever more stridently. He declared that the freedom constitution had removed the legal foundation of the Aquino government. The administration, he reasoned, was a coalition of the forces that had brought it to power, including the armed forces. To remove any one group, including himself, was tantamount to a collapse of the government. Enrile missed no opportunity to warn that the Communist menace was growing and that Pimentel's appointees were sympathetic to the insurgents. Privately, he joked to his RAM associates that the government appeared bent on its own destruction.[17]

17. Robles to Reid, May 10, 1991.

Enrile's criticism was attracting headlines and making him the focal point of the conflict between the armed forces and President Aquino. That, however, obscured the roles played by the RAM officers themselves, especially the charismatic lieutenant colonel, Gregorio "Gringo" Honasan.

Tall for a Filipino, Gringo had a trim, athletic build and macho swagger that made him appear younger than his forty years. His narrow face and dark moustache gave him a rather roguish appearance, in contrast to a squeaky voice that, when he became excited, reminded listeners of a bird's chirping. Legends of his exploits abounded in the armed forces. He was fond of parachuting with a pet snake wrapped around his shoulders and was rumored to have a collection of human ears cut from the bodies of Muslim rebels.

Gringo Honasan was more than a swaggering cult figure. Associates described him as keenly intelligent, with a sharp analytical mind and strongly held views that bordered on megalomania. He was an admirer of Mustafa Kemal, the Turkish general who modernized his country at gunpoint after the collapse of the Ottoman Empire in World War I.

Gringo and his colleagues believed Philippine society must go through a cleansing by fire if it were to free itself from the shackles of poverty, oppression, and injustice. Most of the RAM leaders came from the lower middle class, and they viewed traditional politics and traditional politicians as manifestations of all that was wrong with Philippine society. To them, the duty of the armed forces was to defend the nation not only from foreign aggressors and internal subversion but from ruinous government as well. RAM gave them an organization with the discipline and force to serve as a vehicle for change. Gringo and the others thought they had taken a step toward change in February, 1986, when they mutinied against Marcos. Instead, Cory Aquino and her gang of squabbling, opportunist politicians had snatched the power they thought was rightfully theirs.

They viewed the "February Revolution" not as a glorious affirmation of popular will but simply as a military coup with hundreds of thousands of spectators playing supporting roles. During meetings with foreign reporters, members of the clique spoke openly of their admiration for the Indonesian military, which guided political life in that country after crushing an abortive Communist uprising in 1965.[18]

18. Material on Honasan and his colleagues comes from the Almonte interview by Reid, April 3, 1991, and the Montaño interview by Guerrero, April 9, 1991.

The motives of Honasan and the other RAM Boys are likely to remain the subject of controversy for decades. Critics dismiss them as megalomaniacs who missed the power and privilege Marcos bestowed on the armed forces during martial law. Retired Brigadier General Jose Almonte, who once served as an unofficial RAM adviser, told one of the authors in a 1991 interview that their motives, if not their tactics, were admirable: "To lessen the gap between rich and poor. This was the usual line but we really meant it. These are not just motherhood statements. . . . Some of them [RAM members] were just too inflexible as to what they perceive as good government."

Although RAM was supposedly an alliance of equals, Honasan occupied a special place because of his relationship with Enrile. "Enrile thought he could develop Honasan into his protégé," Robles said. "Enrile admired Honasan, and it was almost like father and son."[19]

At the same time, Honasan and the others used Enrile, playing on his ego, ambitions, and paranoia about Joker Arroyo to support their grandiose plans. Although he shared their misgivings about the direction of the Aquino government, Juan Ponce Enrile was a wealthy man, an establishment figure, and a product of the same political system that had created the traditional politicians whom the RAM Boys despised. "It was not Enrile who manipulated Gringo," recalled Montaño. "It was Gringo who manipulated Enrile."[20]

As events unfolded, Enrile found himself pressed by his RAM Boys into ever more strident positions, which won him international headlines but isolated him from the political mainstream. In August, 1986, Enrile endorsed the government's peace overtures to the Communists and even volunteered his personal assurances for the safety of rebel negotiators. A few weeks later, he was traveling throughout the country, sounding the alarm over the "Communist threat."

He openly called for the dismissal of several left-wing cabinet colleagues, among them Labor Minister Augusto Sanchez, who in turn demanded that Aquino fire Enrile. "Maybe these people are not aware that when I lose my patience, I am like Rambo," Enrile told reporters on September 9. Privately, however, he was growing more and more concerned over his position in the administration. He traveled throughout the coun-

19. Robles to Reid, May 10, 1991.
20. Montaño interview by Guerrero, April 9, 1991.

try seeking support from field commanders, delivering a message that Aquino was surrounded by leftists bent on destroying the armed forces.

The key to Enrile's strategy was General Ramos. It was Ramos who had brought over military commanders during the February revolt against Marcos, and only Ramos could prevent Enrile from exerting control of the senior ranks. Even though he shared many of Enrile's concerns about the direction of the government, Ramos knew the armed forces was so factionalized that a full-scale putsch would probably destroy the institution. He also knew the United States would never sanction a military coup and would cut off aid if Aquino were ousted. On the other hand, Ramos understood the depth of hostility in the ranks toward the president and her administration. His strategy was to buy time, to keep his links to Enrile's clique, and to dissuade them from launching a coup. Ramos urged RAM and senior commanders to give him time to win over Aquino and convince her to make changes in her government.[21]

The palace knew the risks of confronting Enrile head-on and was unsure how the chain of command would react in a showdown. It was a time of great tension and uncertainty. "Many a day, we didn't know whether we would be around the next day," Saguisag recalled.[22]

On October 21, Aquino attended a late-night meeting with Enrile, Ramos, and Vice-President Laurel at the home of Edgardo Angara, president of the University of the Philippines. Although Enrile and Ramos expressed their concerns about government policy, particularly peace overtures to the Communists, Aquino came away with the feeling that Enrile would hold off on any move against her. The next day, in a gesture toward the armed forces, she told a women's convention that the Communists must accept a cease-fire or face a "declaration of war." After the speech, she told reporters, "There is no falling out between Minister Enrile and me."

Reconciliation proved short-lived, however. Four days later, Enrile appeared before twenty thousand Marcos supporters at a downtown Manila rally, where he vowed that the armed forces would not allow the country to go Communist. It marked the first time that Enrile had spoken before an avowedly pro-Marcos crowd since the February uprising. He stood on the platform as the crowd chanted "Down with Cory."

Enrile's appearance before the loyalists set off alarm bells, both at Ma-

21. Saguisag interview by Reid, April 4, 1991.
22. *Ibid.*

lacañang and in Washington. After the rally, the State Department called Cory Aquino the "best hope" for peace and prosperity and expressed satisfaction over her dealings with the Communists. Congressman Stephen Solarz suggested during a visit to Manila that it was time to call Enrile's bluff and fire him.[23]

Enrile knew his position was becoming untenable. On the night of November 4, he attended a promotion party at Fort Bonifacio, along with commanders of the four branches of the armed forces, and outlined vague plans for a coup. His plan called for selected units to strike at midnight, November 11, a few hours after the president was to leave for a four-day visit to Japan. The plan, known by its code name, "God Save the Queen," called for arresting Arroyo and other "leftists" in the government and reducing Aquino, the "queen," to a purely figurehead role.[24]

General Montaño heard of the plan from informants within Honasan's clique. They told him Gringo had created a strike force of six battalions with another fourteen in reserve. Most of the commanders were Gringo's classmates from the Philippine Military Academy, and he could count on their personal loyalty. Ominously, Montaño was told that Ramos was part of the conspiracy.

Montaño then confronted Ramos after a breakfast meeting and asked if rumors of his involvement were true. Ramos was shocked. He denied any role and asked Montaño for the names of those linked to the conspiracy. As he reeled off names of senior commanders, Montaño says Ramos "nearly swallowed his cigar."[25]

Ramos decided to skip the weekly cabinet meeting and use the time to try to reach Enrile. He sent Montaño and Major General Renato de Villa to the cabinet session as his representatives but with clear instructions to say nothing about any planned coup.

By the time Montaño and de Villa arrived at the presidential compound, coup rumors were sweeping the city, and a Manila newspaper,

23. The Davide Commission, *Final Report of the Fact-Finding Commission* (Makati, 1990), 147. In late 1989, Aquino appointed a presidential commission headed by Hilario Davide to investigate the entire cycle of coup attempts that had plagued her term in office (see Chapter 13). Copies of the commission's report are widely available through bookstores, the National Library, or the PIA.

24. *Business Day,* Manila, November 5, 1986; this was a Manila daily paper that is no longer in business. See also Davide Commission *Final Report,* 148–49.

25. Montaño interview by Guerrero, April 9, 1991.

Business Day, had reported details of the plan, including its code name. "They were all running around like chickens with their heads cut off," Montaño said of the cabinet members. "They kept asking, 'What's going on with the armed forces? What's Ramos doing?' " [26]

The two generals feigned ignorance. "If we said anything, we would just panic them," Montaño said. At Camp Aguinaldo, Ramos confronted Honasan and his lieutenants; after lengthy talks, they promised to postpone a coup. The officers spelled out their demands, including a purge of leftists from the cabinet. Aquino then summoned the four service commanders to her office and asked them point-blank if she would still be president when she returned from Japan. The four pledged their support. [27]

Confident that a coup had been averted, Aquino decided to go ahead with the Japanese visit. "I am confident that when I leave there will be no coup, and even while I remain abroad, there will be no coup," she said. But a stubborn display of bravado on her part nearly unraveled Ramos's efforts to pacify Honasan. On Sunday, November 9, one day before her scheduled departure, the president appeared before a convention of Filipino dentists and denounced the "self-appointed messiahs" and "misguided elements" who were plotting against her. [28]

Enrile was outraged, and Ramos, fearing the coup was back on schedule, summoned Honasan and his followers to an afternoon meeting at Camp Aguinaldo. Confirming Ramos's fears, the officers showed up wearing special scarves, their badge of identification during the February mutiny. Ramos warned them that if they went ahead with their "surgical operation," he and others would resist and the country would plunge into civil war. [29]

Aquino left for Japan the next day, and both Ramos and Enrile sought to convey a sense of calm to the public. Ramos, however, learned that a faction within RAM was still lobbying strongly for a coup. He issued a statement to the newspapers declaring that the situation was stable and the country secure but hurried to his office at Camp Aguinaldo and telephoned Montaño. "You better deploy according to your plan," Ramos

26. *Ibid.*
27. Davide Commission *Final Report,* 149.
28. *Ibid.,* 150.
29. *Ibid.,* 150–51.

said. Montaño asked why. "They are going [ahead with the plan]," Ramos replied. "You better find out what's happening, why it's 'go' all of a sudden."[30]

As Montaño's troops began quietly taking up defensive positions at broadcast stations, power plants, and other strategic points, Ramos resumed his contacts with Enrile, urging restraint. After conferring with his RAM Boys, Enrile assured Ramos the coup was off.[31]

On the day Aquino returned from Japan, another crisis emerged. The body of Rolando Olalia, leader of the left-wing May First Movement labor federation and the left-wing People's Party, was found in a ditch on the outskirts of the capital. His driver's body was found a short distance away. Olalia's family had reported him missing that morning after he failed to come home from a labor meeting. Both victims had newspapers stuffed in their mouths and their eyes gouged out.

Olalia was among the country's most prominent leftist leaders. He had served as a liaison between members of the new administration and the Marxist underground. A few days before his death, Olalia promised to organize resistance if Aquino were overthrown in a coup. His death prompted speculation that the killing was somehow linked to the RAM conspiracy. The National Bureau of Investigation later found evidence that he had been under military surveillance.[32]

Two military intelligence agents were eventually arrested for the Olalia killing, but they were acquitted because the trial judge ruled that it was too dark for alleged witnesses of the abduction to have positively identified the perpetrators. It seemed likely, however, that the killing was carried out by members of the armed forces, perhaps RAM, to instigate a violent response from the left. That, in turn, would have been a pretext for a military coup to restore public order. But the left held back, fearing that any protest would simply play into the hands of the conspirators.

Meanwhile, the RAM conspirators—now uncertain about support from senior commanders—modified their strategy and adopted a course of action that contained some elements used successfully in the February putsch. They would seize the National Assembly building before dawn on November 23, then reconvene the legislature, which Aquino had abol-

30. Montaño interview by Guerrero, April 9, 1991.
31. Davide Commission *Final Report*, 151.
32. *Ibid.*

ished eight months before. With the help of pro-Marcos legislators, the conspirators would proclaim the former assembly speaker, Nicanor Yñiguez, as interim president pending new elections. Such a move would give the putsch the appearance of a "constitutional rescue."[33]

On the morning of November 22, Montaño received word of the plan through his informants and passed along the information to Ramos, who ordered troops to seal off the entrance to Camp Aguinaldo, headquarters of the armed forces and the Ministry of National Defense. Three battalions of loyal troops were sent to protect the National Assembly building, and additional forces were deployed around broadcast stations and Malacañang Palace.[34]

Still, RAM believed it had enough forces outside the camp to launch the coup on schedule. Although the main gate to Camp Aguinaldo was closed, other exits were lightly guarded. All that remained was the "go" signal from Enrile. It never came. As the deadline for launching the coup approached, Enrile passed the word that the putsch was off. His officers were stunned.

At the critical moment, Juan Ponce Enrile had lost his nerve. "We showed him the list of people we [the RAM Boys] were going to hit, maybe thirty of them," Robles said. "Some of them were his friends." Ramos saw his opportunity, and with the conspirators in disarray, he sent instructions to commanders nationwide: disregard the orders of the minister of national defense or Colonel Honasan. The coup attempt had been neutralized without firing a shot.[35]

The next day, a Sunday, Aquino summoned Enrile to her office. He arrived about 1:45 P.M. Gone was the brash, self-confident man who weeks before had threatened to bring down the government. Enrile had been so shaken by the tension of the previous night that he had taken sedatives to sleep and arrived at the palace sullen and groggy. During his meeting with the president, his eyes shifted away from her face as they spoke, and his body jerked slightly when she reached for his shoulder in a personal gesture.[36] Aquino demanded the resignations of all her cabinet

33. Soledad Vanzi, former aide to Imelda Marcos, to Robert Reid, Manila, November 23, 1986.
34. Montaño interview by Guerrero, April 9, 1991.
35. Robles to Reid, May 10, 1991
36. Interview with Aquilino Pimentel by Robert Reid, Manila, May 8, 1991.

members but accepted only one that day: Juan Ponce Enrile. She named his deputy, Rafael Ileto, to succeed him. "Of late, my circumspection has been viewed as weakness, and my sincere attempts at reconciliation as indecisive," she said in a nationwide television address. "This cannot continue." She promised a "fresh start" and "stern measures" against the conspirators.[37]

Her promise turned out to be nothing more than words. The precedent of kid-glove treatment that was set during the Manila Hotel incident was again followed by the government. Enrile was fired but was never charged, and a few months later, he was elected to the senate. Honasan and the others were eventually transferred from their comfortable jobs at the Defense Ministry, but they kept their military ranks. For the second time in six months, rebellion would go unpunished. But the clique of officers who were once lauded as heroes was now denounced for trying the same tactics that had helped bring Aquino to power.

She had won, but her victory was not without a heavy price. In the aftermath, she removed Pimentel and three other cabinet members who had fallen out of favor with the military. Allowing Ramos a free hand to contain the rebellion did little to dispel Aquino's image of weakness and made the president appear beholden to him. That boosted Ramos's public image but at the expense of the full trust of the civilian government.

Enrile's bid for power had failed, and the man who once threatened to "do a Rambo" returned quietly to his villa in Makati's exclusive Dasmariñas Village. That night, Enrile received a few friends from the military who had come by to pay their respects. Ironically, the callers included Ramos and Montaño, who played important roles in quashing Enrile's plans. Rather than looking defeated, Enrile appeared serene and at peace with himself. According to Montaño, it was as if a terrible burden had been lifted from his shoulders.[38]

37. Corazon Aquino, address to the nation, People's Television, November 23, 1986.
38. Montaño interview by Guerrero, April 9, 1991.

5 PEACE CHARADE

ENRILE'S DISMISSAL AND Aquino's ultimatum to the left to accept a cease-fire broke the logjam in talks between the government and the Communists and produced a truce accord four days later. But months of bitter political feuding within the administration over its policy toward the left had sapped the peace process of its vitality. Both parties went into the talks like teenagers in a shotgun marriage, forced by circumstances into an arrangement neither expected would succeed.

The crisis between Malacañang and the Ministry of National Defense made Cory Aquino reluctant to do anything that might alienate Ramos and his clique of loyal generals whom she had depended upon to save her people power revolution. Other influential forces had little interest in offering the Communists more than an honorable surrender. The Roman Catholic hierarchy was preaching peace and national reconciliation, but clearly on Cory's terms. Since Aquino took power, Cardinal Sin had been urging "our brothers in the hills" to lay down their arms and to give her government the chance to prove it was sincere. It was a pious way of telling the rebels to give up the struggle at a time when they were in no imminent danger of defeat and when they had no guarantees the administration's "sincerity" would produce programs acceptable to them.

Meanwhile, the business community and its champions in the cabinet, Ongpin and Concepcion, were urging implementation of economic programs that the left could not accept. The business community wanted to deregulate private enterprise and to open the country to foreign investment, not a Marxist agenda. Ongpin strongly opposed the left's demands for repudiating "unfair" foreign debts and for placing limitations on foreign investment.

Despite anticommunist propaganda from the Marcos camp and the uninformed fears within the military establishment, Cory Aquino had no intention of accommodating the left on issues of policy and principle. A conservative Catholic upbringing had left her with no sympathy for "godless Communism." The decision by the Communists to boycott the 1986 election reinforced her conviction that the left was an unreliable ally.

She was willing to talk with the Marxists, but on her terms, and her candid remarks revealed little personal sympathy for the rebels. Soon after assuming office, she was asked to comment on recommendations that soldiers be withdrawn from villages where drinking sprees and other abuses had produced friction with the civilian inhabitants. "They cannot just be sent back to the barracks because I do not want the insurgents to take over," she told the Manila *Chronicle* in an interview.

She would offer peace to those who wanted it and deal harshly with the hard-liners who refused. "My government is willing to negotiate with the top leadership of the Communist Party," she said in a speech in April, 1986. But she added that if the rebels refused to accept "an honorable peace," they would no longer face the "old, dispirited army of Marcos" but that of a government with popular support.[1]

Two months after she made the peace offer, U.S. Secretary of State George Shultz visited Manila and gave Washington's blessing to her initiative. Shultz came away from a meeting with Aquino on June 25, satisfied that she would limit the negotiations to a cease-fire and some form of amnesty but that substantive issues, such as power sharing and the fate of U.S. military bases, would not be placed on the table. "It's not about power sharing but about the return of the people to the normal stream of life and an ability to take part in the political process if they want," Shultz told reporters after the meeting. Shultz added that he had been assured the government would not begin serious negotiations on the agenda offered up by the insurgents.

What was this Marxist agenda that Aquino and the United States

1. Corazon Aquino, commencement speech at the University of the Philippines, Quezon City, April 20, 1986.

deemed unworthy of discussion? The list included some demands the government could not be expected to accept. The National Democratic Front (NDF) wanted formal recognition as the representative "of all democratic forces engaged in armed struggle." Front guerrillas were to be considered combatants under the Geneva Convention, rather than common criminals, which would mean captured rebels could no longer be placed on trial for crimes such as rebellion, murder, or illegal possession of weapons. Instead, the government would be required to treat them as prisoners of war subject to visits by the International Committee of the Red Cross.

Many of the rebel demands, however, came straight from Cory Aquino's own campaign platform. These included land reform, reorganization of the armed forces, punishment of soldiers guilty of abuse of human rights, compensation for victims, and the transfer of police from military to civilian control. Naturally, terms like "genuine land reform" and "respect for human rights" are subject to interpretation. Nonetheless, the mere fact that both sides shared the same slogans indicated there were areas where they might reach limited agreements if only they were serious about doing so.

"There were some reasonable expectations," said Romeo Capulong, a left-wing lawyer who advised the Front during peace talks. "Remember, the Aquino government enjoyed tremendous support from our people. So the NDF proposed that the military be purged of human rights violators and other undesirable elements . . . who committed crimes against the people and who were closely associated with and utilized by the Marcos government."[2]

In return, the NDF could offer the administration an end to years of warfare and a base of support against Marcos and the armed forces. Those in the Front's leadership who supported peace talks, including Ocampo and Zumel, believed the prospect of an end to the fighting might embolden Aquino to implement controversial programs despite resistance from the armed forces and other conservative elements in Philippine society. But the Front was not prepared to lay down its arms on the basis of promises alone.

Ultimately, the Communists accepted Aquino's offer of peace talks because they had no choice. Opposing her on the basis of ideology or doubts

2. Interview with Romeo Capulong by Eileen Guerrero, Makati, May 14, 1991.

about her good intentions was not good politics in the Philippines of 1986; a hard-line stand would have damaged the movement's support among its own constituency. Local rebel commanders in the Cordillera Mountains, Kalinga-Apayao province, and elsewhere were already considering laying down their arms after Marcos was ousted. The boycott of the presidential election was seen within the party as a blunder, and to have refused the olive branch would have been a second, perhaps fatal, error in judgment.

After months of informal contacts, rebel negotiators Saturnino Ocampo and his wife Bobbie Malay held their first formal meeting with Jose Diokno, the government's chief representative, in his rambling, two-story home on a quiet, tree-lined street in Quezon City. The talks dealt in broad terms with a possible agenda, as well as the mechanics of future negotiations. Ocampo insisted on safe-conduct passes so the negotiators could move about freely for consultations without fear of arrest. He also wanted to make sure his bodyguards were covered by the passes and could retain their weapons, a prudent demand considering the high number of unsolved murders in Manila.[3]

But Ramos was insisting on tight controls. He demanded that the rebel bodyguards register their firearms and that negotiators be limited in the areas of the country they could visit. Diokno was a strong-willed figure with a deep distrust of the military. He was convinced the civilian leadership had to bend the rules if the talks were to succeed. After listening to Ocampo, Diokno wrote out in longhand a safe-conduct pass for Ocampo, his wife, and their bodyguards.

Diokno left that same day for medical treatment in San Francisco. A chain-smoker, the sixty-four-year-old Diokno had suffered from lung cancer, but his doctors believed the disease was in remission. In California, however, they found that his cancer had reappeared; six months later, Diokno died. His daughter, Mariss Diokno, took his place on the panel, and Ramon Mitra assumed the leading role.

Mitra was a controversial choice. NDF members and some of his colleagues complained that he was disorganized and came to the sessions poorly prepared. He would sit through lengthy sessions without taking a single note and then show up for subsequent meetings having forgotten what had already been discussed or decided.[4]

3. Interview with Mariss Diokno by Eileen Guerrero, Quezon City, May 13, 1991.
4. *Ibid.*

A former journalist, Mitra's main goal was to revive his political career, which had been interrupted by martial law. He relished talking to journalists, and as the talks progressed, he would appear from time to time on the ground floor press room of the Ministry of Agriculture, sidle up to favored reporters, and ask: "You want a story? Don't quote me, 'Sources said' only, right?" He would then usher them to his second floor office and regale them with his version of the confidential talks. The three Communist negotiators had themselves been reporters and had no trouble figuring out the source of the leaks. Mitra's habits only served to reinforce their doubts about the government's sincerity.

On August 5, Mitra met for three and a half hours with the rebel representatives in what the administration described as the first "official" round of talks. Afterward, Mitra appeared before reporters and was upbeat about the results. The two sides had discussed broad objectives and details such as safe-conduct passes for the rebel representatives. "Throughout our conversation, I heard none of that Communist rhetoric that you usually hear," Mitra told reporters. "You know, statements about 'running dogs of the Americans.'"

The rebels left the meeting less sanguine. They told Mitra they wanted to set up office and operate openly without fear of arrest. They also wanted safe-conduct guarantees for consultants and advisers who would assist them during the negotiations. The National Democratic Front consisted of twelve outlawed organizations scattered across the country, and all would have to be consulted during the course of the talks. In addition to the party itself and the New People's Army, the NDF included organizations of youth, clerics, teachers, farmers, and others. Although they were required to follow policies set down by the party central committee, each Front organization had its own priorities and programs that would have to be considered in reaching decisions. The rebels said they would accept no cease-fire until their requests were satisfied. Ocampo, however, told friends in the press corps that Mitra spent most of the meeting reminiscing about the days when the three of them worked on competing Manila newspapers.

Aquino, meanwhile, was preparing to visit the United States in September and would no doubt face questions about her overtures to the Communists. Shultz had given her strategy the blessing of the U.S., but there were still doubts in Washington about the firmness of her resolve. What the trip needed was a publicity stunt, and Mitra provided one on September 6, just nine days before the president's scheduled departure. During a meeting with the National Democratic Front, Mitra proposed a sixty-day cease-fire to take effect immediately.

Mitra knew there was little chance the rebels would accept. For months, the National Democratic Front had been insisting that a cease-fire be part of a broad agenda for discussion, including reorganization of the armed forces and the future of U.S. bases. The government had not even responded to the Front's proposal on its negotiators' security and working conditions.

But the offer made headlines, portraying the president as resolute in her quest for peace despite pressure from all sides. That image was hardly tarnished at all when the rebels finally rejected the offer on the eve of her departure. While in Washington, Aquino drew thunderous applause when she told a joint session of Congress that if the rebels refused peace, "I will not hesitate to unsheathe the sword of war."

In fact, Aquino herself was displaying little personal leadership in the peace talks. In his prime, Marcos—whose photographic memory and attention to detail were legendary—would carefully supervise every step of a sensitive project. Cory's style was to delegate authority to subordinates and then allow them wide latitude to carry out broad guidelines. Such a management style requires not only competent subordinates but clear and detailed marching orders from the top. Instead, government negotiators were operating in a factious government with a detached chief executive. Just as she had deferred to Ramos in maneuvering against Enrile, Aquino had turned over the peace negotiations to Mitra.

But Mitra did not have a free hand either. Although military representatives were not included in the negotiating panel, the armed forces was making its influence felt.

With Enrile gone, Ramos had become the spokesman of the defense establishment. Instead of criticizing the wisdom of negotiations, which was a matter of presidential policy, Ramos cleverly raised numerous questions on virtually every point under discussion, often in the press. Ramos said he was willing to accept a cease-fire "in place," meaning that combatants would stay in the areas where they were before the truce, but he insisted that such a cease-fire did not apply to "routine" police operations against common criminals.

At the time, however, the national police was an integral branch of the Armed Forces of the Philippines, virtually indistinguishable from the army. Ramos also demanded that the definition of a "hostile act," which would be forbidden during the cease-fire, be expanded to include collection of "revolutionary taxes" by the insurgents in areas they controlled. Such "taxes" were a major revenue source for the insurgents.

Many, if not all, of Ramos's concerns were understandable, given his position as military chief of staff. The armed forces had been fighting the Communists for seventeen years and was not prepared to hand over to the rebels what they had failed to win on the battlefield. Raising objections, however, served to delay the talks and drain them of momentum. The government negotiators lacked the military expertise to resolve many of Ramos's issues on their own. "It was very difficult to get the agreement going because they [the military] had so many requirements, so many constraints they wanted to impose on the talks," Mariss Diokno recalls. "None of us on the panel were military people, so defining an agreement, what was or was not a hostile act, was difficult."[5]

At one point, the National Democratic Front considered trying to overcome the obstacles by appealing personally to Cory Aquino. They asked Jose Yap, a close associate of her brother Peping Cojuangco, to go to the president and ask for a face-to-face meeting at the presidential palace. Yap came away empty-handed. He told the NDF lawyers, Romeo Capulong and Arno Sanidad, that Aquino did not want to bypass her own negotiators. When she asked Yap about Mitra's skills as a negotiator, he relayed the opinions he had heard from the NDF: "He's bad. He goes to the negotiations without his notes, with no agenda." Although she listened patiently, she said there was nothing she could do. Yap told the two lawyers that she claimed "the Americans imposed Mitra as a negotiator."[6]

The talks suffered a major setback in September with the surprise arrest of Rodolfo Salas, the chairman of the Communist Party of the Philippines. Salas, a thirty-nine-year-old former student activist, was picked up by military intelligence agents on September 29, as he was leaving the Philippine General Hospital in downtown Manila with his wife and bodyguard. Salas, who was also the commander of the New People's Army, had gone to a cousin on the hospital staff for medical treatment.

5. *Ibid.*
6. Capulong interview by Guerrero, May 14, 1991.

Salas's arrest shocked the Front negotiators, who considered it a military provocation to undermine the talks. The rebels had planned for Salas to join their negotiating panel, but at the time, he had no safe-conduct pass. To the rebels, that seemed a petty technicality compared with the greater issue of war or peace. After the military refused to release Salas, the NDF walked out of the talks and stayed away for six weeks.

The arrest also surprised many urban, middle-class Filipinos, who did not have the same personal experience with the insurgency as their rural countrymen. Aquino and her stalwarts had been talking of rebels "coming down from the hills" and "rejoining society," as if they were living in physical isolation, unaware of the "new democracy" that Cory Aquino had restored. Salas, however, had been arrested in the heart of the capital.

Talks resumed October 19, but the Front was growing impatient over what it considered the government's stalling tactics. The rebels announced they were ready for a one-hundred-day cease-fire, three times as long as the truce offered by Mitra, but they wanted to talk about substantial changes in Philippine society. "We want basic changes in our society, not just a piece of land for me, for Satur, and our other comrades," Zumel said. He called on the government to disband its militia, the Civilian Home Defense Force, and to remove the police from military control as a condition for a truce.[7]

Both conditions were contained in Aquino's campaign platform. The CHDF had been organized to provide defense for villages threatened by rebels, but it had degenerated into an armed rabble frequently used as enforcers by local landlords and politicians or to protect plantations from squatters. Marcos had incorporated the Integrated National Police into the armed forces during martial law to solidify his control over the internal security apparatus. Although Aquino had promised to return the police to civilian control, Ramos strongly supported maintaining and even expanding the CHDF, and the administration needed his support against RAM.

The government told the Front it needed time to study its proposals. Mitra admitted to the rebels that his panel was having trouble convincing "others in government"—notably the military—to support the peace program. In a letter to Mitra, Ocampo responded that the government must

---

7. Diokno interview by Guerrero, May 13, 1991.

"obtain a working consensus" within its own ranks if the country were to resolve "our tragic civil war."[8]

Four days after Enrile's dismissal, the negotiating panels representing the two sides signed a cease-fire agreement at Club Filipino, where Aquino had taken her oath as president ten months earlier. The cease-fire was to go into effect at midnight on December 10, the International Human Rights Day, and last for sixty days, subject to extension if the two sides so agreed. In addition, a national committee under the chairmanship of the Right Reverend Antonio Fortich, the left-wing bishop of Negros Island, was established to monitor the cease-fire and investigate alleged violations. Regional committees of military commanders, clerics, and civilian officials were also established throughout the country to supervise the truce and discuss local issues.

The announcement was greeted by a widespread sense of public relief. It finally appeared that the new government had managed to overcome the threat from the armed forces and take a significant step toward peace. On the day the truce went into effect, church bells pealed throughout the nation to usher in the long-awaited era of peace. Prayers were offered in churches and mosques, and celebrations marking the event took place all over the country. In Bacolod, the main city on rebel-infested Negros Island, the local NPA commander, Nemesio Demafiles, played the guitar for thousands who turned out for festivities in the town square. Rebels who had spent years in hiding walked freely through the streets of their hometowns and made plans to spend Christmas with their families, some for the first time in nearly twenty years.

After the Christmas holidays, the government and the Front made preparations for the "substantive phase" of peace talks, scheduled to begin January 6, 1987. Mitra stepped down as chairman of the government panel and was replaced by Teofisto Guingona, a lawyer who also served as chairman of the government's auditing commission. The change had been agreed upon when the cease-fire discussions began and did not signal any shift in policy. In fact, the government's position appeared to be hardening.

The administration had made clear it would not agree to a coalition government or to the immediate closure of the six U.S. military bases.

8. Diokno referred to the letter in her interview, *ibid.*

The government commission established to prepare a new constitution had completed a draft national charter and made plans for a national plebiscite on February 2. Aquino had declared that any agreement with the rebels must be within the framework of the new constitution, which the NDF had played no role in drafting.

On the eve of the January 6 talks, the government-run People's Television broadcast a commentary that said the "hardline faction" of the rebel movement remained "single-minded in its quest for power. . . . If the people begin to see that meaningful change can begin without armed struggle and the CPP, then the latter will lose large segments of its mass base," the commentary declared. This was a clear expression of the government's goal in the talks: to isolate the doctrinaire Marxist leadership from the rank and file and to win over the latter with promises of reform. The administration had virtually closed the door on the rebels' demands by drafting a new constitution without participation by the Communists or the Muslim rebel organizations. The draft constitution included a liberal bill of rights, reestablished the pre–martial law senate and house of representatives, and mandated a single, six-year term for the president. It left little room for the extensive political, economic, and social changes the rebels had been seeking.

Before the January talks, Zumel said in a television interview that the two sides were "poles apart" and could not even agree on a framework for discussions, which he believed made a peaceful settlement beyond reach at that time. Nonetheless, the Communists saw advantages to continuing the process, even if it proved to be nothing more than a charade. The cease-fire and safe-conduct passes enabled Zumel, Ocampo, and other leaders to move about freely after nearly two decades of constriction. They were well known to a generation of television commentators, newspaper editors, and others who had worked with them in journalism before martial law. The articulate Zumel, Ocampo, and Malay were sought out as guests on television shows and as speakers before university audiences, civic clubs, and other forums. They joined in labor rallies, where red flags and Communist banners were displayed openly for the first time in a generation. As former journalists, they knew how to use the media to espouse their views and, also for the first time, to give a human face to a rebel movement that had operated in the shadows.

In the countryside, the New People's Army was using the cease-fire to retrain and regroup its forces for the next phase of the struggle, which its leaders believed was inevitable. In Quezon province, a rebel stronghold southeast of Manila, a twenty-seven-year-old woman fighter, known only by her nom de guerre, *Ka* [Comrade] *Abed,* told visiting reporters: "There's more work now [during the cease-fire] because we have to consolidate." Rebels invited reporters to camps on Mindoro Island, where they watched young trainees working out with makeshift equipment and firing their M-16 rifles just like any basic training recruit.

The government and NDF panels held their first meeting in the Commission on Audit building, a brick structure on the outskirts of Quezon City. The three NDF negotiators arrived with a detailed list of priority demands, which they asked the government to implement immediately as a sign of good faith. These included a substantial reorganization of the armed forces; release of all remaining political prisoners; repeal of Marcos-era laws that violated human rights; punishment of soldiers and police guilty of abusing human rights; compensation for victims of such abuse; abolition of the CHDF militia; removal of the police from military control; an end to torture; and adherence to international covenants on human rights.

Government negotiator Mariss Diokno read the rebel demands and knew immediately where they came from. They were the same principles that her father had outlined as chairman of the Presidential Commission on Human Rights. That, in fact, made them part of President Aquino's official national policy. But Guingona said only that the government was moving on those policies but needed time. During a briefing for reporters, Guingona described the rebel demands as a matter of "continuing concern."[9]

The government had not bothered to draft its own proposals for the talks. Instead of handing the rebels an agenda to study, Guingona simply referred them to the government's five-year economic development plan, full of dry statistics on growth projections and vague outlines of land reform. Guingona did not even have a copy of the plan, and staff aides scurried to type out a summary so the rebels would have something to take away from the talks. After the meeting, Ocampo pulled Diokno aside. "Are you serious?" Ocampo asked her. "Mariss, is that really all

9. *Ibid.*

you are going to give us?" Diokno was speechless, and deeply embarrassed as a member of the government panel. [10]

At best, the development plan fell far short of the minimum NDF demands. The land reform portion, for example, was nothing more than a commitment to push forward with the program initiated by Marcos. Aquino had promised to expand the Marcos program to include all agricultural lands but had decided to defer a new, broader reform program until the constitution was ratified and a new congress elected.

After the first session, Diokno approached Guingona and suggested that they organize an interagency committee to help them study issues raised by the NDF. The rebels were asking detailed questions on a broad range of subjects, from agriculture to industrial policy, foreign relations, and the status of the armed forces. The government needed a response to these. Guingona accepted the recommendation and a committee was formed, but it proved ineffective because of lack of direction from the president.

At the first committee meeting, members spent most of the time fretting about how good Zumel and Ocampo looked on television and how articulately they performed compared to the drab Guingona and the overweight Diokno. "Unfortunately, there's nothing we can do about that because God gave us these faces," the portly Diokno snapped at her colleagues. "It seemed to me that there was no clarity and direction," she later complained. [11]

Meanwhile, the negotiations were becoming sidetracked by the issue of cease-fire violations and internal bickering within the government. Some of the violations by the rebels were clear breaches of the agreement, but others appeared manufactured by the military in an attempt to discredit the talks. In one of the first reported violations, the military claimed Communist rebels hurled a grenade into a dance hall in southeastern Luzon, injuring several people. Bishop Fortich and his panel flew to the area, only to discover that the grenade was thrown by a jealous lover. "How dare you waste the panel's time with this?" Fortich shouted at the military commander. [12]

10. *Ibid.*
11. *Ibid.*
12. The Right Reverend Antonio Fortich in the presence of reporters, Bicol, December, 1986, Agence France Press news agency.

Ramos refused to acknowledge that there was any area of the country, no matter how isolated, under rebel control. He protested vehemently when Ocampo appeared along with armed rebels during a parade through a town in Bataan province, scene of the historic battle during World War II. Ramos also insisted that the police, which were legally part of the armed forces, had the right to patrol anywhere they chose in their campaign to curb "criminality."

Aquino had established the negotiating panel as the sole voice of the government in the talks. But that did not stop Ramos, Laurel, and others from using the press to promote their own views of the negotiations and terms of the cease-fire. The Front's negotiators did not know who was speaking for the government and who was voicing his own opinion. "Every day Ramos would talk," Diokno said. "We would meet with the NDF, and they would make us accountable for every single thing that a government official had said because Cory designated the panel as her representative of the government of the Republic of the Philippines. So Ramos would talk, make a headline, and later they would say at the meeting, 'Why did he say that? It's not what we agreed upon.'"[13]

At the same time, Front negotiators had set up an office at the National Press Club and were holding their own daily news conferences, often denouncing what Ramos or others had said in the press and listing their own complaints about truce violations by the military. "Propaganda blurred the issue," Diokno said. "We were so preoccupied with the cease-fire that we had little time to spend on substantive issues."[14]

Two days after talks resumed, Zumel began warning that they were on the verge of collapse. The NDF issued a statement urging the government to repeal immediately all presidential decrees imposed by Marcos that still remained on the statute books under the Aquino administration. These included decrees that banned persons convicted of subversion from organizing public rallies and others that increased penalties for various offenses committed "in furtherance of rebellion." During the struggle against Marcos, human rights lawyers such as Arroyo had roundly denounced the decrees as a violation of civil liberties. Arroyo, however, had recommended Aquino maintain some of the decrees as weapons against Marcos loyalists, mutineers within the armed forces, and other enemies

13. Diokno interview by Guerrero, May 13, 1991.
14. *Ibid.*

of the state. Guingona, meanwhile, threatened to offer peace talks to regional rebel commanders if national-level talks broke down.

By mid-January, the National Democratic Front had given up and was looking for a graceful exit. The opportunity came on Thursday, January 22. A group of militant farmers, led by a prominent leftist named Jaime Tadeo, had been camping out for several days at the Ministry of Agrarian Reform to demand that the government turn over state-owned lands promised to landless peasants. The administration, however, was waiting for the reestablishment of congress before moving on its program.

After getting nowhere in talks with the agrarian reform minister, Heherson "Sonny" Alvarez, Tadeo led his followers to Bonifacio Plaza in downtown Manila and, after a rally, announced the crowd would march on the presidential palace to see Aquino herself. The crowd was clearly in a hostile mood and different from the usual collection of students, intellectuals, and young professionals who normally frequented leftist rallies. This group included wiry farmers, their skins darkened by years of working under the tropical sun, and young, muscular men, who tore down metal staves from fences as they left the square for Malacañang.

When the marchers, now numbering about ten thousand, reached the Mendiola Bridge five hundred yards north of the palace compound, they were met by a phalanx of police and Philippine marines. The new government had removed the barbed wire barricades that blocked off the bridge during the Marcos administration, and so the marchers proceeded right to the first line of defenders. As the protesters surged against the plastic shields of the riot police, marines in the second rank opened fire, killing at least twelve people and wounding nearly a hundred. The toll was higher than during any of the demonstrations that had helped bring Cory Aquino to power.

The shooting erupted at about the same time as NDF and government negotiators were to resume meeting at the Commission on Audit, about ten miles northeast of the Mendiola Bridge. Negotiators and reporters huddled around transistor radios listening to live broadcasts from the scene. The atmosphere was tense. The three rebel negotiators summoned reporters and breathlessly announced they were breaking off the talks.

That evening, Aquino watched video tapes of the shooting, along with Ramos, Montaño, and her advisers. She was stunned by the carnage and deeply concerned about what it would do to her image. Montaño suggested that he should resign his command to deflect criticism from the president. She agreed. [15]

Aquino appeared on television a few hours later to express her sorrow over "this bloody incident." She promised a full-scale investigation and punishment for those responsible. Like her "get tough" statements after the Manila Hotel and Enrile crises, her words proved nothing more than empty rhetoric. The investigation she promised hit a stone wall when the military refused to release weapons for ballistics tests.

No one was ever punished. Aquino announced that Montaño was being removed as chief of the capital command, without mentioning that the general himself had suggested the move. Montaño, however, had proven his loyalty to the president during the Manila Hotel takeover and the God Save the Queen conspiracy; thus, instead of retiring, he was quietly installed as operations chief of the armed forces general staff, a plum staff position. Later, he was promoted to chief of the Philippine Constabulary, or national police. Brigadier General Alfredo Lim, the second-ranking officer at Mendiola, kept his job as Manila police chief and was later named director of the National Bureau of Investigation. He was elected mayor of Manila in 1992.

The cease-fire expired on schedule. Fighting resumed. Aquino offered an unconditional amnesty to rebels who chose to surrender, but her conciliatory speeches were replaced by clarion calls for the military to defend "the people's peace and freedom that the terrorists are trying to destroy." Campaign promises to abolish the CHDF were not only forgotten but the militia force was expanded, albeit under a new name—the Citizens Armed Forces Geographical Unit, or CAFGU.

The peace initiative proved little more than a public relations exercise by the two sides. The NDF needed to respond to the public's clamor for peace, and Aquino needed to promote her image as peacemaker to claim moral authority for the struggle ahead. Even the most cosmetic concession would have incurred the enmity of the armed forces.

The real "winner" in the peace process turned out to be the institution that most opposed it: the Armed Forces of the Philippines. The talks collapsed without the government conceding on any of the rebel demands, including planks in Aquino's election platform. Once again, events had shown how dependent she had become on the armed forces.

15. Interview with Ramon Montaño by Eileen Guerrero, Manila, April 9, 1991.

Once, during the negotiations, Aquino received the government panel, and after discussions, the talk turned to family and mutual friends. The president inquired about Jose Diokno's widow, Nena, whom she got to know when both of their husbands were in prison during martial law. Mrs. Diokno had a reputation for toughness. They all remembered how she defiantly blew cigarette smoke into the faces of military jailers when she visited her husband in prison. "Nena should be the one sitting in the palace," Cory said. "Nena is not afraid of the military."[16]

16. Diokno interview by Guerrero, May 13, 1991.

6 LOYALISTS STRIKE BACK

THE PRESIDENT'S PRESTIGE within the armed forces benefited little from the government's hard-line stand in the peace talks. Whatever gains Aquino could have expected by hanging tough had been lost by her kid-glove treatment of military mutineers. Rather than appearing magnanimous, her decision not to punish the mutineers convinced her enemies that there was little risk in challenging her by force.

Abroad, however, and among the public at large, surviving armed challenges and standing up to the Communists enhanced her stature. *Time* magazine named President Aquino as its 1986 Woman of the Year and in a gushing tribute wrote: "If she can now bring something of the morality play even to a hardened political world, history itself, like most of the forces she has already met, may one day be quietly transformed."[1] Few asked whether her own decisions had contributed to the problems.

Pressure, meanwhile, was mounting on the Marcos camp to move soon if their deposed leader were ever to return to power. The political and military turmoil of the past months had shaken the Aquino government and served to reinvigorate the Marcos forces, but time was running out. Filipinos would vote on February 2, 1987, to accept or reject a new constitution, and a strong "yes" vote would reaffirm Aquino's mandate.

Pro-Marcos military officers began recruiting followers for another

1. "Woman of the Year," *Time*, January 5, 1987, p. 15.

coup as early as December, 1986. Most of the officers in the conspiracy came from the Philippine Air Force and the Philippine Constabulary and had been associated with General Ver's faction of the armed forces. They used the rhetoric of the RAM clique—Communists were influencing the government to destroy the armed forces—but their real goal was to restore Ferdinand Marcos as president.

The recruiting drive caught the attention of General Ramos and Lieutenant General Salvador Mison, chief of the newly organized National Capital Region Defense Command. In mid-January, Ramos placed the armed forces on "red alert" and increased the number of troops guarding Malacañang Palace, the Catholic radio station, and other strongholds.

On the evening of January 20, a group of air force officers met at the Kowloon House, a Chinese restaurant in Makati, to finalize their plans for the coup. The plan called for simultaneous attacks on Villamor Air Base, located near Manila's international airport; the Sangley Point naval air station across Manila Bay in Cavite; armed forces headquarters at Camp Aguinaldo; and the constabulary headquarters at Camp Crame.[2] Most of the troops would come from garrisons in central Luzon north of the capital and from Camp Nakar, the southern Luzon constabulary garrison in Lucena, about fifty miles southeast of the capital.

One week later, the putsch was launched. Shortly before midnight on January 26, a group of officers led by Colonel Bertuldo de la Cruz assembled at the home of Dr. Arturo Tolentino, Jr., son of the leader of the Manila Hotel takeover. De la Cruz, at forty-nine, was chief of staff of the Third Air Division in Zamboanga and a veteran of the Manila Hotel caper. He issued M-16 rifles to about twenty mutineers and then set off with them for Villamor, where they were joined by more than fifty other rebels for an attack on the headquarters of the 205th Helicopter Wing.[3]

General Mison learned the rebels were on the move and ordered the police commander of the Manila area, Brigadier General Alexander Aguirre, to seal off major approaches to the city and intercept the rebels as soon as possible. Aguirre's men caught up with 110 mutineers from Fort Magsaysay about 1:30 A.M. at the Balintawak toll station on the

2. The Davide Commission, *Final Report of the Fact-Finding Commission* (Makati, 1990), 159.
3. *Ibid.*, 159–60.

main road south into the city. They were to have taken over Camp Aguinaldo but surrendered without a fight.

A smaller rebel force under Lieutenant Colonel Reynaldo Cabauatan, another Manila Hotel veteran, managed to slip through the darkened streets toward Camp Crame, headquarters of the national police. They got lost in a neighborhood southwest of the camp, however, and dispersed without ever reaching their objective.

De la Cruz's forces reached the gate at Villamor Air Base about 1:30 A.M., but failed to get inside. The Twentieth Wing commander, Colonel Loven Abadia, had doubled the guards at the gates, and loyal troops refused to allow the mutineers to enter. After trying to bluff their way inside, the rebels opened fire; in a four-hour gunbattle, de la Cruz and fifteen others were wounded and one rebel was killed. The attackers surrendered about dawn, and the threat to Villamor was over.[4]

The rebels at Sangley Point were more successful. About forty of them entered the base and took prisoner the commander of the Fifteenth Strike Wing and his deputy. "This is the day of the return of Marcos, and we are protecting the government from communism," the rebel leader announced. But progovernment troops blocked the runway with armored cars, and after nine hours of negotiations, the mutineers surrendered.[5]

The only objective the rebels managed to seize was the GMA Television station, located in Quezon City northwest of Camp Aguinaldo. Troops from the air force's special reaction force entered the compound about 1:30 A.M. after telling security guards they had come to strengthen the station's defenses. Once inside, the intruders rounded up station employees, herded them into a room, and refused to allow them to leave.

Later that night, about one hundred rebel reinforcements from Camp Nakar arrived at the television station, bolstering the mutineer force to more than two hundred. The reinforcements were led by a forty-five-year-old lieutenant colonel named Oscar Canlas. Canlas was the military intelligence chief for central and southern Luzon and a former protégé of Danding Cojuangco, Aquino's estranged cousin who fled to Hawaii with Marcos. By virtue of his rank, Canlas soon became the most visible figure among the mutineers, although it was never clear whether he was really in command.

4. *Ibid.* 161.
5. *Ibid.,* 161–62.

By sunrise, the coup attempt seemed already to have failed. Militarily, the television station was the least valuable of the mutineers' planned targets. It was located on EDSA Boulevard far from military camps, airports, the presidential palace, and other strongholds necessary to overthrow the government. Loyal troops moved quickly to surround the compound and cut off electricity and water to the mutineers inside.

Early on the morning of January 27, Aquino appeared on television and announced that "certain groups of misguided military personnel" had failed "to seize key installations." She blamed the putsch on "the inability of some elements" to accept the fact that "civilian government is here to stay." Mindful of her reputation for weakness and indecision, Cory talked tough: "Nothing will derail our effort to establish full constitutional democracy in the coming plebiscite. Let me make myself clear on this matter: We shall not treat this like the Manila Hotel incident. I have ordered the chief of staff to proceed against the officers responsible for this act of rebellion in accordance with the manual of courts martial. The full force of the law will be applied to everyone, civilian and military, implicated in this crime. I have ordered their arrest and detention. There is a time for reconciliation and a time for justice and retribution. That time has come."[6]

Despite the tough talk, the government responded as it had before—cautiously. The mutineers could serve as a rallying point for Marcos loyalists, and as long as the siege lasted, there was always the possibility that other units might join them. Attacking the rebels could also be risky. Aquino's image had already been tarnished by the bloodshed at the Mendiola Bridge. Killing rebellious soldiers could further anger a distrustful military.

As word of the takeover spread, more than five thousand Marcos supporters converged on the station chanting, "We want Marcos, we want Marcos." Thousands of Aquino supporters also arrived at the station and began pelting the loyalists with stones. Police fired tear gas to disperse the groups, but they only scattered, regrouped, and came back for more.

By noon, Ramos was confident that the mini-coup had been contained and that no other units would join them. Canlas refused to surrender, however, and appeared to be playing for time. As the afternoon passed,

6. The full text of Aquino's televised speech of January 27, 1987, was published by the PIA.

the standoff began to look like another loyalist "theater of the absurd" production. A pair of has-been porno stars, Alona Alegre and Elizabeth Oropeza, showed up at the station to the cheers and catcalls of government soldiers, who graciously allowed them to pass through their lines and enter the rebel compound.

With no electricity for the air conditioners, the buildings were like steam baths, and the floors were littered with empty plastic food containers and scraps of paper. Canlas appeared relaxed, even confident. "We are fighting communism, and we feel that the influence of communism has grown very fast in the past eleven months," he told journalists.

Ramos's staff learned the names of some of the rebels and brought their wives, mistresses, and children to the station to broadcast poignant appeals to their men over megaphones. One of them was Canlas's mistress, Leah, who was seven months pregnant. "Please, don't die," she cried. "Think of your future."

Ramos, meanwhile, was coming under strong pressure from the presidential palace to end the standoff quickly. Corazon Aquino's image as a leader was at stake, and for her followers, nothing could be more important. Three coup attempts in eleven months were making the Philippines look like a banana republic. Ramos had summoned several advisers, among them Jose Almonte, who had recently retired from the service. Almonte was at Ramos's command center near the station compound when the door suddenly opened and in walked Joker Arroyo. Ramos was conferring with his aides, and Arroyo remained in the room for several minutes before the general took note of his presence. If he felt slighted, Arroyo never showed it. He sat quietly in one corner until Ramos finished with his conference.

Arroyo and Ramos then went upstairs for a private talk. About an hour later, Arroyo returned to the ground floor and left the building without speaking to anyone. Moments later, Ramos appeared, and Almonte asked what had transpired. Ramos told Almonte that Arroyo had ordered him in the name of Cory Aquino to attack the station and "flatten it if necessary," regardless of the casualties. She had to be seen as a woman of courage and decisiveness.[7]

Ramos was horrified. The rebels were positioned on the roof of the

7. Interview with General Jose Almonte by Robert Reid, Camp Aguinaldo, April 3, 1991.

station with machine guns and semiautomatic weapons and had clear fields of fire. A frontal assault would be bloody. Wanting to hear the order from the president herself, he telephoned Aquino, who confirmed what Arroyo had said. Ramos explained the risk of a backlash in the armed forces, especially if the attack caused loss of life. But Aquino was adamant: attack as soon as possible. "All right, Mrs. President, I'll do what you say, but I want a direct order in writing," Ramos told her. She paused, then said, "Well, then, do what you think is best."[8]

Instead of attacking, Ramos "invited" Canlas to a "dialogue," and about 3:00 A.M. on the morning of January 28, the two met in a van parked outside the compound. Government television and private radio stations broadcast the forty-five-minute meeting live, and viewers still awake at that hour were treated to the unusual spectacle of the chief of staff patiently encouraging the rebel colonel to end the standoff. Ramos promised "fair and honorable treatment" if Canlas surrendered but warned him that he would face punishment. Canlas was respectful but firm. No surrender.

The tactic was a shrewd move by Ramos. There was still significant support for Marcos nationwide at a time when Aquino's own image was slipping because of bungling by her government. No one could be sure whether other military units were poised to join the mutiny.

Before the meeting, Ramos had gone jogging with about fifty of his troops, as he often did in times of stress. Before the television cameras, he appeared relaxed, except for chewing incessantly on a large cigar. Canlas, however, was nervous and inarticulate. Although Ramos was nearly fifteen years older than the rebel colonel, he was trim and athletic, whereas Canlas's ample belly rolled over his belt buckle.[9]

Canlas was unyielding. The mutiny was staged to bring the people's attention to the dangers of communism and to protest "unfair" treatment of military officers by the Aquino government, thus the standoff would continue. Ramos left the van and told his aides, "This cannot go on indefinitely."[10] By that evening, his patience was at an end. He knew he could not fend off the palace forever, and no amount of persuasion seemed to move Canlas.

8. *Ibid.*
9. Interview with Colonel Honesto Isleta by Eileen Guerrero, Quezon City, March 27, 1990.
10. *Ibid.*

Rumors spread through the capital that Marcos himself had secretly returned to the Philippines and was hiding out in his home province of Ilocos Norte, awaiting the proper moment to appear. The rumors became so strong that the armed forces issued a formal statement assuring the public that Marcos was indeed in Hawaii.

Meanwhile, Ramos made plans for an attack. On the evening of January 28, he allowed Canlas's mistress to enter the compound to hear a Roman Catholic mass said by an army chaplain. The atmosphere was like the last rites. Canlas read the story of David and Goliath from the Old Testament, and Leah wept throughout the service. Still, Canlas would not surrender.

At 10:00 that night, Brigadier General Aguirre stood on a street facing the camp and barked an order over a loudspeaker: clear out of the station in half an hour or face attack. Over the next thirty minutes, the nation was treated to a tense standoff, a poker game with a quintessentially Filipino mixture of bravado and the bizarre.

A radio reporter at the scene counted down the minutes to the deadline during a live, nationwide broadcast. Government troops armed with semiautomatic rifles and tear gas canisters scampered to positions near the station and crouched into firing positions. Canlas's mistress wailed through a bullhorn for him to save himself.

Inside the compound, mutineers managed to activate a generator and broadcast briefly over the station's AM radio subsidiary. "We're going to die, we're going to die," a woman wailed in the fearsome style of an Irish banshee. Between sobs, she complained that she was menstruating but the government troops were so "brutal" they would not let her leave even "to buy sanitary napkins."

The deadline came with no sign of surrender from the rebels. At 10:31 P.M., a sharp "pop" pierced the silence, and a single tear gas canister soared over the station wall and crashed inside. A second canister was fired, but still no response. Suddenly, a busload of wives and children of the mutineers arrived at the government lines. "To those of you inside the compound, your wives are here, and they want to talk to you," Aguirre shouted. "They want to talk to you, one by one. If you agree to that, get in touch with the command post."

As an officer read out the names of the wives and children, Aguirre gave the rebels five minutes to respond. They refused, and more tear gas was fired. The woman inside the compound came back on the radio: "Why are you doing this to us, Mrs. Aquino?" she asked. "We are not moving out of here. It will be sweeter for you if you kill us with bullets rather than with tear gas. We won't leave the soldiers here because we know they are fighting for the country, for all of us, for you and me."

After firing more than two dozen tear gas canisters, some of which flew harmlessly over the compound, Aguirre suspended the attack and told Canlas to send out an emissary to discuss surrender. Colonel Honesto Isleta, a Ramos confidant, left the scene to telephone Ramos with a status report. As he passed reporters, Isleta said, "We cannot wait until tomorrow. They're waiting for something else. We have to finish it tonight."[11]

Isleta returned a few minutes later but this time rushed past reporters without a word. He headed straight for Aguirre and told him that Ramos wanted to stop the attack. No more tear gas, no live grenades. Something had happened.

What happened was the intercession of Gringo Honasan and the RAM Boys. Honasan and his group had distanced themselves from the coup attempt, but when it appeared the military would attack, Honasan and more than one hundred fellow officers sought a meeting with Ramos and warned him that an assault would tear apart the armed forces. They urged him to settle the standoff peacefully and presented Ramos with five demands: a major reform of the armed forces and a firm, anticommunist stand; removal of officers who had been retained beyond mandatory retirement; equal treatment for all soldiers, including Marcos supporters; permission for civilian supporters to leave the television station; and a guarantee that force would not be used against Canlas and his men. Faced with a crisis in the officer corps, Ramos relented and offered to talk again with Canlas.[12]

At 3:30 A.M. on January 29, Canlas agreed to leave the station; later, he appeared at a press conference at Camp Aguinaldo with Defense Secretary Ileto and Ramos. Canlas insisted that he had no ties to Marcos and had taken over the station to dramatize the Communist threat.

Afterward, presidential spokesman Teodoro Benigno announced that the aborted coup was designed to bring Marcos back from Hawaii. Of-

11. *Ibid.* The description of the scene at the compound comes from notes of AP and other reporters who covered the event.
12. Isleta interview by Guerrero, March 27, 1990.

ficials claimed Marcos had secretly chartered a Boeing 707 from a Lebanese arms dealer, Sarkis Soghanalian, and that the plane was already in
Honolulu. Marcos had simply been waiting for the uprising in Manila to
succeed. Two U.S. State Department officials visited Marcos in Honolulu
and told him he could not leave Hawaii without permission. Marcos
fumed to reporters that he was being treated like a prisoner, but that he
would try to get to Manila "as soon as I can at the risk of my own life."

About 9:00 A.M. on January 29, the porno queens and other civilians
were escorted from the station and taken by bus to a military camp, where
they were fingerprinted, photographed, and released. Before leaving the
station, Miss Oropeza led the group in singing the Philippine national
anthem. Seven hours later, the rebel soldiers left the station and boarded
buses to be taken to army headquarters at Fort Bonifacio. As the rebels
emerged, they cheered "Long live democracy," and many of them em-
braced and joked with friends in the government ranks.

This time, Aquino made good on her threat to punish the mutineers.
Canlas and the other officers as well as senior enlisted men were detained
at military camps and eventually placed on trial. Nearly two years after
the coup attempt, Canlas was sentenced to ten years' imprisonment. Most
of the lower-ranking troops were quietly returned to the ranks. It was
Ramos, not Aquino, who set the pace for resolving the rebellion and later,
for disposing with those who led it.

The January, 1987, coup attempt demonstrated that dissension in the
ranks extended beyond Honasan and his RAM clique. Simply removing
Enrile from the defense ministry had not been enough. "I don't think this
will be the end of it," Deputy Defense Minister Wilson Gamboa warned
in a radio interview. "The military is restive. A lot of mending and a lot
of understanding has to be done by the national leadership."[13]

13. Interview with Wilson Gamboa by DZRH Radio, January 30, 1987, authors'
notes.

7 PUTTING THE HOUSE IN ORDER

AFTER CANLAS SURRENDERED, only five days remained until the plebiscite on a new Philippine constitution, scheduled for February 2. But the campaign for and against the document had already been underway for weeks and was only slightly interrupted by the drama at GMA television. Voters would be asked to give a simple "yes" or "no" to a seventy-nine-page document, which dealt with issues as varied as the definition of the national territory, the system for approving government loans, tenure of elected officials, citizens' rights, the budget process, and standards of official conduct.

It was a complicated document, longer and more detailed than the U.S. Constitution or other national charters. Fearful that another Marcos might emerge, the framers sought to preclude any move to reestablish authoritarianism. The draft accepted that a future president might have to declare a national emergency, such as during foreign invasion, but required the president to seek congressional ratification of such a declaration.

Rules requiring presidential appointees to be certified by the Philippine congress were also spelled out, as well as limits on the number of posts any one person could hold. Guidelines were also established to prevent a president from appointing close relatives to government posts, as Marcos had done when he named Imelda governor of Metro Manila and minister of human settlements.

The draft reestablished the pre–martial law system of a bicameral legislature, with a senate and house of representatives, despite widespread feelings during the 1960s that the system was too slow and cumbersome. A vocal minority on the constitutional commission argued strongly that a unicameral system was more efficient and better suited for a country that needed rapid social change.

Bicameralism prevailed by a single vote in the commission. Supporters argued that a president would find it more difficult to control two chambers than one, and sensitivity about the emergence of a new strongman proved stronger than the desire for legislative speed. The commission members and Aquino herself were anxious to dismantle anything that smacked of the Marcos era.

The charter also included articles that contained the seeds of future disputes with the United States and other foreign powers. Chief among these was the thorny question of the future of U.S. military bases, one of the most contentious and divisive issues in the Philippines since independence.

Aquino's longtime supporters, including Lorenzo Tañada, Saguisag, and Pimentel, wanted the bases closed as an affirmation of national independence. To many Filipinos in academia, the media, and other professions, the six U.S. military installations represented an unwanted vestige of colonial rule.

During the Convenors' deliberations in 1985, Aquino had signed a manifesto pledging the opposition to work for removal of the bases.[1] But because undermining Marcos's support within the Reagan administration was central to her political strategy during the 1986 election, she quickly abandoned the antibases position and declared she was keeping her options open on the future of the installations.

As a compromise, the draft constitution provided a formula to extend the bases' tenure if such extension were provided for in a formal treaty ratified by two-thirds of the senate and, if congress so chose, a national referendum. Aquino personally approved the wording of the formula.[2]

1. Declaration of Unity, Manila, December 26, 1984, p. 4, AP files. Copies of the manifesto, signed by members of the anti-Marcos coalition, were widely disseminated and can be found in the National Library and other collections.
2. Teodoro Locsin, oral communication to Robert Reid and Eileen Guerrero, Manila, September 14, 1991.

Passing judgment on such a complicated, far-reaching document required careful and sober study. Serious implications for the nation's future lay within the language of the document. For example, Aquino had promised autonomy for the six million Filipino Muslims, and the document enshrined that principle. But Mindanao Island, the Muslim homeland, was predominantly Christian. How would the interests of the two communities be reconciled? Setting a structure of government in place precluded acceptance of many demands, not only of the Communists but of non-Marxist social reformers as well. The new constitution curbed the powers of the presidency to the extent that effective government would perhaps become impossible.

In the weeks before the plebiscite, few copies of the draft were available to the public. Thus, the debate boiled down to one question: Do you still support Corazon Aquino? Support Cory, support the constitution.

Both the Aquino administration and the opposition focused on that single issue. Enrile, now recovered from the shock of his dismissal, argued that if the constitution were rejected, Cory Aquino would have no choice but to call for new national elections. For her part, Aquino maintained that rejection of the constitution would threaten democracy. The nation, she argued, needed to return to a constitutional base as soon as possible to attract foreign investment and deal with the challenges from left-wing and right-wing extremists.

As the date for the plebiscite drew near, Aquino's appearances on behalf of ratification took on the character of a personal reelection campaign. Little was said about details of the draft. She loved to describe herself as "not a typical politician," but as she stumped for ratification, she handed out land titles, cash grants for local development, and other pork-barrel favors in a style reminiscent of Ferdinand Marcos.

At the same time, questions were being raised about the independence of the commission that had drafted the charter. Aquino had appointed the commission members rather than having an election. She promised a hands-off approach to the deliberations, and in fact appointed commissioners from a broad political spectrum, including avowed leftists and former Marcos supporters. Two weeks before the referendum, however, a Mindanao Island politician named Homobono Adaza made public an eleven-minute tape of a three-way telephone conversation the previous September between Aquino, Teodoro Locsin, and Arroyo in which they discussed commission deliberations.

. The conversation was taped secretly by RAM members when the president and Locsin were in the United States for her first visit as president. Arroyo, who stayed behind in Manila, could be heard briefing the two on the commission's decision to include a provision banning nuclear weapons from the Philippines. The provision would have certainly offended Washington because it would restrict movement of such weapons at Clark Air Base and the Subic Bay naval base.

Aquino had gone to Washington to seek economic aid. Her reputation in the United States was at its zenith, and Congress was eager to get off to a good start with her government after the bitterness of the Marcos era. A $200 million economic assistance package for the Philippines was pending in the Senate, and the last thing she needed was a dispute with her hosts.

As the gleeful Adaza played the tapes, reporters could hear Aquino telling Arroyo: "I was thinking, Joker, this thing of mine in the Senate might be dead," referring to the U.S. aid bill. Arroyo then promised to meet the following day with commission member Francisco Rodrigo. The tape contained no smoking gun, no unequivocal promise to strong-arm the commission. But soon afterward, the commission adopted a supplementary resolution giving the president authority to make exceptions to the antinuclear policy.

The nuclear issue was not the only instance where the Aquino administration had steered the drafting of the constitution. In fact, the administration had systematically guided its formulation from the very beginning. The conduit for the palace's positions on various issues was a group of wealthy, business-oriented, establishment figures known as the "Esperanza Group," named for the fashionable Quezon City restaurant where they met informally. Three members of the group, Christian Monsod, Jose Bengzon, and Ricardo Romulo, had close relatives in the Aquino cabinet.

The Esperanza Group became the dominant faction on the commission, ensuring that the conservative views of the Catholic reform bloc responsible for Aquino's candidacy in the first place were incorporated as much as possible into the final document. The Esperanza bloc was opposed by six left-wing members, appointed as representatives of nongovernmental organizations, the so-called cause-oriented groups. They included film director Lino Brocka; farm labor activist Jaime Tadeo;

Mindaluz Quesada, a nurse and president of the leftist Alliance of Health Workers; human rights lawyer Jose Suarez; and two university professors, Wilfrido Villacorta and Ponciano Bennagen. Aquino had appointed them to the commission to fulfill a promise to choose representatives from all sectors of society, but in fact, the deck was stacked against these "progressives."

As deliberations began, the leftists sensed that the administration's supporters on the commission were trying to railroad provisions on the economy, foreign relations, and other issues with as little discussion as possible. "We wanted more time for deliberations on the provisions and for an independent policy, especially on the economy," recalls Quesada. "They were not willing and were rushing the talks to a vote."[3]

Finally, the six walked out of the deliberations, complaining that the proadministration bloc was exercising a "tyranny of the majority" by railroading provisions through the commission. All eventually returned except Brocka. "We were the only ones coming out with different views from the rest," Quesada said. "Otherwise there was no debate. We gave color and life, otherwise it was all rigged beforehand in favor of the U.S. and big business."[4]

As the campaign for ratification progressed, it became clear that the right-wing opposition, led by Enrile, was fighting a losing battle in trying to derail the charter. The people and the politicians by and large wanted a constitution, regardless of its flaws. Enrile and his followers had no issue except Cory Aquino herself, and at that time, her prestige was still high. Even politicians who were opposed to Aquino had an interest in seeing the constitution ratified. A "yes" vote would pave the way for congressional elections as well as for regional and local offices. Many of the mayors and governors unseated by Pimentel were eager to win back their jobs.

On the day of the vote, more than 80 percent of the twenty-five million registered voters cast their ballots. When the tally was complete, about 70 percent had said "yes" to the constitution and, by extension, to Cory Aquino. One of the leaders of the anticonstitution Coalition for Democratic Action, Rene Espina, blamed the defeat on the government's prop-

3. Telephone interview with Mindaluz Quesada by Eileen Guerrero, Manila, June 7, 1993.
4. *Ibid.*

aganda campaign, lack of unity among the opposition, and, most likely, "the desire for basic constitutional stability." [5] Most of the "no" votes were cast in Muslim areas—where Islamic separatists claimed the constitution fell short of demands for self-rule—and in the Marcos strongholds of northern Luzon. Ominously, "no" votes were also strong in precincts located on military bases.

Ratification of the constitution paved the way for congressional elections, the next step in restoring the trappings of democracy. Voting was to take place on May 11, 1987.

Even before the constitution was ratified, however, Aquino and her advisers had begun screening potential candidates for the senate and house. In this task, she relied heavily on her brother, Jose "Peping" Cojuangco, and brother-in-law, Paul Aquino. Cojuangco was hardly a people power idealist; rather, he was an old-style, back-room wheeler-dealer, just the sort of traditional politician Cory claimed to disavow.

Peping realized that the administration's political base was too narrow and that many of Pimentel's appointees had little chance against established regional politicians whom his sister had fired. Her tenure had been too brief and too challenged by the RAM Boys and the Marcos clique to have built a strong national movement.

Peping also understood that Filipino politicians are by and large non-ideological opportunists who need the president's support to gain the pork barrel funds necessary for political survival. He was more than willing to cut deals with former Marcos supporters to bring them under Aquino's standard and guarantee administration majorities in both houses of congress.

Although Peping's strategy was good politics, it required compromising with those who did not sympathize with the ideals of the people power revolution or the promises of social change. Fielding an administration ticket also required considerable horse-trading within the ruling coalition, which included six registered political parties. For the senate, the coalition agreed to a single list of candidates under the banner *Lakas ng Bansa,* roughly translated as "People Power." Each party drew up its own list, and these were submitted to the palace for final approval. Paul Aquino would organize the campaign and serve as its manager.

5. Interview with Rene Espina, DZRH Radio, Manila, February 3, 1987.

On February 20, Aquino presented her candidates for the twenty-four senate seats at a televised press conference. Eight of the nominees were from her cabinet, including Jovito Salonga, chairman of the Presidential Commission on Good Government, and the following secretaries: Alberto Romulo (budget); Neptali Gonzales (justice); Aquilino Pimentel (local governments); Victor Ziga (general services); Heherson Alvarez (agrarian reform); the chief auditor, Teofisto Guingona; and special counsel Rene Saguisag.

Two of the nominees had been dropped from the cabinet under pressure from the military: the former labor secretary, Augusto Sanchez, for his leftist sentiments, and the former natural resources secretary, Ernesto Maceda, for alleged corruption. But Sanchez appealed to labor, students, and the cause-oriented groups—the liberal social activists who had been prominent in the struggle against Marcos.

Maceda had served as Marcos's executive secretary until he fell out with Imelda and was replaced. He then moved to New York, where he practiced law and became a confidante of Ninoy Aquino. Although Cory Aquino personally disliked Maceda, who had a reputation as a shifty politician, he lobbied strongly for a place on the ticket and was ultimately brought on board in hopes of using his acknowledged political skills.

Butz Aquino, who had been so effective in mustering crowds at EDSA, was included, along with two women, Leticia Shahani, the undersecretary of foreign affairs and Fidel Ramos's sister, and Santanina Rasul, a little-known educator from a prominent Muslim political clan. Raul Manglapus, a courtly former senator and prominent martial law exile, was chosen for his opposition credentials. John Osmeña, member of a powerful Cebu political family and grandson of the late President Sergio Osmeña, was selected to give the ticket muscle in the central Visayas Islands.

Rounding out the list were Mamintal Tamano, a Muslim lawyer; television personality and former leftist student leader Orlando Mercado; university president Edgardo Angara; Doy Laurel's younger brother, Sotero Laurel; education undersecretary, Art Defensor; customs director, Wigberto Tañada; the acting governor of Manila, Jose Lina; labor leader Ernesto Herrera; and businessman Vicente Paterno.

Most of the candidates were solid establishment figures, and the ticket hardly looked like a commitment to far-reaching reform. The senate and house tickets were formed according to the old-style rules of politics.

Some of the candidates were new faces, and some of them, such as Saguisag, Tañada, Sanchez, and Mercado, were reform minded. But others, such as Osmeña, Ziga, Tamano, and Laurel, were selected because of their links to powerful regional clans.

Family connections played important roles in the selection. Framers of the new constitution recognized the pernicious role that family connections traditionally play in Philippine politics. In an attempt to create a new political order, they approved a provision that "the state shall guarantee equal access to opportunities for public service, and prohibit political dynasties as may be defined by law." But this phrase meant that the provision had no effect until legislation would be enacted to define a "political dynasty." Aquino could have issued her own executive decree under the freedom constitution defining a political dynasty, but six of her relatives were running in the congressional elections, including her brother Jose; her uncle Francisco Sumulong; cousin Egmidio Tanjuatco; her brother-in-law Butz Aquino; a sister-in-law, Tessie Aquino-Oreta; and her husband's uncle, Herminio Aquino. She would leave a decision on political dynasties, as on other reforms, to the new congress.

Aquino maintained that she did not have control over her relatives and that the people themselves should decide who would represent them. She repeated that position eight months later, when other presidential relatives were seeking office in regional elections, even though there was legislation pending in congress to give the provision the force of law. As an opposition leader, Corazon Aquino had held Marcos accountable for his family's activities. Selective disregard for provisions of the constitution, especially one she had so strongly influenced, was a bad precedent for a president who promised to respect the rule of law.

The opposition, meanwhile, was struggling to put together its own ticket. Enrile and Blas Ople were urging the New Society Movement to join in presenting a joint senate ticket under the "Grand Alliance for Democracy." But the process bogged down over the insistence by Marcos's allies that they be given half the slots. Enrile realized that the presence of so many avowed Marcos stalwarts would weaken the alliance's public appeal. Eventually both the Grand Alliance and the New Society Movement announced their own, twenty-four-member tickets, with a few candidates nominated by both groups.

The most radical departure from old-style politics was offered by the

Partido ng Bayan, or "People's Party," an alliance of leftists with ties to the Communists. The party was founded in August, 1986, by Sison, Bernabe Buscayno, and other former political prisoners; it offered a broad agenda for social and economic change, including agrarian reform based on redistribution of land.

Opposition groups from both the left and the right knew they were fighting an uphill battle. Aquino's prestige was still high, and the public tended to identify anyone from the opposition as either tainted by Marcos or a dangerous leftist.

The president's supporters also used the bureaucracy to promote their own candidates, a tactic they had denounced when they were in the opposition. Cabinet members and other appointed officials who wished to stand for election were required to resign before the campaign, but the secretary of local governments, Jaime Ferrer, publicly threatened to fire any local official who refused to support the administration ticket. All those affected were Aquino appointees on the public payroll. The order gave the administration ticket a considerable advantage and smacked of unfair politics.

As in the constitutional referendum, the congressional campaign turned into a contest between Cory Aquino and the ghost of Ferdinand Marcos. Little was said about the grave problems facing the nation: Communist insurgency, Muslim restiveness, the economy, and social justice. Instead, the issue was who supported Marcos and who was loyal to Aquino.

On election day, May 11, nearly 80 percent of the voters went to the polls in what the government hoped would be a quiet election in contrast to the brutality and disorder of the February, 1986, presidential contest. Soon after the polls closed at 3:00 P.M., Cory Aquino announced, predictably, that the elections had been the cleanest and most peaceful "perhaps since independence." As evidence, her government noted that "only" thirteen people had been killed in election day violence.

Most of the cheating in Philippine elections occurs during the laborious counting phase. When the sun set that evening, electric power failed in parts of Manila, Davao, and elsewhere. The opposition claimed their candidates tended to lose votes when the power was restored. As NAMFREL's unofficial "quick count" showed twenty-three administration candidates headed for a senate landslide, the Grand Alliance charged fraud and claimed NAMFREL had rigged a sophisticated computer system to add one million votes to each of Aquino's candidates. The result, the alliance charged, was a "statistical impossibility" in which obscure administration candidates rolled up huge margins in areas where they were barely known.

The official count dragged on for months. In Manila's Navotas-Malabon district, numerous allegations of cheating were filed against Aquino's sister-in-law, Tessie Oreta. Oreta was running against a prominent leftist, Leandro Alejandro, who had been born in the district. Although Oreta was eventually certified as the winner, the election commission listed Navotas-Malabon as one of the areas with the largest number of protests.

The senate contest was not resolved until August 12, three months after the balloting, when the supreme court finally ordered Juan Ponce Enrile certified as the winner of the twenty-fourth and last seat. That gave twenty-two seats to the administration and two to the Grand Alliance opposition. The People's Party and New Society Movement were shut out.

The opposition fared better in the house of representatives, winning about fifty of the two hundred seats. Most went to former Marcos supporters, but the leftist People's Party also won two seats.

Despite opposition claims, the election appeared generally fair and orderly, at least when measured against contests in the Marcos era. More likely, the Grand Alliance and the New Society Movement simply could not shake the Marcos stigma, except in the house districts in the Ilocano north. The election also demonstrated the shallowness of the people power revolution, which had promised to usher in a new era in Philippine politics. A study by the left-wing Institute for Popular Democracy found that 129 of the 200 house members had either held elected office before or were members of established political clans.[6]

Throughout the country, it was clear that whatever winds of change had accompanied the rise of Corazon Aquino had blown themselves out. In the southern city of Zamboanga, where she won 59 percent of the vote in the presidential election, voters chose a pro-Marcos politician, Maria Clara Lobregat, as their representative in the house. The pro-Aquino bloc was split between two rivals.

In Negros Occidental province, Aquino's appointed governor, Daniel

6. *Far Eastern Economic Review* (Hong Kong), July 12, 1990, p. 36.

Lacson, had forged an alliance with former Marcos supporters, enabling powerful sugar planters to reassert their power. All seven elected congressmen were from landowning families, and they were later to work strongly to curb the effects of agrarian reform.

The congressional elections represented a first step in the successful reemergence of traditional political forces that had long dominated Philippine politics. Distinctions between the administration and opposition were increasingly blurred.

Once congress convened in July, 1987, Aquino lost the power of rule by decree that she had held under the freedom constitution. From then on, any reforms initiated by her would have to win the approval of a legislature heavily weighted in favor of special interests and the elite. The opportunity for sweeping change was gone.

The resilience of establishment political forces, the need for political stability, and the threat from the armed forces contributed to this development. So did the character and background of Corazon Aquino. Despite those challenges, however, there was no Filipino on the political stage with her prestige and popularity.

She could have used her enormous prestige to rally the public around an agenda for change and to face her opponents head on. That advice had been given to her by the late Jose Diokno, who urged her to use the network of people's organizations—farmers, social activists, workers, and others—as an alternative political force apart from the traditional parties. Many of those groups, however, espoused "progressive" or leftist views that she could not accept. Despite populist rhetoric, her roots were in the elite, and her sentiments lay with the conservative Catholic hierarchy and their reformist allies in business, academia, and the professions.

Thus, she fell back on the time-tested style of politics based on patronage and personality, even at the expense of the spirit of her people power promises.

A typical peasant home, made of clapboard and *nipa*, on the southern island of Tawi-Tawi. It is the norm for millions of rural Filipinos.

Photo by Robert H. Reid

This is the house in Concepcion, Tarlac province, where Cory and Ninoy Aquino lived soon after their marriage in 1954. Ninoy served as mayor there, launching his political career that ended with his assassination in 1983.

Photo by Robert H. Reid

Aquino flashes the "L" sign—Tagalog for *laban* or "fight"—during the 1986 election campaign. Others (left to right) are Francisco "Soc" Rodrigo, an adviser and later a member of the constitutional commission; Salvador "Doy" Laurel, her running mate and vice-president; Eva Estrada Kalaw, a supporter who later turned critic; and Francisco "Kir" Tatad, Marcos's information minister who supported Aquino but broke with her after she took office.

Photo by Jose Galvez

Juan Ponce Enrile shakes hands with Lieutenant Colonel Gregorio "Gringo" Honasan shortly after they succeeded in leading a military revolt that ultimately toppled Marcos in 1986. Honasan later led several coup attempts against Aquino.
Courtesy AP/Wide World Photos

Imelda Marcos's famous shoe collection in the basement of Malacañang Palace.
Courtesy of the authors

President Aquino chats with her executive secretary Joker Arroyo (center) and peace negotiator Teofisto Guingona in late 1986.
Courtesy AP/Wide World Photos

General Fidel Ramos with Vice-President Salvador Laurel and President Aquino in 1986.
Courtesy AP/Wide World Photos

Leftist protesters rally against threats of a military coup in 1986.
Courtesy of the authors

Defense Minister Enrile (left) talks with General Ramos in 1986 before Enrile was fired for his opposition to Aquino.

Courtesy AP/Wide World Photos

The Manila Hotel, scene of the first coup attempt against Aquino.

Courtesy of the authors

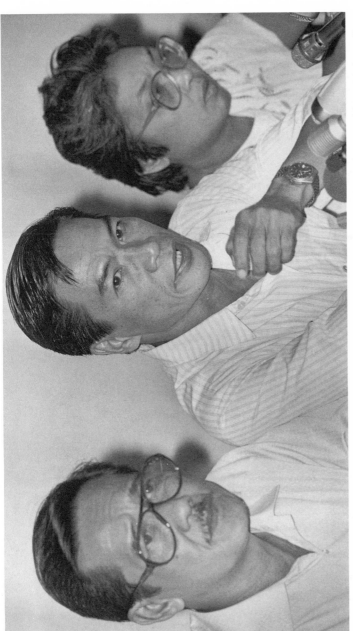

Communist rebel negotiators Antonio Zumel (with glasses), Saturnino Ocampo, and Carolina "Bobbie" Malay talk to reporters during the 1986 peace talks between the government and the NDF.

Troops loyal to the Aquino government man positions at Camp Aguinaldo, headquarters of the Armed Forces of the Philippines, during the December, 1989, coup attempt.

Rebel soldiers loyal to Gringo Honasan during the December, 1989, coup attempt.

Opponents of U.S. military bases in the Philippines burn Uncle Sam in effigy during a protest rally in front of the American Embassy, 1990.

Courtesy of the authors

Remains of a concrete bridge destroyed by volcanic mud avalanches during the June, 1991, eruption of Mount Pinatubo. The volcano dumped so much ash and debris that the river silted up and people could walk across it; the snowlike coating is actually ash. Picture was taken a few weeks after the eruption.

Photo by Eileen Guerrero

Roman Catholic nuns in Zambales province examine a statue of the Virgin Mary buried in volcanic ash from Mount Pinatubo. The local shrine stood nearly ten feet high on its pedestal.

Photo by Eileen Guerrero

Imelda Marcos parties at the Philippine Plaza Hotel, Manila, in January, 1992, two months after returning from exile in the U.S.

Photo by Eileen Guerrero

Imelda Marcos shakes hands with voters during her campaign for the presidency, May, 1992.

Courtesy of the authors

Vice-Admiral Robert Kelly, commander of U.S. naval forces in the Pacific, boards a navy plane at Subic Bay on November 24, 1992, the date the base closed, ending nearly a century of U.S. military presence in the Philippines. Kelly was the symbolic "last man" to leave the base, which had been the navy's largest overseas garrison.

Photo by Eileen Guerrero

President Aquino appearing before a civic group in Manila.

Courtesy of the authors

8 FALSE STARTS AND FUMBLING

THE COLLAPSE OF the peace talks with the Communists left Aquino with little alternative but to fulfill her promise made before the U.S. Congress in September, 1986, to "unsheathe the sword of war" if the rebels refused her offers of reconciliation. Within days after the cease-fire expired on February 7, 1987, the military reported the first clash with the New People's Army. An official report said troops battled about forty Communist rebels near the village of Lupao in Nueva Ecija province ninety miles north of Manila and that one lieutenant and eleven rebels were killed.

But villagers told a different story.[1] According to survivors, an army patrol entered the village early on the morning of February 10 looking for insurgents. A guerrilla unit had spent the night in the village; when government forces appeared, a rebel sniper picked off the patrol leader, Lieutenant Edgardo Dizon, killing him with a single bullet to the head.

Angry over the killing, the soldiers rounded up the villagers, forced them inside a dwelling, and then sprayed them with automatic fire. Seventeen civilians, including women and children, were slain. Manila newspapers bannered the survivors' accounts as the "Lupao Massacre," and

---

1. Guerrero and other reporters visited Lupao and talked with survivors; even though the villagers were probably sympathetic to the rebels, nonetheless, the first, official version released by the AFP was clearly inaccurate.

commentators in the liberal press roundly denounced the incident as a gross violation of human rights.[2]

Aquino's clumsy handling of the Lupao Massacre managed to alienate both human rights advocates and many within the armed forces. She waited nearly two weeks before visiting the site, then helicoptered to the area and, with a large press contingent in tow, consoled the survivors and promised justice. "After the cease-fire ended, I stressed clearly the protection of civilians like you who have no other intention but to live in peace and earn a living for your families," she told them.[3] Soldiers grumbled that the gesture was another sign that Cory Aquino's sympathies lay with the rebels.

As in the Mendiola Bridge incident, the president's words were not matched by action, and the result was a bitter disappointment to her liberal constituency. Although human rights organizations and most of the Manila press demanded swift punishment for the soldiers, such action would have enraged the armed forces at a time when Aquino needed all the support she could get. Instead, the case was referred to a military tribunal. Aquino had retained a Marcos-era presidential decree that gave military courts full jurisdiction over crimes involving soldiers, even those committed against civilians. The military stalled. The twenty-three soldiers were transferred from the province and were eventually court-martialed; three years later, after the country had all but forgotten the massacre, all of them were acquitted.

Meanwhile, the rebels wasted no time in resuming their own military operations after the cease-fire expired. On February 17, rebels used a land mine to blast a troop train as it traveled through the Bicol Peninsula of southeastern Luzon, about two hundred miles southeast of Manila. As cars careened off the tracks, rebels hiding in the underbrush sprayed the train with automatic weapons fire, killing one soldier before swiftly retreating. It was the first time the rebels had ever attacked a train, and the incident was widely seen as a sign that the New People's Army was prepared for a major escalation of the conflict.

On Mindanao Island, fighting escalated so rapidly in the Davao area

---

2. The *Philippine Daily Inquirer* and the Manila *Chronicle* were especially aggressive in criticizing the military for abusing the villagers' rights.

3. Corazon Aquino, speech at Lupao, February 22, 1987.

that more than twenty-three thousand people fled rural villages to escape the conflict. Several refugees interviewed at a banana plantation north of the city said they were mostly afraid of indiscriminate attacks by army helicopters strafing suspected rebel positions. In Misamis Oriental province, also on Mindanao, eighteen soldiers were killed during an ambush on March 17.

The rapid series of attacks was widely reported in the Manila media and painted the picture of a nation careening headlong into civil war. Clearly, the promise of democracy and reform would not be enough to quell the insurgency, despite the hopes of Aquino's human rights advisers and liberal-minded supporters.

As fighting escalated, the Philippine military's performance gave little cause for optimism. Although some units, including the marines, the constabulary Special Action troops, and the army's Scout Rangers performed effectively, many others displayed glaring deficiencies in tactics and training. Troops in convoys often sat in the back of trucks facing one another, which delayed their reaction time during ambushes. In some units, more than 40 percent of the vehicles were deadlined for lack of spare parts. Weapons jammed because of improper maintenance.

Training and discipline in the armed forces were spotty. In April, two months after the truce expired, the military reported a major clash in Bulacan province just north of the capital. When reporters arrived, residents told them that there had been no rebels in the area at all. Instead, two military patrols—one from the army and the other from the constabulary—had chanced upon one another and opened fire before realizing they were shooting at fellow soldiers.[4]

The government's ham-fisted response to the rebel threat began to cause concern in Washington, which had publicly supported Aquino through the peace talks and her political battles with Enrile. Assistant Defense Secretary Richard Armitage told an open session of the House Subcommittee on Asian and Pacific Affairs that the Aquino government was clinging "to the forlorn hope that the insurgents will fade away"

---

4. The assessment of the AFP's fighting skills comes primarily from private conversations Reid held with various U.S. army officers who were military attachés with the U.S. Embassy. Their comments, made on the promise of anonymity, appear accurate based on the AFP performance; they were privately echoed by senior officers, including former defense secretary and vice-chief of staff, Rafael Ileto.

because of her popularity. "Counterinsurgency strategies are developed and then discarded, military advice is often ignored," Armitage said.

It should be pointed out that a difference of opinion existed between the U.S. Department of Defense and the State Department regarding Aquino, with the Pentagon's assessment tending to be more critical. U.S. military attachés at the time maintained close ties with Honasan and the RAM group, before they went underground after the August, 1987, coup attempt, and the attachés' views of Aquino were somewhat colored by the association. State tried to offset this with more upbeat assessments because, although she was not ideal, she was the only viable prospect for acceptable change. David Lambertson, deputy assistant secretary of state for East Asia and Pacific Affairs, stated on September 10 that during the previous six months, insurgency-related military activity had increased steadily, with approximately the same number of casualties for the AFP as a year earlier. Nevertheless, he said, "It is important to bear in mind the situation which existed when the Aquino government took office and the considerable progress that has been made in the past eighteen months."

Much was made of this apparent split at the time, but to say that State supported Aquino and Defense opposed her is too strong. On December 2, 1987, Karl Jackson, deputy assistant secretary of defense, commented before the House Asian and Pacific Subcommittee: "I am quite frankly tired of hearing Defense views misrepresented. The United States and the Philippines are allies. . . . Our policy is to support Philippine democracy and President Aquino, period."[5]

The insurgency was spreading into the major cities, bringing what had been a largely rural conflict into the streets of Manila, Cebu, and other urban centers. During the cease-fire, about two thousand New People's Army guerrillas had slipped into Manila from central Luzon and were secretly living in hideouts in the districts of Tondo, Pasay City, and Santa Cruz. They organized themselves into small assassination cells known as "sparrow units," and after the truce expired, they launched a series of attacks on policemen and soldiers throughout the city. During the first six

---

5. The quotes from Armitage, Lambertson, and Jackson were all made in open hearings of the House Subcommittee on Asian and Pacific Affairs, which were covered by the AP.

months of 1987, forty-five policemen and soldiers were slain by these units in metropolitan Manila, including eight in five days beginning June 4.[6]

The government's counterinsurgency program lacked focus. Officially, it had a three-pronged approach: military action, amnesty for those who surrendered, and a resettlement program so that former insurgents could begin new lives. In practice, there was hardly a program at all. Ramos complained publicly and often that local officials, most of them Pimentel appointees, were not cooperating with the regional military commanders. Officials themselves complained that the military could more effectively win over the people if soldiers refrained from drunken brawls with the locals.

The government was determined at least to win the propaganda war. After the cease-fire expired, Aquino announced a six-month amnesty and resettlement program for the rebels and earmarked $50 million to help former insurgents with housing and jobs. Every day, the government's press organs reported that hundreds of rebels here and a hundred more there had "returned to the folds of the law."

The program quickly proved to be little more than a publicity stunt. The government was so strapped financially that it released only about $1 million of the $50 million allocated for the program. Those rebels who did surrender often found themselves without the housing, food, and support that had been promised.

In a clumsy attempt to make the program appear effective, military and civilian authorities organized numerous "mass surrender" ceremonies, where hundreds, sometimes thousands, of so-called rebels would stand under the sun and take oaths of allegiance to the constitution for the benefit of television crews flown in from Manila. Generally, however, reporters discovered that most were not guerrillas at all. Some were doubtless rebel sympathizers, but the majority appeared to be peasants dragooned into the ceremony at the request of their local village leaders. These barangay captains soon discovered that the best way to keep mil-

6. The source for all figures on insurgency-related casualties is, in the final analysis, the AFP Civil Relations Office, although all journalists—ourselves included—strongly suspect its figures. Common crimes could be hidden as battle deaths, and many suspected that the AFP adjusted figures to suit political goals, increasing casualties when it wanted to promote the notion of a Communist threat. In addition, blaming Communists for a killing was a good way to cover up something else.

itary patrols out of their communities was to take part in a surrender ceremony.

The most accurate accounting of genuine rebels who surrendered came from the number and quality of firearms turned in. Four months into the program, the government claimed that 1,382 New People's Army "regulars" had surrendered, but it admitted that only 155 firearms had been given up.

During a "mass surrender" ceremony held on June 25, 1987, on Negros Island, seventy-eight so-called Communist regulars took their oaths of allegiance. After the ceremony, a social worker arrived to distribute bread to them, nearly provoking a riot as the scrawny "rebels" clamored for the food. Negros Island was, at the time, among the poorest areas of the Philippines, and many of the group appeared not to have had a decent meal in weeks. Later, a group of the "surrenderees" approached Mayor Ernesto Tingson and told him: "Our problem is how to find food. Can you help us?" Tingson promised 150 sacks of cement to build waterpumps. "There are a lot of food-for-work projects, but they have been suspended now," he explained to them.[7] Aquino's government, saddled with huge foreign debt payments and an economy ravaged by years of corruption, simply lacked sufficient funds.

The local military commander admitted to one of the authors his doubts that any who surrendered were genuine rebels but instead were impoverished peasants hoping to get food if they pretended to be guerrillas. After his remarks appeared in Manila newspapers, the officer, Lieutenant Colonel George Moleta, was transferred to northern Luzon.

At the same time, the government was coming under strong criticism for the slow pace of agrarian reform. The Aquino government and the Manila press talked a lot about agrarian reform during the first two years of her administration. The program was seen as a necessary step to improve economic conditions in the rural areas, where more than 60 percent of the population lived, and to wean the peasantry away from Marxist insurgents.

Land ownership, however, was the foundation of the entire Philippine social class system. There were also wide differences within the administration over the structure of a future program, such as whether to pro-

7. Guerrero was invited by the local congresswoman, Hortencia Starke, to attend this "surrender"; when she arrived, she realized it was essentially a hoax.

mote redistribution or to focus instead on profit sharing among tenants. Whereas the Marcos land reform program covered only rice- and corn-producing areas, Aquino had promised to include all croplands, including sugar. Given the administration's own lack of consensus, she simply pursued Marcos's program, distributing land titles for corn and rice farms while trying to work out details of an expanded program.[8]

The Reverend Joaquin Bernas, an Aquino stalwart since the Convenor days, and other churchmen urged her to enact some sort of new program as soon as possible to show her commitment to social change, but she was firm: the final decision on the details would be left to the new congress. The result, however, was to create a public impression that nothing was being done on land reform. Aquino's priorities were on building institutions of questionable effectiveness rather than on taking urgent steps toward fundamental reform.

On the economic front, the new administration reversed the downward spiral that crippled the Marcos government, and the gross national product registered 0.13 percent growth for 1986. Using its reservoir of international goodwill, the government signed an agreement in March, 1987, with 483 commercial banks to reschedule $10.3 billion in debts, but at interest rates less favorable than the bankers gave Mexico and Argentina. That led to criticism of Finance Secretary Ongpin by those who claimed he should have been tougher in talks with the banks.

Ongpin was already growing more and more frustrated with government, in particular his dealings with Arroyo and his allies, who favored selective repudiation of the debt.[9] Ongpin had no background in politics or in dealings with the Philippine press, which seized upon repudiation as an easy answer to the country's cash problems. He chafed at suggestions that he was the "bankers' friend" in the administration and did not hesitate to lecture reporters, which only served to produce more and more unfavorable stories about him.

Little progress was being made also in efforts to resolve the complaints of the six million Muslims. After Aquino's meeting in 1986 with Muslim

8. For more on the agrarian reform program, see James Putzel, *A Captive Land: The Politics of Agrarian Reform in the Philippines* (Quezon City, 1992), and Richard J. Kessler, *Rebellion and Repression in the Philippines* (New Haven, 1989).

9. Ongpin's frustration with his cabinet colleagues is discussed in detail in Nick Joaquin, *Jaime Ongpin: The Enigma* (Makati, 1990).

rebel leader Nur Misuari, the government had held on again–off again talks with the Moro National Liberation Front regarding terms for autonomy for Muslim areas of the southern Philippines.

Misuari agreed to drop his demand for an independent state in favor of autonomy based on a 1976 formula that Marcos accepted but never implemented and that would have granted Muslim self-rule in thirteen southern provinces. But immigration since World War II had changed the religious character of much of Mindanao and other traditional Muslim areas, and Christians now dominated the populations of many provinces Misuari wanted to include in his autonomous region.

Even though many Christians shared Misuari's view that Mindanao, despite its wealth in agricultural and natural resources, had been short-changed in development in favor of Luzon, they had little interest in living under Islamic rule. As with the Communists, the government insisted that the Muslims accept an agreement within the framework of the new constitution, which limited the scope of self-rule.

In the meantime, Aquino allowed Misuari to travel throughout Mindanao, ostensibly to confer with his supporters after ten years in exile. The military, as well as Misuari's rivals in the Muslim community, however, claimed he was using the opportunity to reorganize and re-equip his forces, which numbered about ten thousand. Critics argued, with some justification, that Misuari's position had deteriorated during his long exile and that the peace process had served only to resurrect him from political obscurity.

The peace talks finally broke down in May, 1987, raising fears the government might face a two-front war. But the MNLF never revived the war, mostly because of disunity and war weariness in its ranks. Scattered fighting erupted from time to time, especially in the Cotabato area, but the combatants were usually Muslims from rival factions angry at what they considered government favoritism toward Misuari.

The result of all the disorder, the policy fits and starts, and the seeming lack of progress on so many fronts all contributed to a palpable sense of national drift by the middle of 1987. True, the economy was growing, although improvements in living standards were slow in trickling down to the masses. Figures from the National Statistics Office at the time showed 60 percent of the Filipino people lived below the poverty line and

70 percent of the nation's children lacked proper nutrition. Such statistics, as well as the definition of "poverty," are highly subjective in the Philippines, however. In terms of income and based on world standards, the poverty rate was probably even higher. "Nothing has really changed under Cory for the people," Negros Bishop Antonio Fortich complained in a February, 1987, interview. "In the countryside, it's still the same."[10] Aquino was moving to reestablish the institutions of democracy, but there appeared to be no plan, no sense of national direction beyond those institutions themselves. Richard Kessler, a former staff member of the U.S. Senate Foreign Relations Committee, wrote: "In effect, Aquino has projected no vision for the country's future beyond the simple one of rewriting the constitution and reestablishing the semblance of democratic institutions with elections."[11]

Aquino's response to these charges was that the government simply lacked the resources to address all the various demands at the same time. From an economic point of view, there could be little doubt she was correct. At the time, nearly 40 percent of the government's revenues were going for debt service, both foreign and domestic. Nevertheless, campaign hyperbole and her "all things to all people" image, so carefully crafted by her closest advisers, had raised unrealistic public expectations: the people expected change sooner than later.

Filipinos wanted some idea of Aquino's priorities now that democracy had been nominally restored. "The disenchantment over what's happening in Philippine society today is a natural offshoot of the people's high hopes after the fall and flight of the Marcos regime," wrote commentator Arturo Borjal in the pro-government *Philippine Star*. "The perception grew that the Cory government lacked the leadership qualities demanded by the times."[12]

For many Filipinos, simply restoring democracy was not enough. They yearned for a sense of national purpose, a vision for the nation that Cory Aquino was not giving them. Senator Leticia Shahani alluded to this when

---

10. Telephone interview with Bishop Antonio Fortich by Eileen Guerrero, Manila, February 22, 1987. The bishop was an outspoken champion of the poor, earning the nickname "Ka Tony" (short for *kasama* or "comrade") or the "Red Bishop" in conservative circles.

11. Kessler, *Rebellion and Repression,* 148.

12. Arturo Borjal, *Philippine Star,* September 5, 1987.

she said in a radio interview in 1987, "I think the moderate Filipinos need an ideology which can match the dedication of the ideology of the extreme right and the extreme left." [13]

Butz Aquino believes that his sister-in-law simply failed to understand the inertia factor so prevalent at all levels of Philippine society. "She tells you something once, and she expects it to be done," he said. "She didn't realize at first that to accomplish anything in the Philippines, you have to push and push and push." [14]

What her critics had forgotten was that Cory Aquino had actually promised virtually nothing beyond removing Marcos and reestablishing democracy. Collectively, the anti-Marcos opposition had made lavish, often-contradictory promises encompassing land reform and social justice before the 1986 election. What was uncertain was Aquino's personal commitment to any single issue once in office. She represented the conservative wing of an essentially conservative opposition movement that at best was prepared to promote modest socioeconomic reform.

The Aquino presidency early on was composed of leftist, centrist, and conservative elements, and all shades in between. During the 1986 campaign and the first months of the administration, the reformist group was most prominent: Saguisag, Arroyo, Jose Diokno, Bernas. Both Saguisag and Arroyo had much interaction with the press, and they tended to present an image of Aquino that reflected their own beliefs as reformers. The president, however, shared their views only to an extent, and when Arroyo left, Saguisag moved to the senate, and Diokno died, they and other, more left-leaning figures were replaced by more conservative, establishment ones. By the end of her term, she was surrounded by persons with Catholic church or military ties, such as Jesus Estanislao (her last finance secretary), Jose Cuisia (the last Central Bank governor), or Fidel Ramos, who did not represent a reform agenda. This shift in the ideological spectrum is why she eventually opposed her former aides on the U.S. bases' issue.

World opinion about Aquino, however, had been shaped by those early image-building efforts, and when reforms did not materialize as expected,

13. Interview with Leticia Shahani, DZRH Radio, Manila, September 4, 1987. Shahani was part of the Philippine UN delegation in New York in 1986 and was one of the first diplomats abroad to break with the Marcos administration. After serving briefly as Aquino's deputy foreign minister, she was elected to the senate in 1987, where she is currently president pro tempore.

14. Interview with Agapito Aquino by Robert Reid, Manila, May 8, 1991.

the consensus was that she had failed to accomplish "her" goals, primarily because of lack of experience and political expertise. In reality, she could be as shrewd and cunning as she needed to be, and the authors believe that her one goal in running for the presidency was to get rid of Marcos, which she accomplished. Filipino society and political culture are highly personal, and institutions, parties, and ideology are often secondary to an individual's personal agenda. As the months, then years passed, it became clear that Cory Aquino's personal agenda was very limited.[15]

Indeed, the essence of democracy for her seemed to lie in the absence of an ideology, especially one directed from the top. She seemed to believe that it was up to the people, through their elected representatives in the congress, to set the national agenda. "Some complain of a sense of drift under my administration and urge me to do something about it," she said during an appearance at Ateneo University in 1987. "Not too long ago, they complained of a sense of being pushed around and dragged into disaster."[16]

As the Aquino presidency moved through its second year, signs of disaffection were everywhere: labor unrest, political infighting, armed insurgency, and government indecision. It seemed only a matter of time before armed opponents would strike again.

15. Kessler, *Rebellion and Repression,* 148.
16. Corazon Aquino, speech to the Integrated Bar of the Philippines, Ateneo de Manila University, June 19, 1987.

9 GUNS OF AUGUST

CORY AQUINO AND her supporters had hoped that ousting Enrile from the defense ministry and taking stern measures against the mutineers at the GMA station would end open rebellion in the ranks. But six weeks after Canlas surrendered, a bomb exploded at the Philippine Military Academy parade ground, killing four people and injuring thirty-nine. The blast occurred a few days before the president was to attend commencement exercises there. The military first blamed the Communists, then admitted the bomb was probably planted by dissident soldiers. Although an explosives instructor at the academy, Major Wilhelm Doromal, was questioned, he was never charged and was retained on the faculty. Later, Doromal was implicated in two other coup attempts.

The crisis in the military was not limited to individuals such as Johnny Enrile, Gringo Honasan, and their followers. Many members of the armed forces viewed Aquino and the state of the country very differently from how she was seen abroad. On December 2, 1987, before an open hearing of the U.S. House Subcommittee on Asian and Pacific Affairs, Karl Jackson, deputy assistant secretary of defense, said that while most Filipinos applauded Aquino's restoration of democratic institutions, "Many in the military perceived her accomplishments as marginal to the AFP [Armed Forces of the Philippines] as an institution. To some of these persons, 'restoring democracy' meant tolerating communist violence while subjecting the military to a different set of human rights standards and returning the Philippines to 'politics as usual.'"

Signs of military restiveness were everywhere. On April 18, the Saturday before Easter, thirteen enlisted men broke into Fort Bonifacio before dawn and tried to free prisoners held at the stockade since the GMA coup attempt. The attackers failed to get past the guards but managed to take over the army headquarters building, where they held out until they surrendered about noon.

Coup rumors abounded. Despite signs of trouble, little attention was paid to the activities of Gringo Honasan and the remnants of the Enrile clique. Gringo appeared to accept defeat gracefully. He and others in the RAM clique told Ramos and Defense Secretary Ileto that they were ready for reassignment, even, if necessary, to training units, normally considered a career dead end. Honasan's opponents in the command thought that with Enrile gone, the RAM power base had been broken.

If Honasan wanted to command a training unit, Ramos was only too happy to oblige. He sent the youthful colonel to the Special Operations school at Fort Magsaysay, seventy-five miles north of Manila in Nueva Ecija province. Red Kapunan, whose wife had led the computer operators' walkout during the 1986 election, was transferred to the Philippine Military Academy in Baguio.

But Honasan's offer was like throwing Br'er Rabbit into the briar patch. His job at Fort Magsaysay was to train elite Scout Rangers, the Green Berets of the Philippine Army, while Kapunan's assignment put him in contact with the young, idealistic cadets who would be the future leaders of the armed forces—the perfect jobs for those who wanted to inculcate future generations of leaders with their ideals.

Gringo made no secret of his disdain for Aquino. He brazenly sent signals to the palace that he was planning something. In mid-1987, Honasan contacted Teodoro Locsin, her speechwriter and presidential adviser, and told him: "Tell Cory we're going to launch a coup against her." Locsin, a witty, urbane man with an abrasive sense of humor, was perplexed. If Honasan wanted to overthrow the government, why tell the president beforehand? He decided to call Honasan's bluff. "Why don't you launch your coup first, then she'll know," Locsin replied.[1]

1. Teodoro Locsin, oral communication to Eileen Guerrero, Manila, September 15, 1991.

The upsurge in fighting with the Communists after the cease-fire collapsed provided Honasan with a compelling message: Aquino's weak government had no counterinsurgency strategy and the Marxists were gaining the upper hand. The president had dismissed a few cabinet members
to appease Ramos, but she stubbornly refused to fire Arroyo and Locsin.
The previous November, Ramos thought he had a deal with Cory: Enrile
would go, but so would Arroyo and Locsin. Months had passed, and the
two still held positions of influence.

Ramos was not the only official who wanted Arroyo fired. Ongpin and
his business community friends also wanted him removed because of what
they considered his high-handed interference in their departments. Newspapers were replete with stories, leaked by cabinet rivals, that Arroyo was
an administrative disaster. Important memos piled up on his desk, delaying policy decisions. Senior officials who wanted to raise issues with the
president had to get past Arroyo, a formidable hurdle. Calls for his head,
however, only stiffened Aquino's determination to keep him. She trusted
the man the press called "the little president," felt comfortable with him,
and had come to rely heavily on his counsel.

On August 22, Ongpin and his wife Maribel visited Aquino at her
Arlegui residence. Ongpin wanted to apologize for unflattering remarks
he had made to a U.S. reporter about her husband Ninoy. Maribel recalls
that she was gracious until the conversation turned to Joker Arroyo. "We
elected you president, not Joker Arroyo," Ongpin told the president. Mrs.
Ongpin added, "Yes, Cory, you can make your mistakes, but don't make
Joker Arroyo's mistakes." Silently, Aquino turned and walked away. Arroyo had stood by her during the long years of Ninoy's imprisonment.
He was by her side in the flush of the 1986 victory and in the dark hours
when her enemies sought to overthrow her. She owed much to Joker
Arroyo and could not abandon him. [2]

Aquino's friendship with Bernabe Buscayno also convinced disaffected
soldiers that the president's heart lay with the left. On June 8, 1987, the
former rebel commander was leaving a television station in Quezon City
after appearing on a panel show. Shortly before midnight, three assailants
wearing fatigue uniforms opened fire on Buscayno's car with semiautomatic weapons. Buscayno, a veteran of hundreds of shoot-outs, threw

    2. Nick Joaquin, *Jaime Ongpin: The Enigma* (Makati, 1990), 315.

himself forward at the first crackle of gunfire, and a bullet struck him in the back. Two of his companions were killed, and two others, including his pregnant future wife, were wounded. Her daughter was born months later with a facial scar from a bullet in the mother's uterus. No one was ever arrested.[3]

When the president heard of the attack, she telephoned Buscayno at the Philippine Heart Center and told him she would soon visit. Buscayno thanked her but advised against a visit. He knew such a gesture would only increase the anger of police and soldiers, whose support she needed to stay in power.[4]

Widespread talk of drift in the Aquino government convinced Honasan that a new coup would stand a good chance of public support. The Communist killings in Manila may have been tame compared with the daily violence in the countryside, but the Philippine media rarely reported rural violence in the same graphic detail as killings in the capital. The country appeared to be on the verge of civil war.

This perception was dramatically heightened on the evening of August 2, 1987, when the secretary of local governments, Jaime Ferrer, was ambushed near his home in Parañaque, a suburb south of Manila. Ferrer was heading home after evening church services when five gunmen opened fire, killing him and his driver.

The seventy-year-old Ferrer was a leading anticommunist figure in the government and had been supervising the organization of civilian vigilante groups to fight the Communists. U.S. diplomats wept at the news of his death. Jaime Ferrer had been closely associated with the Central Intelligence Agency since the 1950s, and speculation about his murderers centered on the Communists.[5] As local governments' secretary, however, Ferrer had fired numerous local officials, sometimes in a demeaning manner. He humiliated one official by ordering him to publicly recite Joyce Kilmer's poem "Trees" to atone for cutting down an ancient tree on state property without permission. Ferrer had a lot of enemies.

3. Interview with Bernabe Buscayno by Eileen Guerrero, Tarlac province, April 11, 1991.

4. *Ibid.*

5. Joseph Smith, *Portrait of a Cold Warrior* (New York, 1976), 296–97, 315–21. Smith describes himself as a former CIA operative who saw duty in Chile and the Philippines. His book, a mea culpa, primarily criticizes the toppling of Allende but also includes chapters on the Philippines. Ferrer's background as local governments' secretary and his prominence in anticommunist movements lends credence to the claim that he worked with the CIA.

Two persons eventually were convicted in the slaying, but they never revealed who hired them. One of the gunmen was actually serving a life sentence for murder at the time but had been allowed out of prison when a corrupt judge issued a warrant for him to testify at a bogus trial.

Political assassinations had become a tragic fact of Philippine life, but Ferrer was only the second cabinet-level official to be assassinated since independence. The Communists publicly denied the killing. Years later, however, party leaders told the rank and file secretly that they had indeed been responsible.[6]

Another factor that figured in Honasan's timing for a new coup was Aquino's mishandling of fuel price increases. The government was subsidizing consumer fuel prices with an oil price stabilization fund, but its assets were dangerously low. Fuel price hikes were a politically volatile issue in the Philippines, where salaries were so low that even a modest increase posed a financial burden for the public. The administration delayed a price increase until after the May elections for fear of giving the opposition a badly needed issue.

On August 14, the president approved increases that boosted the price of gasoline from $1.24 to $1.49 per gallon. The increase was unpopular, and militant labor unions immediately announced plans for nationwide strikes. A few days later, a harried-looking Aquino appeared on television and tried patiently to explain the need for the increase; she then rolled back the price to $1.35 a gallon. The waffling did not dissuade the unions from pushing through with the strike, but it did make Aquino appear to be vacillating and indecisive.

The strike began on Wednesday, August 26, and its effects were devastating. It was clearly the most effective strike ever launched by the left-wing May First Movement. Public transport came to a halt in Manila and other major cities, and government and private offices were virtually empty by mid-day. In Cebu, police fired water cannon at protesters and arrested fifty of them.

When reporters telephoned the Department of Labor for an assessment of the strike's impact, the minister himself, Franklin Drilon, answered the telephone. He apologized for being unable to comment on the scope of the walkout—too few of his employees had come to work to compile an

---

6. This information was revealed to the authors by two party members who are trustworthy but still active in the party, whose identities must be confidential.

accurate picture. Nationwide, 127 people were arrested when police broke up illegal pickets.

The May First Movement planned to continue the strike the following day, but police cracked down immediately. They arrested about seventy people in Manila, including strike leaders, and others went into hiding. "It's about time we enforce the law and maintain peace and order," growled General Lim to reporters near one of the dispersal sites. The show of resolve was too late. Honasan was already on the move.

The attack did not come without warning. Four days before the general strike, Major General Renato de Villa, the Philippine Constabulary commander, told the general staff that he believed Honasan was organizing a new coup attempt. At first Montaño, the general staff's chief of operations, didn't believe him. Bogus coup plot reports were common throughout the first half of the year, and there was no reason to believe this one was valid.[7] Besides, Montaño knew that Honasan's trainees in classes at the Special Operations school only numbered about one hundred, hardly enough for a serious military operation. Where would Honasan get enough troops, Montaño asked himself?

Montaño learned to his horror that instead of graduating classes on schedule, Honasan had been holding them back, ostensibly for more training. Meanwhile, the system had been sending him new batches of students, enabling him to build up his force. By late August, he had about six hundred ranger trainees in his command. Orders were issued to stop sending more students to Fort Magsaysay.[8]

De Villa telephoned Honasan and confronted him with his suspicions, but Honasan denied a coup was in the works. De Villa decided that he and Montaño should go to Fort Magsaysay and talk personally to Honasan, scheduling the visit for the morning of August 28.[9]

An attack on Manila from Fort Magsaysay would require skill, deception, and stealth. The garrison was located in a remote area, and most of the journey to Manila would have to be made on a two-lane road through heavily populated areas. Gringo knew, however, that he could count on his old friend, Lieutenant Colonel Eduardo Matillano, the police com-

---

7. The Davide Commission, *Final Report of the Fact-Finding Commission* (Makati, 1990), 177–78.

8. Interview with Ramon Montaño by Eileen Guerrero, Manila, April 9, 1991.

9. *Ibid.*

mander of Nueva Ecija province, to help in the operation. On August 25, Matillano summoned his company commanders and told them to prepare for combat operations on twenty-four-hours' notice. Troops were to carry enough fuel, food, and ammunition for a three-day operation.[10]

Aquino had scheduled a visit to central Luzon on August 28, and Honasan knew that security around the presidential palace would be reduced because of the trip. The Presidential Security Group, the one-thousand-member guard force, ordinarily sent half its troops ahead of the president to prepare arrangements. Other units would have to be deployed throughout central Luzon to strengthen security for the visit, and Honasan knew he could move his own forces then without attracting undue attention.

On the afternoon of the twenty-seventh, Honasan loaded his troops aboard trucks and buses and left Fort Magsaysay for the Santa Rita tollgate on the North Diversion Road, the main four-lane highway linking Manila with towns in central Luzon. There, they were to link up with other rebel troops, mostly from Scout Ranger commands based in central and northern Luzon. Some of the troops later testified they thought they were to take part in training maneuvers, while others believed they were to defend Manila against the Communists.[11]

At Camp Aguinaldo, the general staff monitored the rebels as they headed south, but, as Gringo had hoped, the command was uncertain which forces were with Honasan and which were deploying for the president's visit. One report said truckloads of troops were "strung along the highway" north of Manila, but the northern Luzon commander, Brigadier General Bayani Fabic, assumed the forces were simply reinforcing for the presidential visit. It was only when the convoy continued south that the command in Manila realized the coup had begun. By that time, it was too late to stop them from reaching the gates of the city.[12]

De Villa and Ramos set up a base of operations at Camp Crame. Across the street at Camp Aguinaldo, Lieutenant General Eduardo Ermita and Montaño manned the AFP general staff headquarters. Senior officers scurried about Camp Aguinaldo, rounding up clerks and anyone else they could find to defend the garrison.[13]

10. Davide Commission *Final Report,* 178.
11. *Ibid.,* 178–80.
12. Montaño interview by Guerrero, April 9, 1991.
13. *Ibid.*

Ramos and his staff were uncertain where Gringo would strike. As a precaution, Ramos alerted Colonel Voltaire Gazmin, the chief of the Presidential Security Group, to prepare to defend Malacañang with those troops still in Manila.

When Honasan's forces reached the edge of the capital, they split into several formations and headed for the palace, broadcast facilities, and other strong points. Some four hundred rebels reached the Malacañang area about 1:45 A.M. and attacked along two fronts: Dr. Concepcion Aguila Street in the direction of Aquino's residence and another down J. P. Rizal Street, which runs in front of the palace compound. Another rebel force, made up of troops from the army's Sixteenth Infantry Battalion, seized the Ayala Bridge west of the palace to prevent reinforcements reaching the compound from the other direction.

Gazmin had deployed two Scorpion tanks near the gates along J. P. Rizal Street; when the rebels approached, the vehicles opened fire with their .50-caliber machine guns. Many of Honasan's troops were still in their buses, apparently not expecting resistance. They returned fire, but their advance on the palace was blocked. Reinforcements from the Philippine Constabulary rushed to the western edge of the compound and drove off the rebels holding the Ayala Bridge.[14]

Cory Aquino was awakened by the crackle of gunfire. Although the military had been bracing for an attack for hours, she had not been warned of the threat. She rushed to the intercom in the second-floor bedroom she shared with daughter Kris and called the duty officer downstairs: "What's going on?" The officer replied, "Ma'am, we'll get back to you. We're contacting our commander."[15]

Aquino then tried to telephone Ramos but was told he had gone to Camp Crame. She called Arroyo but could not reach him either. One of her daughters suggested, "Mom, why don't we pray the rosary in the meantime?" Frightened, Cory and her daughters knelt to pray, but other thoughts were racing through the president's mind. This was very serious, more so than the Manila Hotel incident, the Enrile showdown, or the attack on the GMA television station. This time, the battle had reached the gates of the palace.

14. Davide Commission *Final Report*, 181–82.
15. Interview with Corazon Aquino by Maria Shriver, "Sunday Morning," NBC News, October 6, 1987. The following account of Aquino's recollections during the coup attempt is from this interview.

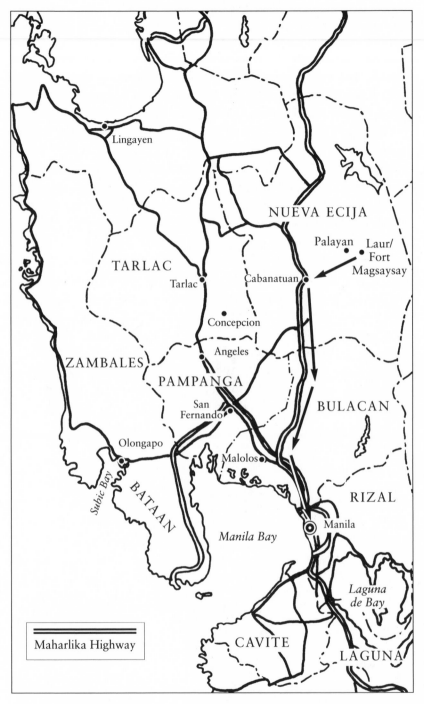

Map 5. Route used by Lieutenant Colonel Gringo Honasan in mounting the August, 1987, coup attempt.

Sometime after the thirtieth "Hail Mary," Gazmin appeared at the residence. "Ma'am, they attacked us, and I think two of the sentries have been shot." When she asked who was leading the assault, the officer replied, "I think it's Honasan." He escorted Aquino and her daughters to the ground floor, where they huddled in darkness, afraid to switch on the lights.

Aquino was scared. Her thoughts returned to another terrible August night four years before, when she learned in Boston that her husband was dead. That night, the news gave her the shivers, but as she faced an even more dangerous personal threat, she remained calm. She brushed aside a suggestion to take a tranquilizer.

Her first concern was for her missing son, Benigno "Noynoy" Aquino III. Her instincts as a mother outweighed those as a president, and although the government was under armed attack, she spent valuable time telephoning around the city trying to find her son. Noynoy, a twenty-seven-year-old bachelor, had slipped out about midnight and was in Makati, one of the centers of Manila's nightlife. He heard radio reports about trouble near the palace and rushed to Joker Arroyo's house in Dasmariñas Village. The mayor of Makati, Jejomar Binay, and others had gathered there to await word of what was happening, but initial reports failed to convey the scope of the attack. "We felt the situation was not that critical because there had not been massive firing," Noynoy told reporters later, "so I felt it was safe to proceed." He and his bodyguards left Arroyo's residence in two cars and headed in the darkness toward the palace. As they approached Saint Jude's Church on the eastern edge of the compound, Noynoy saw armed troops. He assumed they were palace guards because their weapons were pointed toward Gringo's forces.

The cars slowed to a halt, and Noynoy stepped out to identify himself. "We're on the same side. I'm Noynoy Aquino." The troops turned and fired, wounding him in the neck and killing three companions, including a woman. Officially, the troops were said to have been rebels. But the shooting took place close to the palace, and the assailants may well have been presidential guards, nervous and ready to shoot at the slightest provocation.[16]

Other troops rushed forward and carried Noynoy to safety. He tele-

16. Davide Commission *Final Report*, 181–82. Noynoy gave his account of the shooting in a radio interview (transcript on file with AP, Manila).

phoned his mother to assure her he was alive but did not tell her that he had been wounded. It was not until 7:00 A.M., nearly five hours later, that she learned he had been shot. Although his wounds were not life threatening, Cory Aquino would never forgive Honasan for nearly killing her only son.

About 3:00 A.M., the rebels began withdrawing from the palace, heading east down the darkened Ramon Magsaysay Avenue. Several thousand people had gathered there, awakened by the gunfire. As the rebels passed, the crowd began taunting them; some of the troops opened fire, killing about eleven people—including a Filipino news photographer—and wounding fifty-four others. The coup attempt was only in its first hours but was already bloodier than any of the previous uprisings.

Ramos announced over local radio stations that an "apparent attack" on the palace had been foiled. President Aquino was safe. "There is propaganda that operations of mutinous soldiers numbering two hundred to three hundred are supporting a combination of Senator Enrile and General Ramos," he said. "Insofar as General Ramos is concerned, that is not true. We are on the side of the president and we are ensuring her safety."

At 4:00, about an hour after the attack on the palace had ended, Aquino broadcast for the first time from a local radio station to assure the nation she was safe. The palace had been under attack, the government was in disarray, the military was on the verge of collapse, and armed rebels were in control of strong points throughout the city. But her voice was calm, almost jocular. "It's all right here, but it's a little noisy. . . . I want to tell our people that first of all, I am all right, and General Ramos is on top of the situation and is in constant touch with me." [17] In fact, she had not been able to reach Ramos for more than an hour after the attack began. Despite the reassuring tone, Cory Aquino and Fidel Ramos knew that a grave challenge to their leadership was unfolding. The next few hours would be crucial to their very survival.

Although the attack on Malacañang had failed, the mutineers controlled Camp Olivas, the constabulary headquarters for central Luzon, the airport at Legazpi 250 miles southeast of Manila, the air and naval station at Sangley Point in Cavite, and several garrisons in the Cebu area. In Baguio, cadets of the Philippine Military Academy issued a manifesto

17. Both the Ramos and Aquino radio broadcasts were monitored by Reid, and details on shooting near the palace were related to both Reid and Guerrero by eyewitnesses.

supporting the mutiny to establish good government and save the country from communism. The manifesto was delivered to a Baguio radio station by Major Wilhelm Doromal, the man questioned and later cleared in the bombing there five months earlier.

In Manila, strong points were also falling one by one to the insurgents with little or no resistance. About twenty rebel air policemen bluffed their way past the gate guards at Villamor Air Base, surrounded the headquarters building, and trapped the air force commander, Major General Antonio Sotelo, in his office.

Matillano's rebels seized four of the city's five television stations and took over the Camelot Hotel, a garish-looking structure near Camp Aguinaldo that rented rooms by the hour for romantic trysts. A young lieutenant, Ramon de la Cruz, and eight enlisted men remained holed up in one corner of the government television station and refused to surrender. De la Cruz telephoned the general staff headquarters and begged for reinforcements. "We've spent all of our ammunition," he said. "Where's your reinforcements?" Montaño was afraid to tell him the truth: there were no reinforcements. Every available man had been ordered to defend Camp Aguinaldo. To keep up the lieutenant's morale, Montaño lied, telling him that reinforcements were on the way.[18]

In fact, the military within the capital was falling apart. Ramos was having trouble finding enough loyal troops to defend his own headquarters, much less rescue stranded lieutenants. By dawn, Gringo's forces, including those who had attacked the palace, rolled into Camp Aguinaldo with no resistance. Government forces blocked one gate, and one officer, Colonel Pedro Juachon, told Gringo to return to Fort Magsaysay. "No way, sir," Honasan replied. "We came here and we decided to stay." Juachon persisted. He threatened to attack Honasan with tanks. "It's all right, sir," Honasan replied calmly. "We are prepared to neutralize your tanks."[19]

Honasan's troops simply drove to the back of the camp, where about thirty troops under the command of a rebel officer had overpowered guards and opened the gate. The rebels quickly fanned out across the sprawling camp without serious resistance. Although Montaño had ordered the chief of the camp's security command to reinforce the garrison's

18. Montaño interview by Guerrero, April 9, 1991.
19. Davide Commission *Final Report*, 183.

three-story general headquarters building as well as other strong points, the officer, a classmate of Honasan, ordered his men to stay in their barracks instead.

Three companies of the National Capital Region Defense Command's headquarters battalion were ordered to Camp Aguinaldo. Instead of fighting, the troops parked their vehicles near the camp's parade grounds and took seats in the grandstand. Some even joined the rebels.[20]

Once inside the camp, Honasan's troops headed straight for the Department of National Defense building, which faces the parade field perpendicular to the general staff headquarters. The rebels established a command post at the defense building, where Honasan had worked during Enrile's time. Ileto, Enrile's successor and a friend of Honasan's father, had disappeared and was nowhere to be found.

Rebels milled about freely at the camp, unconcerned for their safety. There was little sense of a garrison under siege, and reporters had no trouble getting through the gates. They found Honasan, dressed in combat fatigues and a flak jacket, smiling and bubbling with nervous energy. "This is not a military coup," he told reporters. "All we are fighting for is the children—our children and the children of the Filipino people."

Across town at Malacañang, the civilian leadership was in disarray. Arroyo left his Makati home before sunrise but had to reach the palace by barge across the Pasig River because he was unsure which side controlled the bridges. He tried to telephone Ileto on a special hot line, but the circuit was dead.[21]

The palace wanted Ramos to launch an attack and finish off Gringo as soon as possible. Aquino appeared on television and issued a blunt warning: surrender or die. Gone was the light-hearted tone of her earlier radio address. She promised there would be "no terms" to "these traitors." "Speaking as your president, let me assure our people that the government is in firm control of the situation," she said. "We are at this very moment moving to destroy this threat."

Teodoro Locsin rushed to Ramos's headquarters at Camp Crame to

20. Montaño interview by Guerrero; eyewitness accounts.

21. Joker Arroyo, official statement to the Philippine House of Representatives, Quezon City, September 8, 1987, AP files, Manila. Reid made notes from the live broadcast of the hearings by DZXL and DZRH radio stations, and Arroyo later released a text of his testimony.

convey the president's order. Sending Locsin as an emissary to the military was like asking Lester Maddox to negotiate with the Black Panthers. A brilliant but temperamental figure, Locsin pressed Ramos and de Villa: "Why don't you attack?" The two generals kept saying, "We're making preparations. There are still some things that we have to do." Locsin was adamant. "Snipers, do we have snipers? Call for them." He finally left in disgust. Ramos would act according to his own judgment and timetable, not those of the palace. [22]

Ramos alerted the marines in Zamboanga, five hundred miles to the south, to prepare a force to come to Manila. The air force had no jet transports, however, only slow-moving propeller planes, and it would take hours for them to arrive. Meanwhile, the rebellion was spreading. At 10:00 A.M., the regional commander in Cebu, Brigadier General Edgardo Abenina, announced over a radio station that he had joined the uprising because "our rights as citizens and policemen have been abridged and trampled upon by the policies of the present government." Cebu was the country's second most important commercial center and the transportation hub of the central islands. Abenina's troops seized government buildings and placed civilian officials under house arrest.

At Camp Aguinaldo, Ermita and Montaño sealed off the general headquarters building. The rebels wanted to talk with the enlisted troops inside, but the two generals were afraid that the mutineers would win over the others to their side. Instead, Montaño and Ermita opened the armory and issued weapons. Most of the soldiers inside the building were clerks, and they refused to take up arms against the elite Scout Ranger mutineers. To the clerks, the mutineers were "brothers in arms," fighting for goals that they themselves supported. Better to sit on the sidelines than to fight and die for Cory Aquino's government. [23]

Montaño and Ermita knew that if resistance did not start soon, the enlisted clerks would probably defect and the general headquarters would fall to Gringo Honasan. Montaño grabbed a submachine gun, stepped to an open window, and fired at the rebels outside. His ploy worked. Honasan's forces returned the fire, and bullets crashed into the walls and ceilings of the building. The clerks then rushed to take up weapons to defend

22. Interview with Colonel Honesto Isleta by Eileen Guerrero, Manila, March 27, 1991.

23. Montaño interview by Guerrero, April 9, 1991.

themselves. The battle lines were drawn. There would be no more talking.[24]

Observers from the military attaché's staff of the U.S. Embassy fanned out to the camps early on the morning of the twenty-eighth and reported that the situation appeared desperate. Many military commands throughout the capital were "sitting on the fence," waiting to see which side would prevail. It appeared that Ramos could not count on any major command to defend the government.

The Americans realized that a gesture of support from Washington was critical. Honasan and other RAM Boys had had close personal ties to U.S. military officers since the Marcos years, and many of them shared Gringo's misgivings about Aquino's effectiveness. Official United States government policy, however, remained solid behind Cory Aquino. A display of support would dissuade other senior officers from joining the mutiny.

The newly appointed ambassador, Nicholas Platt, telephoned Honasan at Camp Aguinaldo and warned him the United States would cut off all aid to the Philippines if Aquino were overthrown. Honasan listened but made no firm commitment.[25]

As the hours dragged by, most of the streets in the sprawling capital were largely deserted. Schools were closed, as were many private companies. The government ordered state offices to open as usual, but few workers ventured out to them. Thousands of others converged near Camp Aguinaldo, the broadcast stations, and other rebel strongholds to watch the drama unfold.

The crisis was deadly serious, and the democracy so widely hailed a year and a half earlier was facing its gravest test. But for thousands of Filipinos, the drama was grand entertainment, an action movie played out before their very eyes. They stood on the streets, watching the creaky armored vehicles pass by and scampering for cover as occasional volleys of gunfire burst forth from the combatants.

At noon, a young rebel officer, Navy Lieutenant Robert Lee, arrived at IBC Television, which was held by the mutineers, and broadcast a statement in the name of the insurgents. As about a dozen armed rebels stood behind him, Lee told the people that the country was suffering from

24. *Ibid.*
25. Statement to media from U.S. Information Service, Manila, August 28, 1987, AP files, Manila.

an "overindulgence in politics" and that the military would "initiate the struggle for justice, equality, and freedom which our senior officers have failed to do." Lee claimed the mutineers would be in control of the entire country by nightfall.

But the tide had begun to turn. Except for General Abenina, none of the other regional commanders had thrown their support publicly to Honasan. No large crowds of civilians had turned out to support the mutineers, as in the EDSA uprising against Ferdinand Marcos. Police and constabulary units had already begun recapturing broadcast stations, and it would be only a matter of time before marines from Zamboanga were ready to attack Camp Aguinaldo.

Inside the camp, the rebels were sniping at the general headquarters building from upper floors of the Department of Defense. As the bullets crashed downward into the walls, tables, and even the floor, Montaño crawled to his radio and called Ramos at his command center at Camp Crame. "Sir, you have them [planes], you have to assault the DND building." When Ramos asked why, he told him: "They're the ones firing at us. General Ramos, you have to attack now." [26]

No attack came. Loyal troops were still trying to regain control of Sangley Point, where the air force kept its T-28 bombers, known in the Philippines as *tora-tora* planes because they resembled Japanese aircraft from World War II. At mid-afternoon, the rebels decided to set fire to the headquarters building to flush out Ermita and Montaño.

As smoke billowed through the cavernous building, Montaño was back on his radio, shouting at Ramos for help. The battery in the radio was dying, and it appeared their last link to the outside would soon be gone. Ammunition was running low. "The rebels assaulted in the morning and it's already afternoon and you haven't counterattacked," Montaño shouted. "We're on fire. There are now seventeen wounded here." [27]

This time, Ramos responded. Troops from the military's logistics command attacked rebels near the Defense Department, and three V-150 armored personnel carriers cleared rebels from a main gate leading to the parade field. But the attack appeared confused and disorderly. At Camp Crame, loyal troops fired twelve rounds from a recoilless rifle toward Aguinaldo to relieve pressure on the troops in the general headquarters.

26. Montaño interview by Guerrero, April 9, 1991.
27. *Ibid.*

Brigadier General Braulio Balbas calmly radioed Ermita and Montaño to reassure them and find out whether the recoilless rounds had hit their mark. "Did you hear a second explosion?" Balbas asked. Montaño shrieked, "What second explosion are you talking about?" Perplexed, Balbas replied, "But I fired twelve rounds." Most of them were so far off the mark that they soared over the camp and crashed into neighborhoods outside the compound. [28]

Meanwhile, two aging tora-tora planes took off from Sangley Point, flew over the city, and dropped bombs over the camp. The thirty-year-old planes were notoriously inaccurate and were flying so high that most bombs missed their targets, apparently because the pilots did not want to inflict casualties on fellow troopers, even mutineers. One bomb landed on the middle of EDSA Boulevard. Another crashed into a civilian neighborhood northwest of the camp. Meanwhile, hundreds of civilians, mostly young men, had gathered along the streets near the camp and cheered each explosion as if they were watching a basketball game.

The air strike convinced Honasan that his gamble had failed and that Ramos was prepared to use extreme force. Marines had already arrived from Zamboanga and were poised for the attack. Early that evening, a marine platoon entered the main gate of Camp Aguinaldo and moved forward amid only scattered sniping. Honasan slipped away from the camp just before the assault.

Ramos promptly denounced Honasan as a coward for having abandoned his men. He repeated the accusation a few days later during a television panel show, in which another guest was the young lieutenant who had led the marine assault. The program's host, Ricardo Puno, Jr., turned to the young officer and asked if he considered Honasan a coward. "Oh, no, sir," the lieutenant replied in respectful tones. "He's Gringo the Great." [29]

Honasan remained at large until December, when he was captured in a Manila neighborhood while giving an interview to American free-lance writer Steve Le Vine. Gringo was taken to a ship with about three hundred other mutineers but escaped four months later, in April, 1988, with the

28. Ibid., see also Davide Commission Final Report.
29. Reid notes from Ricardo Puno program, "Viewpoint," GMA Television, August 31, 1987.

help of his guards. His charisma proved stronger than the discipline and loyalty of his jailers.[30]

Realizing they had been beaten, rebels abandoned the camp. Most simply changed into civilian clothes and disappeared into the crowds. By midnight, the last of the rebels holding television stations had surrendered and abandoned Villamor. Nearly two thousand rebel troops were eventually rounded up and taken to detention centers at military camps throughout the city.

As word of the government victory spread, Abenina and others in the provinces also abandoned the revolt. Abenina was taken to Manila and placed under limited house arrest, but he was never tried. He remained on active duty because of his rank and prestige; like many others, he was kept in limbo, with no command or post. He joined another revolt against Aquino in December, 1989.

Cory Aquino and her government had survived, but the cost was devastating. By the end of the coup, fifty-three people were dead and about three hundred had been wounded. The armed forces' general staff headquarters was a smoldering ruin, and the military was again in turmoil. Ermita and House Speaker Mitra rushed to Baguio to meet with rebellious military academy cadets, including Mitra's own son, and convinced them to give the government another chance.

Politically, the fallout was nearly as severe. Enrile claimed he had played no role in the latest coup but refused to condemn it. Three days afterward, he told a civic club luncheon that the uprising was due to the "fundamental inability of this government to arrest the gloom and drift of this nation, its lack of statecraft, and its unwillingness to carve a sound political direction."

Coming from Enrile, the charges may have seemed self-serving, but similar views were being expressed by business leaders, journalists, and thousands of ordinary Filipinos. Cardinal Sin, among Aquino's staunchest supporters but a shrewd political analyst, blamed the coup attempt on "an erosion of hope" and accused the administration of "indifference to the plight of the poor." "That there is widespread corruption and dishonesty is the theme of daily common talk," the Cardinal said.[31] The Filipino

---

30. The account of Honasan's arrest was related to Reid by Steve Le Vine, who was present when it happened.

31. Cardinal Jaime L. Sin, statement to reporters, Manila, September 6, 1987.

people may not have abandoned the president during the coup attempt, but they clearly were distressed at her lack of leadership.

The coup attempt sabotaged what had been an encouraging economic revival. It frightened foreign investment and convinced international businessmen that the time was not right for investing in the Philippines. Hotels reported significant declines in occupancy, and tourism plummeted.

A few days after the coup attempt, Vice-President Laurel volunteered to visit military camps and discuss complaints of the soldiers. With Aquino's sanction, he visited a dozen camps and surveyed fifty-eight hundred officers and enlisted men. Laurel's tour seemed opportunistic because during conversations with soldiers, he appeared to be championing their disgruntled views as well as soliciting their opinions. In his report to the president, Laurel identified their major complaints as inadequate salaries, conditions in the armed forces, favoritism toward the left, and Communist influence in the government. He claimed that 73 percent of the majors and colonels surveyed believed there were Communists serving in the administration. Most of the troops, Laurel said, disapproved of Honasan's methods but nearly all sympathized with his views, especially regarding the Communists.

In the wake of the coup attempt, congress rushed through bills granting an across-the-board pay increase to the armed forces, in an effort to squelch charges that the government was disregarding military complaints.

The clearest winner, once again, was Fidel Ramos. Ramos had saved Cory Aquino, and he emerged with an unassailable grip on his post, despite complaints from the RAM clique and its sympathizers within the armed forces about his leadership.[32] Ramos was widely perceived as the second most powerful figure in the government, if not more powerful than the president herself.

At the same time, Arroyo's position had become untenable. Joker Arroyo had become the very symbol of everything that was wrong with the administration. To the troops, he was the "closet Communist" seeking to destroy the armed forces. To the business community, he was the bum-

32. The RAM Boys' complaints were that Ramos was guilty of favoritism in promotions; he was indecisive; he tended to favor the Philippine Constabulary over the army; he had not been vigorous in upgrading training with the military; and he was too close to Aquino.

bling incompetent blocking urgent decisions. Human rights groups wondered why he had not been more aggressive in dismantling the institutions of the Marcos regime.

But Arroyo would not leave quietly. On September 8, he appeared before the house of representatives, which was investigating the coup attempt, and used the forum to vent all the anger and frustration that had been welling up inside him. He blamed his troubles on back-stabbing businessmen disappointed because he would not grant them favors. He named names—Cesar Buenaventura, president of Shell Oil's local subsidiary; Roy Navarro, president of a leading accounting firm; and Raul Concepcion, twin brother of the secretary of trade and industry.

Joker denied he was a Communist. He praised General Ramos but accused others in the armed forces of disloyalty to constitutional government. True, he said, Vice-President Laurel had been authorized by the palace to seek the opinion of soldiers "but as to whether he was authorized to foment dissension, no."[33]

The next day, Jose Concepcion appeared at a meeting at the palace and demanded an explanation for Arroyo's attacks on his brother. The session quickly degenerated into a shouting match until Aquino decided she had had enough. She quickly summoned all twenty-five cabinet members and demanded their resignations.

Laurel, in turn, announced he would no longer serve as foreign secretary or in any other cabinet post because Aquino was too soft on the Communists. The man who had once expected to run the government now had no role at all. On September 16, Aquino accepted the resignation of Jaime Ongpin, Arroyo's principal rival in the cabinet and the man who had played such a prominent role in bringing the business community to back her in 1986. A few months later, a despondent Jaime Ongpin took his own life.[34]

The following day, she dismissed Arroyo and Locsin. Whereas the others had been let go with a brief announcement, the president appeared on television and lavished praise on Joker Arroyo as one who had "stood by my husband, and by the cause of democracy." She then told him, "For all you have done for me and for our country, I thank you, Joker, from my heart."

33. Arroyo to the House of Representatives, September 8, 1987.
34. See Joaquin, *Jaime Ongpin*.

10 LISTING TO THE RIGHT

THE AUGUST 28, 1987, coup attempt was a watershed in the political evolution of Cory Aquino and the people power revolution. With Arroyo gone and Aquino under siege by military opponents, her government moved inexorably to the political right.

It is questionable whether Arroyo's exit changed the philosophic character of the Aquino government. It remained what it had been before: a conservative, establishment government with reformist tendencies. Arroyo's presence had done nothing to prevent incidents such as the Lupao Massacre, nor had he been vigorous in promoting agrarian reform. But Arroyo had been a voice in the cabinet for liberal ideals, including human rights. Progressives considered him a spokesman for their views such as the closing of U.S. bases, limitations on foreign business penetration, and selective repudiation of debt.

Arroyo, however, had become a lightning rod for criticism of the Aquino government, and his enemies in the business community were quick to use the August 28 turmoil to vent their frustration about the government's direction. "I think what is happening today is that the moderates are, I hate to say, very restless," observed industrialist Raul Concepcion, whom Joker had denounced before congress. "They would like to see dramatic change in government. They would like to see a stronger and more decisive president."[1]

The challenges from the armed forces and the Marcos camp had created a siege mentality at the palace. A president who admitted from the start that she despised unsolicited advice seemed unable to distinguish between constructive criticism and subversion. "I think the government will have to engage again in consultation and listen," said Christian Monsod, the former NAMFREL secretary-general and husband of Aquino's economic development secretary. "It cannot be thin-skinned to the opinion of the people."[2]

Arroyo was replaced by his friend Catalino Macaraig, a low-key corporate lawyer. Macaraig was better organized than Joker, and paperwork flowed more smoothly. But Macaraig lacked Arroyo's long association with the Aquino family, something Cory considered essential in building trust. With Arroyo gone, she began to take a more personal, visible role in managing her government.

She signaled the shift in direction on October 20, when she appeared before a convention of businessmen at the Manila Hotel. During the speech, the president defended her record in office, especially the restoration of democratic institutions, but she made no attempt to conceal the frustration welling up inside her. "The Cory who could do no wrong in those early invigorating months after February, 1986, is seen as having government by consultation, which I hoped would get your understanding and support, has disappointed you, has given you a sense of drift. Henceforth, I shall rule directly as president."[3]

She gave Mayor Gemiliano Lopez of Manila one week to clean up the garbage piled along the street, ordered the Department of Public Works to fix potholes in the downtown area within seven days, and canceled plans by the National Power Corporation to raise electricity rates. After a flurry of "brushfire" activity, however, the garbage piled up again, and the potholes reappeared after the monsoon rains washed away the poor-quality asphalt.

1. Interview with Raul Concepcion, DZRH Radio, Manila, September 5, 1987, Reid notes of broadcast.
2. Interview with Christian Monsod, DZRH Radio, Manila, September 5, 1987, Reid notes.
3. Corazon Aquino, speech to the Philippine Business Organizations, Manila, October 20, 1987, OPS, PIA.

But for the moment, the businessmen were enthusiastic. The president was finally getting tough. The freewheeling, almost anarchic style that had prevailed when Arroyo and the human rights lawyers were at their zenith was over. Aquino promised that regulations against unauthorized strikes would be enforced, and hours later, police began dismantling the barricades erected behind illegal picket lines set up outside factories and offices during the August general strike.

The words were pure Cory—tough and stubborn, with little sign of accommodation to those she despised. "I expect sniping from yesterday's men, passed over as they are, by the march of history," she said. "To all other Filipinos, though, I say, the tide is with us."[4]

Aquino accelerated the crackdown on the left, even though the gravest challenges had actually come from the right—Marcos supporters and dissidents in the armed forces. In 1987, she still enjoyed a degree of support among left-wing labor, human rights, and church groups, even after the breakdown of peace talks with the hard-line leadership of the underground. Legal left-wing organizations such as Task Force Detainees and the Philippine Alliance of Human Rights Advocates considered themselves the true guardians of the reformist spirit of the people power revolution.

Cory Aquino, however, was bedrock establishment: a member of the social elite and devoutly Roman Catholic. She distrusted the left. She had offered the Marxists peace, albeit on her terms, and they had rejected it. With the exigencies of the military challenge and without the restraining influence of Arroyo, the break with the left became inevitable.

Aquino's dilemma was how to combat the armed guerrillas without plunging the nation into a bloodbath and trampling on human rights. The so-called national democratic movement, as the left broadly referred to itself, was not limited to armed guerrillas and secret Communist cadres. The left also included numerous student, labor, peasant, feminist, and human rights organizations that operated legally, although many of them were strongly influenced by the illegal Communist Party of the Philippines.

Against the backdrop of armed insurgency, drawing the line between subversive activity and legitimate political dissent is difficult. It presents

4. *Ibid.*

a special dilemma for a government that used tactics of protest in its own rise to power and that made respect for human rights a cornerstone of its public image.

Zealots in the armed forces, however, drew little distinction between dissent and subversion, and in the polarized climate following the August, 1987, coup attempt, bloodshed was inevitable. The price Aquino set by sanctioning a crackdown on the left was an escalation of violence and abuses of human rights.

Alarmed by the implications of the August coup attempt, the legal left struck back. On Saturday, September 19, twenty-seven-year-old Leandro Alejandro, president of the *Bagong Alyansang Makabayan,* "New Nationalist Alliance"—popularly known by its Tagalog acronym, *Bayan* or "Nation"—announced plans for a rally the following Monday to protest "the resurgence of fascist rule" that he feared the coup attempt would produce. Alejandro, who had run unsuccessfully for the house against Aquino's sister-in-law four months earlier, suggested that the administration should arm the legal left-wing organizations to defend itself against another coup.

After his press conference, Alejandro drove back to Bayan's headquarters in Quezon City with his chauffeur and two women colleagues. As the car slowed at the driveway, a white van pulled alongside. A passenger rolled down the window, pointed an automatic shotgun directly at Alejandro, and fired. The blast blew off half his face. No one was ever arrested in the killing, but intelligence sources believed the attack was carried out by Marcos supporters in the armed forces.

Ten days later, more than ten thousand people turned out for Alejandro's funeral. As the casket was taken through the streets, angry mourners raised clinched fists and shouted "Down with the U.S.-Aquino regime." When the procession reached Alejandro's old neighborhood, the fishing district of Malabon, the crowd swelled so large that mourners were pressed against the fronts of buildings by the dense mass of humanity.

At the same moment, Salvador Laurel was appearing before a senate committee investigating dissent in the military. In a style reminiscent of Joseph McCarthy, he claimed to have a list of Communists serving in government and demanded a purge. The vice-president, embittered over his ostracism by the palace, was seeking a constituency and was gambling that he would find one in the ranks of the armed forces. Talk of a "Red scare" filled Manila newspapers for months.

The large turnout at Alejandro's funeral and Laurel's simultaneous performance dramatically illustrated the polarization of Philippine society in the wake of the August coup attempt. The dreams of national unity and reconciliation that arose at EDSA in February, 1986, were being swept away in a tidal wave of violence, vendetta, and political intrigue.

No sector was spared, including the large U.S. community, which numbered nearly 140,000. Americans had enjoyed a privileged position in their former colony, despite a growing clamor to shut down the six U.S. military installations. Although the military community numbered about forty thousand, including wives and children, the rebels had not attacked any U.S. citizens since an ambush near the Subic Bay naval base in 1974.

In late September, a Philippine Constabulary patrol clashed with rebels in a barrio of Mabalacat, one of the towns hugging the perimeter of Clark Air Base about fifty miles north of Manila. Several Filipino troopers were wounded, and their commanders asked the Americans for help. A U.S. Air Force ambulance retrieved the wounded and took them back to the Clark dispensary for treatment. Rebel sympathizers saw the operation and notified the local New People's Army command. To the rebels, the presence of Americans at the ambush site confirmed their suspicions that the United States was taking an active role in the war.

At about 3:45 P.M. on October 28, 1987, Airman First Class Steven Faust of Pasadena, Texas, walked out of the McDonald's restaurant a mile from the Clark main gate and strolled across the street toward his car. Suddenly, three young men approached, pulled out .45-caliber pistols, and shot him dead. Two other Americans were killed in separate ambushes, along with a Filipino of U.S. descent who had wandered inadvertently into an ambush site.

The Clark attacks emboldened the rebels. Six months later, on April 21, 1988, they struck at the Americans again, assassinating U.S. Army Colonel James "Nick" Rowe as he drove to his office at the Joint U.S. Military Assistance Group headquarters in Quezon City. An expert in counterinsurgency, Rowe had spent five years as a Vietcong prisoner before escaping after killing a guard with his bare hands. He had been recently assigned to the Philippines to coordinate training and logistical support for the Armed Forces of the Philippines. Rebels threatened more attacks against U.S. citizens.

On the day of the Clark shootings, a Manila police captain, Eduardo

Mediavillo, was climbing into his car at his home in suburban Mandaluyong when three young men approached and opened fire, killing him and his driver. As Mediavillo's body lay in state at the Manila police headquarters, his embittered colleagues milled about in the courtyard, grumbling openly about the government allowing Communists to "run free" and kill policemen. Some of them spoke openly of "roasting" human rights advocates, whom they considered apologists for the Communists.

Aquino could not afford to lose the support of the police, who had stood by the government during the August military rebellion. At the funeral, after paying her condolences to Mediavillo's widow, she met privately with Brigadier General Lim and told him to step up his campaign against the rebels.

That was all Lim needed. He stood in front of Mediavillo's flag-draped casket and, with his voice choking, promised, "We will get your killers, no matter what it costs." On November 10, a few days after Mediavillo's wake, Lim unveiled "Manila's Crusaders for Democracy," a force of one thousand youths who volunteered for what was effectively a vigilante group to neutralize Communist influence in the barrios.

Allowing an expansion of such vigilante organizations marked a significant shift in the domestic policy of Cory Aquino, who had promised to disband paramilitary groups during her election campaign. The Marcos-era Civilian Home Defense Force and similar outfits had been organized to supplement government regulars in the fight against Communist and Muslim rebels. The paramilitary forces had also been accused of widespread human rights abuses, as well as extortion, theft, rape, and murder. Such groups continued to operate in rural areas after Marcos was ousted, and the military stubbornly resisted calls to disband them.

Within the military itself, there were misgivings about using armed civilian militia. On November 5, 1987, Defense Secretary Rafael Ileto admitted to the Philippine Senate's Committee on Justice and Human Rights that the government might be unable to disarm the estimated two hundred armed groups nationwide. On March 10, 1988, Ramos, as military chief of staff, warned commanders on Mindanao—where sixty of the armed groups were operating—that vigilantes represented a threat to public security if they were not strictly controlled. A year earlier, the *Philippine Daily Inquirer* had observed that the use of vigilantes demonstrated that "the government as a whole has not yet made up its mind on how

to deal with the insurgency." It appeared that both the civilian administration and the military as well were stumbling into a policy that accepted
vigilantism because each lacked a coherent, realistic alternative. Events
had created their own dynamic.[5]

The Crusaders were modeled after a vigilante organization in Davao
known as *Alsa Masa,* or "Masses Arise." Alsa Masa first appeared in 1985
in Davao's Agdao district, a foul-smelling slum area of dilapidated, tin-
roofed shacks near Davao Bay. At the time, Agdao was so heavily infiltrated by the Communists that it was known as "Nicaragdao." The military described Agdao as a laboratory for the Communists to refine urban
warfare techniques.

Although its origins are somewhat uncertain, Alsa Masa was apparently organized as a neighborhood watch force by a district ward leader
named Wilfredo "Baby" Aquino. Aquino (no relation to Cory) was a
shady character involved in prostitution and illegal gambling. He was
protected by police because he would allow them to take suspects to a
motel he owned for the kind of interrogation that is best conducted beyond the view of defense lawyers.[6]

Baby Aquino was eventually murdered by the Communists, but his
group was taken over by the new Davao police chief, Lieutenant Colonel
Franco Calida. Calida, a short, stocky figure, nurtured a tough-guy mystique by keeping a pistol on his desk and a poster of Rambo on his office
wall. He transformed Alsa Masa into a vehicle for stamping out rebels
and extending his control over Agdao.

Alsa Masa's activities were generally unknown outside Davao until
December 10, 1986—International Human Rights Day—when local human rights activists organized a march to Agdao. Alsa Masa members
attacked the procession, killing one of the marchers and chasing others
through the streets. After that, unfavorable reports of Alsa Masa's activities began appearing in the Manila press, including stories of intimidation

5. Philippine News Agency dispatch, No. 113, November 5, 1987; *Philippine Daily
Inquirer* editorial, March 12, 1987.

6. Task Force Detainees, *Human Rights in the Philippines,* pamphlet (Quezon City,
1989). TFD is an avowedly left-wing organization established by the progressive wing of
the Roman Catholic church to monitor human rights abuses during the Marcos era. It
continues to operate and periodically issues reports. It also contributed to a two-year study
from which this account of the Alsa Masa origins is drawn. See Lawyers Committee for
Human Rights, *Vigilantes in the Philippines: A Threat to Democratic Rule* (New York,
1988), 23–36.

and extortion—an embarrassment to a government committed to human rights and to disbanding private armies. Three months after the Davao incident, government television reported that Aquino had ordered all private armies and the CHDF disbanded, including Alsa Masa and a clone called Nakasaka that operated in a nearby province.

The administration, however, was under pressure to crack down on the left. Thus the following day, the palace announced that the order did not apply to Alsa Masa because it was "unarmed." The description was absurd. Anyone who visited Davao could see checkpoints manned by armed Alsa Masa members. Calida made no secret of the fact that he was arming Alsa Masa; during interviews, reporters watched him hand out pistols to "volunteers" who wandered into his office.

Ramos ordered curbs on the issuance of firearms and required the vigilantes to operate only under "strict supervision," but the standards of supervision varied widely throughout the country, depending on the whim of local commanders. By the end of 1987, nearly two hundred vigilante groups were operating throughout the nation. Many were little more than Latin American-style "death squads."[7]

Aquino went along with the vigilante plan so as not to alienate Ramos and other loyal officers. It was clear, however, that it was a difficult decision for her. On a visit to Davao on October 23, 1987, she praised Alsa Masa as a model in the struggle against Communism. "What is necessary is unity between the military and the civilians and the cooperation against Communist insurgents," she said during her speech.

Two days later, back in Manila, she repeated that the vigilantes should not be armed and should operate under military supervision. And in December, she told BBC Television: "I think what saddens me so much is that we are being forced to choose between the NPA [New People's Army] on the one hand and the vigilantes, or Alsa Masa, on the other. And surely we didn't fight the dictatorship just to end up with these two choices."

In Manila, the crackdown escalated with a series of police raids aimed at rooting out Communists and their sympathizers. During such "saturation drives," police fanned out through crowded urban neighborhoods, rounding up hundreds of persons, mostly men in their twenties who fit the military intelligence profile of a Marxist assassin. Suspects were then

7. TFD, *Human Rights.*

herded into courtyards of schools or government buildings, where hooded informants would wander through the crowd pointing out the Communists. The tactic was designed not only to root out individual guerrillas but to make life so difficult for ordinary people in the barrios that they would turn against the rebels and deny them sanctuary to avoid trouble from the police.

The tactic raised a firestorm of criticism, even from Filipinos who were stridently anticommunist. Older Filipinos recalled that the Japanese secret police used the same tactic during the World War II occupation. The arrests reached a climax in November, 1987, when police raided the downtown campus of the Polytechnic University of the Philippines and arrested thirty-nine persons who had taken refuge there. The refugees had come to Manila from Leyte Island, where some of them were wanted by police as Communist rebels.

The president of the university was Dr. Nemesio Prudente, a prominent leftist who had been released from detention by Cory Aquino. Prudente reportedly once headed a Marxist underground group known as *Gerilya Anak Pawis,* or "Guerrillas of the Poor," which had been responsible for assassinating police and soldiers during the Marcos era.[8]

On the day after the raid, police returned to the university and arrested twenty-four more persons, despite protests from Prudente that the suspects were simply fleeing vigilante violence. Lim insisted the suspects were Communists, and he warned publicly that if Prudente persisted in his complaints, he would be arrested for harboring fugitives.

A local congressman, Pablo Ocampo, offered to mediate the dispute and invited both Lim and Prudente to a reconciliation meeting at his home on the evening of November 10. Prudente arrived and waited a few hours for Lim, but about 10:00 P.M., Lim's office called and said the general was attending a social function and could not make it. Prudente and three associates left the house about 10:30. As their car approached a bridge, gunmen opened fire, wounding Prudente and killing his lawyer. No one was arrested for the attack.

Seven months later, Prudente was again the target of an ambush, this time a daytime attack as his car was approaching the PUP campus. Pru-

8. Although Prudente has not publicly acknowledged his leadership of the Gerilya Anak Pawis, as far as the authors know, several former members of the Marxist underground have stated he was believed to have been the leader.

dente was wounded and three of his bodyguards were killed. Four policemen assigned to Lim's command were eventually arrested in the second attack.

As violence escalated, Filipino human rights organizations such as Task Force Detainees and the Philippine Alliance of Human Rights Advocates tried to rally public opinion in the Philippines and abroad against human rights abuses. TFD, which was led by left-wing clergy, reported that in 1987, 8,367 people were arrested without warrant on suspicion of links to the rebels, more than the 5,967 arrested in the last full year of the Marcos administration.[9] Regardless of the accuracy of the figures, it was clear that human rights abuses were continuing. And regardless of the victims' political views, their treatment was hardly in keeping with the rule of law or the campaign promises of Cory Aquino.

On the evening of March 19, 1988, seven youths were plastering posters on walls along Taft Avenue in downtown Manila calling for dismantling U.S. military bases in the Philippines. The youths belonged to a leftist organization called Kabataan Para Sa Demokrasya at Nasyonalismo, or "Youth for Democracy and Nationalism," known by its Tagalog acronym, KADENA.

Suddenly, a police car appeared, and its occupants began chasing the youths through the darkened streets. Two of them, Hilario Bustamante and Reynaldo Francisco, were captured. According to Bustamante's testimony, they were taken to the headquarters of the Presidential Security Group, where they were beaten and tortured. After several hours, they were driven by car to a deserted field. Bustamante was dragged from the car and made to kneel. The last thing he remembered was a sharp blow across the back of his neck.

The next day, a security guard found Bustamante, nearly dead, lying in the tall grass. Francisco's lifeless body was found nearby. Bustamante was rushed to a hospital where doctors found deep knife wounds throughout his shoulders and back of the neck. His assailants had apparently tried to decapitate him but gave up, thinking he would soon be dead. Bustamante told reporters of his ordeal, and the report was widely published.

The National Democratic Front's office in the Netherlands began citing

9. TFD, *Human Rights*.

the case as a flagrant example of Aquino's lack of zeal in defending human rights. Human rights organizations in Western Europe began writing letters to the Philippine government urging a resolution of the case.

Bustamante, meanwhile, was receiving anonymous death threats. In April, 1989, human rights organizations invited him to visit Western Europe to speak on civil rights under the Aquino government, and he eventually turned up in the Netherlands, which granted him political asylum. On July 7, on the eve of Cory Aquino's visit to West Germany, the National Bureau of Investigation announced that one soldier had been arrested and two were sought on murder and attempted murder charges in the Bustamante incident. By the end of the Aquino administration, however, no one had been convicted because Bustamante, still fearing for his life, refused to return to the Philippines to testify. [10]

Staffers of the government's own human rights commission found themselves at risk if they dug too deeply into abuses. After Commissioner Leticia Buenaseda, a lawyer, began investigating the disappearance of civilians on Samar Island, soldiers ransacked her office. "They say Samar is number one in insurgency so they think everyone is a Communist," she said. [11]

Aquino did little or nothing to stop the abuses. "While there were attempts to fulfill promises, I believe she was shocked into submission by the series of coups d'état," commented Arnel de Guzman, secretary-general of the liberal Ecumenical Movement for Justice and Peace. "She is a hostage of the military." [12]

In desperation, many ordinary Filipinos turned to their local parish priests as their advocates with the elite. Brother Rafael Donato, chairman of the liberal Association of Major Religious Superiors, became so alarmed at the reports he was receiving that he sought a meeting with President Aquino, Defense Secretary Ramos, and General de Villa, now chief of staff. Donato outlined several significant cases of human rights abuse and begged for action. He came away disappointed. "All of them said, 'We will investigate, we will investigate,'" he said. "There is no

10. Guerrero interviewed Bustamante several times, and before he left for Holland, he went to the AP office in Manila, where the staff saw his wounds.

11. Interview with Leticia Buenasada by Eileen Guerrero, Manila, April, 1989.

12. Interview with Arnel de Guzman by Eileen Guerrero, Manila, April 14, 1989.

satisfaction in the way these cases are investigated. Justice is not felt. The legitimate grievances are not given their due course." [13]

Despite Aquino's promises of firm leadership after the August coup attempt, there was little sign that words were being matched by deeds. Her leadership deficiencies were revealed dramatically in the events that began unfolding on December 20, 1987, less than three months after her "get tough" speech. On that evening, a 2,215-ton passenger ferry, the *Doña Paz,* collided with an oil tanker, the *Vector,* in the Tablas Straits off Mindoro Island. The two vessels burst into flames. A passing ship, the *Don Claudio,* managed to rescue twenty-six survivors, all but two of them from the *Doña Paz.* No one knows how many people perished in the disaster, but the Philippine government later estimated that at least 3,563 persons were aboard the two ships. That would place the death toll well above the 1,503 who lost their lives aboard the *Titanic* in 1912.

The Philippine Coast Guard was supposed to have a radio network to report disasters, but it was in such poor condition that officials were unaware of what had happened until the following morning when the *Don Claudio* entered Manila Bay.

Subsequent investigations revealed appalling negligence. Coast guard investigators found that when the collision occurred, the *Doña Paz* captain was watching a video and the chief mate was drinking a beer. An apprentice seaman was alone on the bridge. The *Vector* had defective steering and no radio operator on board. The skipper of the *Vector,* who was among the dead, lacked the required master's license. [14]

The *Doña Paz* was authorized to carry 1,380 passengers and 60 crew members, far fewer than the number believed aboard. For years, however, interisland ferry operators routinely paid off coast guard inspectors to allow them to take on more passengers than could be safely carried.

Following the disaster, Cory Aquino suspended the permit of the *Doña Paz*'s owners, Sulpicio Shipping Lines, pending a safety check of its twenty-two ships. Soon, however, the firm was back in business. One year later, a second Sulpicio ship, the *Doña Marilyn,* sank during a typhoon off Masbate Island with hundreds of fatalities.

13. Interview with Brother Rafael Donato by Eileen Guerrero, Manila, March 31, 1989.

14. Report on the *Doña Paz–Vector* collision by the Board of Inquiry, Philippine Coast Guard, January 4, 1988, AP files, Manila.

Although the president visited the *Doña Paz* survivors and promised them compensation, there was little follow-up. Because the manifest was incomplete, it became difficult to prove who was on board. Sulpicio Lines paid compensation to families of 3,130 victims, although the company never officially acknowledged that more than 1,583 people were aboard.

The survivors eventually received $250 each in compensation from a special government fund controlled by the president's staff. One of the victims, sixteen-year-old Arnel Galang, refused to accept a larger sum from Sulpicio because he would have had to waive further claims. There was no psychological counseling, job training, or government-organized support group to help him or the others recover from the ordeal. Like many survivors of traumatic ordeals, young Arnel blamed himself for not saving his family, and for years after the tragedy, he could see their anguished faces in his dreams. Because there were so few survivors and Galang was among the youngest and had lost his family, Aquino referred him to a pharmacy chain for a job; he was not hired, however, because he lacked training. Too poor to afford school, he drifted from job to job. "We have been denied justice," he complained to the authors years later. [15]

The coast guard commander, Commodore Carlito Cunanan, fared better, however; he was promoted to commander of the Philippine Navy. The Cunanan family was close to Aquino, and such personal ties were very important to her.

The pattern of placing the interest of family and friends ahead of the broader national interest had been set early in the administration and persisted throughout its tenure. From the very beginning of Aquino's term, the new government had hailed agrarian reform as its centerpiece. It was seen as the most effective way to break the feudal grip of the rich and powerful over millions of impoverished peasants. By 1987, 35 percent of the agricultural population were landless tenants, up from 9 percent a generation before. [16]

In truth, land reform was never treated as a priority issue by Aquino. She and her conservative allies preferred the term "agrarian" reform, which connoted the idea that the program need not be based on redistribution of property as demanded by the Communists and other left-wing

15.   Interview with Arnel Galang by Eileen Guerrero, Quezon City, December 21, 1987. Guerrero interviewed Galang on numerous occasions as follow-up to the disaster.

16.   *Far Eastern Economic Review,* March 5, 1987, p. 33.

advocates. She, as well as Ongpin, had scrupulously avoided any unequivocal commitment to break up large estates. [17]

Aquino was receiving strong pressure to proceed slowly with land reform. Her brothers Pedro, who managed the family estate, Hacienda Luisita, and Peping were unenthusiastic about any program that would cause dismantling of profitable estates, including their own. The elite had a vested interest in delaying agrarian reform, and there were serious questions about how the government would finance a far-reaching plan.

On July 21, 1987, a few days before she was to lose her legislative powers, the president had signed a land reform decree covering all agricultural holdings nationwide, including her family's sugar plantation. But the decree left most of the implementing details to congress, including the timetable for distribution of titles and the amount landlords would be able to retain.

At the time, little attention was paid to Section 10 of the decree. It gave landowners the right to sell shares of stock in corporate farms to employees in lieu of actual land titles, reflecting the agrarian reform philosophy of Ongpin and the conservatives. The provision was especially beneficial to Aquino and her brothers and sisters. In 1957, the Cojuangcos had borrowed $2.1 million from the Central Bank and another million from the Government Service Insurance System to purchase Hacienda Luisita, on condition that they would eventually sell the property to small farmers.

For years, the government tried to get the Cojuangcos to comply with the agreement, but they refused. In December, 1985, a court ordered the family to transfer the entire estate to the Ministry of Agrarian Reform to be divided into lots sold at low costs to peasants. The Cojuangcos appealed, but Cory became president before the Court of Appeals could hear the case.

Aquino's land reform decree changed everything. Section 10 of the decree removed the legal necessity of breaking up the estate, and in May, 1988, the government dropped its case to regain ownership of Hacienda Luisita. A decree that was supposed to provide "land to the tiller" enabled the president's family to retain control of an estate it had purchased on the understanding that the workers would own the land some day. [18]

17. James Putzel, *A Captive Land: Politics of Agrarian Reform in the Philippines* (Quezon City, 1992), 196–202.

18. Renato Constantino, *Demystifying Aquino* (Quezon City, 1989), 149–51.

As soon as congress convened, Ramon Mitra, the former peace negotiator and now speaker of the house of representatives, boasted that his
chamber would pass a land reform bill within thirty days. Instead, it took
three weeks before a bill managed to reach the floor. The initial house bill
was a radical departure from the previous Philippine agrarian reform
programs. Drafted by left-wing representative Bonifacio Gillego, the measure would not have allowed landowners to retain any property at all.
Furthermore, landowners would have been entitled to receive compensation only for the first 122.5 acres seized.

The debate over land reform continued for nearly a year as legislators
wrangled over virtually every aspect of the bill, including the compensation formula, exemptions, and definitions of tenancy. On June 7, 1988,
more than ten months after Aquino's decree, the two houses of congress
finally hammered out a compromise formula. The bill allowed landlords
to keep twelve acres for themselves and another seven acres for each of
their children if they agreed to till the land. The legislation also exempted
lands designated for industrial use or as agricultural training schools.
Government-owned lands were to be parceled out over ten years. The bill
also included the stock option formula provided for in Section 10 of Aquino's 1987 decree. Gillego was so disenchanted that he wound up voting
against the final version of his own bill.

The Comprehensive Agrarian Reform Program, as it was officially
known, was so cumbersome and difficult to administer that scandal was
inevitable. The secretary of agrarian reform, Philip Juico, believed the
program could achieve fastest results by encouraging landowners to sell
their holdings voluntarily and receive payment under a complicated formula averaging the property's value based on tax declarations and three
recent sales of similar property in the same area. The system offered landlords several ways to overvalue their offering.

In May, 1989, Manila newspapers reported that the Department of
Agrarian Reform[19] had agreed to buy a 5,100-acre tract of land in Ca-
marines Sur province, known as the Garchitorena Estate, for $3 million,
or about $700 per acre. But the Land Bank of the Philippines objected to

19. Under Marcos, all cabinet departments were designated as "ministries," which was
retained by Aquino until the new constitution was ratified on May 2, 1987. At that time,
they were all automatically redesignated "departments," thus, for example, the Ministry of
Agrarian Reform became the Department of Agrarian Reform.

the purchase after determining the property was low-priced pastureland worth no more than $100 an acre. The estate was also located in a remote area without adequate roads and near New People's Army strongholds.

The government agreed to buy the land from a little-known company, Sharp International, Inc. The deal looked like a scam by corrupt officials to bilk the government of a substantial sum of money. There was no evidence that Juico himself profited from the sale, but he was responsible not only for the department but for its emphasis on voluntary sales. [20]

After the story broke in the press, about twenty department officials were suspended; most were later charged with various administrative and criminal offenses. Juico, however, remained on the job. He had worked in the media bureau of Aquino's campaign staff during the 1986 election, and his wife Margie was her appointments secretary and personal friend. Nevertheless, although she refused to fire Juico, the public outcry became so strong that she had no choice but to ask him to resign. In announcing his departure, Aquino lavished him with such praise and sympathy as to appear to exonerate him, even without a full investigation.

Regardless of the issue of Juico's personal culpability, Aquino's handling of the issue reinforced the suspicion that, despite all her promises, she would not take action against friends and relatives. One week after taking office, the president had promised to be uncompromising in combatting "corruption, graft, nepotism, usurpation, and abuse of powers and authority." [21] But when allegations of high-handed conduct by members of her family, including her brother Peping and brother-in-law Ricardo Lopa, began appearing in the Manila press, her response was to demand proof but do little personally to seek evidence.

One official did step forward. In 1989, Jose "Linggoy" Alcuaz, the telecommunications director, complained publicly that Aquino's sons-in-law were pressuring him not to implement government policy to break up the monopoly of the Philippine Long Distance Telephone Company, effectively controlled by her cousin. Alcuaz sought a meeting with Aquino to discuss the problem. As Alcuaz spoke, she placed her hands over her ears. Later, she asked aides, "Why is Linggoy implicating my family?" Alcuaz was pressured into resigning. [22]

20. Putzel, *Captive Land*, 312–16.

21. Corazon Aquino, commencement address, St. Scholastica College, Manila, March 26, 1986.

22. Interview with Jose Alcuaz by Robert Reid, Makati, March 19, 1991.

The gossipy Manila press made little distinction between fact and fiction when it came to reporting allegations of corruption, and Aquino could not be expected to respond to every unsubstantiated charge. Some allegations were doubtless fabricated by the opposition seeking to discredit her by association. Nevertheless, her lack of zeal in stamping out corruption disappointed those who had helped place her in power. Among them was the venerable Joaquin "Chino" Roces, the newspaper publisher who had gathered a million signatures in 1985 to convince her to run.

In July, 1988, the government presented the seventy-five-year-old Roces with the Legion of Honor in recognition of his service to democracy. Chino, who was dying of lung disease, used the occasion for an eloquent, subtle indictment of the moral tone of the government he had helped install. "A new moral order is best appreciated in terms of our response to graft and corruption," he told the audience, which included the president. "We cannot afford a government of thieves unless we tolerate a nation of highwaymen." A little more than a month later, Chino Roces died.[23]

By mid-1989, public outrage over corruption reached the point that the Catholic Bishops Conference could no longer remain silent. In August that year, the bishops issued a strong statement expressing their dismay that corruption "has become so widespread and has gone largely unpunished." Aquino was not criticized by name, but the statement was a clear indictment of the administration for failing to root out corruption with vigor and impartiality.

People power as practiced by Aquino had brought little change in the daily life of millions of Filipinos, nor had it eliminated the evils of Philippine society. The promises of reform and reconciliation appeared to have been forgotten. Instead of reform and social progress, the nation was adrift. Tensions were again building in the country, and the stage was being set for another national explosion.

23. Joaquin Roces, acceptance speech for the Legion of Honor, reported in Manila *Chronicle*, July 26, 1988.

II A CHRISTMAS SURPRISE

ON THE CRISP autumn morning of November 9, 1989, President George Bush stood beside Corazon Aquino in the White House Rose Garden and declared: "Your leadership has made the Philippines a beacon of democracy, worthy of imitation throughout the world. . . . America," George Bush declared, "loves Cory Aquino."

America may have still loved Cory Aquino, but the same could not be said of George Bush. Privately, Bush detested her. He was irritated with her noncommittal attitude toward the continued presence of U.S. bases and her government's endless carping about money. Before Aquino's visit, the U.S. ambassador to Manila, Nicholas Platt, suggested that Bush invite her to his retreat at Camp David for a family weekend, the sort of thing she loved. Bush turned down the idea cold.[1]

Aquino had gone to Canada and the United States seeking investments. During a stop in Dallas, she told a group of oilmen that the Philippines was well on its way to prosperity and that coup attempts were "a thing of the past." Two weeks later, her government would be fighting for its life, as plans for a massive coup were already in their final stages back in the Philippines. Coup preparations had been underway for nearly a year, spearheaded by Gringo Honasan.

Since his escape from the prison ship in April, 1988, Honasan had

1. Stanley Schrager, oral communication to Robert Reid, Manila, August 21, 1991. Schrager was the official spokesman of the U.S. Embassy at the time.

been busily planning for another coup. He sensed that disenchantment with Cory Aquino was growing, and he was optimistic that this time he would succeed in ousting her.

In early 1989, Honasan began contacts with pro-Marcos followers, led by renegade Brigadier General Jose Maria Zumel, in order to broaden his base. By mid-year, a working alliance had been forged between Marcos loyalists and the very same clique of young military officers that had helped overthrow their leader only three years earlier.

After nearly two years underground, Honasan resurfaced in November, 1989, for a clandestine interview with some Filipino reporters, which was published in the *Inquirer*. "There is obviously anarchy, disunity, injustice, too much politics, rampant graft and corruption, and total disregard for the laws because of the absence of a viable government," Honasan told the reporters. He claimed Aquino was simply "pretending to be president by issuing directives."

By that time, the military's intelligence services were receiving reports from its agents that rebel officers were recruiting followers. On the night of November 29, a flash report said thirteen Scout Rangers had raided the military communications facility in Tagaytay, thirty miles south of Manila.

The raid on Tagaytay was a mistake. It was to have taken place the following day as a signal for the coup to begin. Hearing of the raid, Cory Aquino telephoned the army commander, Major General Manuel Cacanando, and asked him what had happened at Tagaytay. Cacanando was visiting the military academy in Baguio, about 130 miles north of Manila, and was planning to leave soon for a visit to the United States. President Aquino told him to cancel his plans and return to Manila at once. [2]

The next day, November 30, posters appeared on walls in Makati and Quezon City denouncing corruption in government and inefficiency in the armed forces. The posters were signed in the name of the heretofore unknown Young Officers Union, or YOU.

The extent of the YOU's influence within the ranks of junior officers may never become clear because of the nature of the organization and the absence of knowledgeable, nonpoliticized sources. Self-styled YOU members claimed that a majority of lieutenants, captains, and majors

2. The Davide Commission, *Final Report of the Fact-Finding Commission* (Makati, 1990), 262–63.

were either members of YOU or sympathized with its goals. The organization was modeled after the Communist movement. Members belonged to small cells, usually numbering fewer than ten. Only one cell member would have contacts with other cells to prevent an arrest that might compromise the entire organization.[3]

The chief of staff, General de Villa, appeared on national television to announce that a coup attempt by "the forces of Honasan" had been aborted at Tagaytay. In fact, the coup was just beginning. Major General Rodolfo Biazon, the capital regional commander and a marine officer, ordered the Fourth Marine Battalion Landing Team to strengthen defenses at Camp Aguinaldo. The order was never carried out. Biazon did not know it at the time, but the Fourth Marines had joined the mutiny.

The key to the rebel operation was Fort Bonifacio, a sprawling garrison on a hill in suburban Makati that contains the largest U.S. military cemetery in the Pacific. Fort Bonifacio, headquarters of the Philippine army, controlled access roads leading south to Villamor and west toward Camp Aguinaldo and included the largest ammunition depot in the Philippines. Most of the combat units stationed in the capital were based at Fort Bonifacio, including the First Scout Ranger Regiment.

Honasan had used Scout Rangers in the 1987 coup attempt, and this time they were to be the major strike force in the mutiny. By the time the command learned of the Tagaytay raid, Scout Ranger officers were already issuing ammunition to their troops and preparing for the attack.

At 9:00 P.M. on the night of November 30, Scout Ranger teams fanned out from their barracks at Fort Bonifacio and quietly took control of key command and control facilities. Cacanando had just returned from Baguio and was meeting his staff when jeeploads of armed insurgents arrived and announced they were taking control. There was no resistance. Cacanando ducked out the backdoor and hid in the bushes to avoid being taken prisoner.[4]

After Cacanando disappeared, de Villa and Ramos, now defense secretary, did not know who was in charge and who could be counted on to rally a defense in the first critical hours of the putsch. Once in control of

---

3. Information on the cell organization of the YOU was given to Reid by a navy lieutenant who was a member; his identity must remain confidential because he is still in active service.

4. Davide Commission *Final Report*, 266.

the communications center, rebels sent messages under Cacanando's name to major subordinate commands nationwide, claiming that the army leadership supported the coup.[5]

A few miles to the northwest at Camp Aguinaldo, de Villa was becoming alarmed. He tried to contact army headquarters but there was no answer. De Villa telephoned General Montaño, the constabulary commander at Camp Crame, located across the street from Camp Aguinaldo. "Mon, have you got troops there?" de Villa asked. Montaño said he did and asked why. "We can't contact the army," de Villa replied. He told Montaño that rebel marines were already besieging Villamor Air Base and had trapped the air force commander.[6]

With the government's forces in disarray, the rebel plan unfolded like clockwork. Truckloads of mutineers wearing white arm bands and red flags swarmed over the city. At Villamor Air Base, the air force commander, Major General Jose de Leon, had placed his troops on alert and summoned commanders for a conference after word of the Tagaytay raid. De Leon began his briefing with the words, "Gentlemen, there is fantastic news about . . ." He never finished the sentence. Staccato bursts of gunfire echoed through the headquarters building. Rebel marines were rushing through the gates and soon controlled most of the garrison. De Leon stayed behind and was trapped, but most of his staffers scampered for the doors and got away.[7]

Elsewhere, mutineers seized the Sangley Point naval air station across Manila Bay in Cavite, while others established checkpoints throughout the Santa Mesa district east of Malacañang Palace to prevent reinforcements from reaching the area.

In Cebu, 350 miles south of Manila, Brigadier General Jose Commendador also joined the mutineers and seized the aircraft, including F-5 jet fighters, helicopters, and transport planes, at Mactan Air Base next to the city's international airport district. In northern Luzon, Rudolfo Aguinaldo, a former lieutenant colonel who had been elected governor of Cagayan province, called private radio station DZRH and said he was supporting the coup and was heading south to the capital with artillery and armor.

5. *Ibid.*, 267.
6. Interview with Ramon Montaño by Eileen Guerrero, Manila, April 9, 1991. "Mon" is Montaño's nickname within the armed forces.
7. Davide Commission *Final Report*, 290–91.

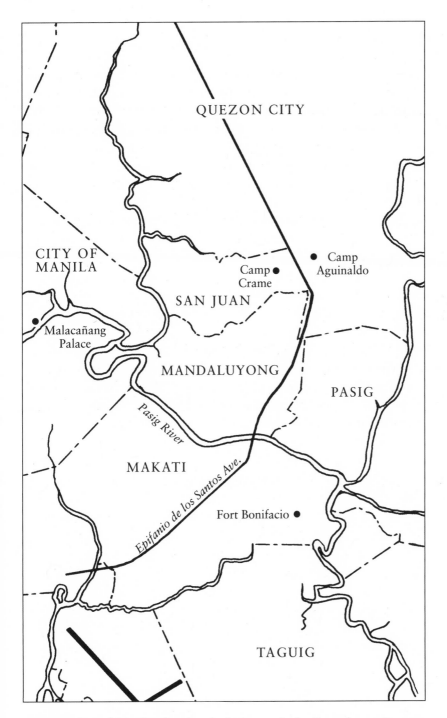

QUEZON CITY

CITY OF
MANILA

Camp
Crame ●

● Camp
Aguinaldo

SAN JUAN

● Malacañang
Palace

MANDALUYONG

PASIG

Pasig River

MAKATI

Epifanio de los Santos Ave.

Fort Bonifacio ●

TAGUIG

Map 6.   Central Manila, showing the key areas in the December, 1989, coup
attempt.

In the early hours of December 1, the Manila area command was disintegrating. Troops felt greater loyalty to their fellow soldiers than to Cory Aquino and refused to fire on mutineers. Montaño reported to de Villa about the situation near Camp Aguinaldo. "They're just waltzing with each other," Montaño said. "There's no firing." [8]

About 6:30 A.M., three T-28 propeller planes took off from Sangley Point, flew low over Manila Bay, then bombed and strafed Malacañang Palace. Even though the attack was mostly symbolic and caused only minor damage, it was a psychological blow to the government and a boost to the rebels, believed to number about twenty-five hundred men. The troops holding the government television station began cheering "Cory Aquino is dead" as the planes delivered their payloads.

At the beleaguered palace, frightened presidential aides scurried for cover. Aquino, ironically, took refuge in the basement amid all of Imelda Marcos's shoes. [9]

The T-28s roamed unchallenged over the skies of the city. They blasted the constabulary headquarters at Camp Crame, setting the building on fire. The planes then bombed de Villa's own home, and the building exploded in flames. Meanwhile, a Sikorsky helicopter from Villamor machine-gunned government forces at Camp Aguinaldo.

There seemed to be little response from the government. With the National Capital Region Defense Command crumbling, Montaño ordered constabulary units from southern Luzon to reinforce loyal troops. But their commander, Brigadier General Alejandro Galido, had been part of the conspiracy, and Montaño had to replace him early on December 1 before the troops could move. [10] What response there was to the rebel threat was pitifully weak. Private radio stations were broadcasting constant reports of the rebel air attacks, defections by government soldiers, and the number of strong points in insurgent hands, giving the impression to the public that their government was collapsing.

Senator Rene Saguisag heard the radio broadcasts at his home in Quezon City and decided to go at once to Malacañang Palace. Saguisag had

8. Montaño interview by Guerrero, April 9, 1991.
9. Interview with Lourdes Siytangco, former deputy press secretary, by Eileen Guerrero, Manila, April 12, 1991.
10. Montaño interview by Guerrero. He insists that Galida was part of the mutiny, although later, de Villa claimed he had been a government spy. Galida did offer testimony about the coup before he died of cancer in 1990.

been with Aquino during the long struggle against Marcos and in the turbulent early months of her administration. As the government seemed to be in its final hours, Saguisag told his family: "If Cory is going down, I'll go down with her." When he arrived at the palace, the atmosphere was grim. Presidential staff members were quaking with fear, some weeping. The calmest person at the palace was Cory Aquino. Her fatalism and strong Catholic faith had seen her through so many crises. She would not surrender.[11]

Ramos and de Villa, however, knew the situation was desperate. Loyal units held most of Camp Aguinaldo and the constabulary headquarters at Camp Crame. But Villamor Air Base, Sangley Point, and Fort Bonifacio were in rebel hands. Unless the government could mount a credible defense, other major military commands might decide to throw their support to the rebels.

In a desperate hour, Ramos decided to take a drastic step. He turned to the United States. After the air attack on Malacañang, Ambassador Platt telephoned Aquino and offered Washington's help on his own initiative. He had spent the past two years in the Philippines trying to convince Washington that for all her faults, Cory Aquino was the best option, not only for the Philippines but for U.S. interests as well.[12]

After Aquino told Ramos of Platt's offer, the defense secretary telephoned the ambassador. Ramos wanted U.S. jets to bomb rebel positions. At the time, the United States Air Force maintained a squadron of aging F-4 Phantom jets at Clark, only a few minutes from Manila by air. Platt, however, opposed the idea of Americans killing Filipinos. Filipino nationalism was at an all-time high and the public would have been outraged.[13]

Ramos was insistent, and the situation was disintegrating. A request for military support was relayed to Washington. The message arrived while President Bush was en route to Malta to meet Soviet President Mikhail Gorbachev. Vice-President Dan Quayle, who had visited Manila the previous September, convened a White House meeting to discuss the request. General Colin Powell, chairman of the Joint Chiefs of Staff, and

11. Interview with Rene Saguisag by Robert Reid, Pasay City, April 4, 1991.

12. Schrager to Reid, August 21, 1991, Montaño interview by Guerrero. Although Ramos insists that he never asked for U.S. intervention, it seems unlikely the U.S. would have responded without some sort of request from Philippine authorities.

13. *Ibid.*

Brent Scowcroft, chairman of the National Security Council, recommended against using U.S. aircraft to attack the T-28s or their bases. Both men shared the same concerns as Platt about bloodshed. "The Pentagon people wanted to know who was winning," said one U.S. diplomat familiar with the deliberations. [14]

Finally, it was decided that American jets would make "symbolic" flights over Manila and the air bases in rebel hands. The recommendation was forwarded to Bush, who authorized use of two F-4s from Clark Air Base. Before the Americans could respond, however, the Philippine Air Force had already begun to mount attacks. At 12:45 P.M., a Philippine Air Force F-5 destroyed the fuel dumps used by the T-28s at Sangley Point, although on the final attack run the plane crashed and the pilot, Major Danilo Atienza, was killed. Two other F-5s strafed Sangley's airfield and bombed the hangar.

About an hour later, two U.S. Phantoms roared over Manila. Throughout the day and until 6:00 A.M. the next morning, the jets flew wide, circular patterns over the city, low enough for their markings to be clearly seen. Although they never fired a shot and were not enough to stop the rebellion, the presence of U.S. warplanes in the skies gave a badly needed morale boost to Cory Aquino's government when it appeared on the verge of collapse.

The rebels had planned for nearly every contingency except one: U.S. intervention. They could not be sure whether Bush was prepared for additional actions to the "persuasion flights," such as dispatching marines from Subic to defend Malacañang. As a result, rebel units converging on Manila from southeastern and central Luzon stopped for hours before deciding to proceed, and there was a marked lull in rebel activity until the evening. Commanders backed off on promises to commit troops to the revolt.

Ramos has denied that he ever asked the U.S. to bomb the mutineers, but informed American and Filipino sources insist that he did. "I don't know what Ramos was thinking of," one U.S. diplomat said. "Maybe he was worried about his own skin." [15] Ramos's friend, retired Major General Montaño offers another explanation: "Ramos had to show that the U.S. was still backing up this government. The flights were more or less

14. *Ibid.*
15. *Ibid.*

to show the rebel forces and the rest of the Armed Forces of the Philippines that the U.S. was with us. And they believed it too, because they stopped, they hesitated."[16]

By December 2, the American demonstration had unleashed a storm of criticism both inside and outside the government at a time when Cory Aquino needed all the support she could get. Progovernment generals openly bristled at "foreign intervention." Opposition parties denounced the decision to call in the United States. The following day, Vice-President Laurel gave an interview by telephone to the British Broadcasting Corporation, in which he denounced U.S. intervention. Laurel, who was stranded in Hong Kong when the mutiny began, expressed sympathy for the rebels. "I condemn the method," Laurel said of the coup. "But I cannot condemn the cause because they have been quoted as fighting for good government." Still bitter at his treatment by Aquino, Laurel suggested she resign to spare the nation further bloodshed.

The mutineers began to shift their strategy in the wake of the U.S. flights. They could no longer rely on the T-28 bombers to blast Aquino into submission. After sundown, the mutineers began to regroup. They abandoned Villamor Air Base about 10:00 P.M. on the night of December 1 and reconvened about ten miles to the northwest in the White Plains area near Camp Aguinaldo, where the battle was to continue.

As the rebellion entered its second day on December 2, the mutineers issued statements by telephone to news organizations demanding that President Aquino resign and turn the government over to Supreme Court Chief Justice Marcelo Fernan pending a national referendum to decide a new form of government. Fernan disavowed the proposal, and in a television address, Aquino was defiant. Using the same stubborn language she had employed against the military rebels two years before, she offered no compromise. "We leave them two choices—surrender or die."

As rebel marines massed near Camp Aguinaldo, mutinous Scout Rangers began infiltrating the diplomatic, financial, and commercial district of Makati, where much of the international community as well as wealthy Filipinos lived. By early afternoon, jeeploads of uniformed rangers appeared on Makati streets. Captain Danilo Lim, a bespectacled West Point graduate and Scout Ranger officer, strolled into the lobby of the Inter-

16. Montaño interview by Guerrero.

continental Hotel with a handful of armed men. Vice-President Laurel's Nacionalista Party was holding a press conference there to denounce the government for seeking U.S. help against the mutineers. After chatting briefly with reporters and some of the politicians, the Scout Rangers politely asked everyone except for staff and registered guests to leave the hotel. Rebel snipers then took up positions on the rooftop.

Meanwhile, other small groups of Scout Rangers were entering about twenty other nearby buildings in Makati, including the Japanese-owned Nikko Garden Hotel. Quietly and without great fanfare, hundreds of foreign visitors and Makati residents found themselves hostages.[17]

Recapturing Makati presented formidable tactical problems. Rebels held the upper floors of some of the country's tallest buildings and enjoyed unobstructed fields of fire. The Scout Rangers were the toughest and best soldiers of the Philippine army; by contrast, the Philippine Constabulary had a reputation as a poorly trained and corrupt force.

As the Scout Rangers consolidated in Makati, a major battle for control of Camp Aguinaldo was shaping up. Rebel marines prepared for an all-out assault on the garrison, and about 1:00 A.M. on December 3, they unleashed a thunderous barrage from 105-millimeter howitzers, recoilless rifles, and heavy machine guns. Throughout the night, marine infantry raked the garrison with semiautomatic weapons fire, and armored personnel carriers probed the defenses but were driven back by recoilless rifle fire.[18]

After sunrise on the third, a rebel armored personnel carrier broke through Gate Four and entered the camp near the parade field. As the vehicle approached, a twenty-five-year-old corporal, Robert Salvador, aimed his bazooka and fired. The vehicle burst into flames. "Got him," he shouted, and sprang up and raced for the vehicle. Inside, he discovered the lifeless body of his brother, a sergeant who had joined the rebels.

About two hundred marines also managed to enter the camp behind the burning vehicle but were trapped in three small buildings near the gate. After four hours of negotiations, they surrendered. At 4:00 P.M. that day, Ramos and de Villa announced that the attack on Camp Aguinaldo had failed. More than fifty troops from both sides had been killed in the assault.[19]

17. Davide Commission *Final Report*, 227.
18. *Ibid.*, 227–28.
19. *Ibid.*, 319–20.

After failing to capture Camp Aguinaldo, the battle-weary marines began drifting away; many changed uniforms for civilian clothes and simply left the ranks. In Makati, however, the Scout Rangers showed no signs of giving up. Their commanders boasted they would fight on until Aquino resigned. The country's most fashionable city took on the appearance of a war zone. Makeshift barricades were erected along streets to prevent cars from entering the besieged area. The crackle of sniper fire echoed constantly through the streets. Signs warned, "Stop, War Ahead" and "Danger: Men at Fight."

Early on the morning of Tuesday, December 5, the U.S. Embassy began telephoning its citizens still remaining in Makati and urged them to evacuate as soon as possible by any means at their disposal. De Villa had decided to end the standoff as soon as possible and was preparing to launch an attack against the Intercontinental and other rebel strong points. Aquino had ruled out any negotiations and kept repeating her demand for the rebels to surrender or die. The prospect, however, of a bloodbath in what was unofficially the "foreign quarter" of the capital alarmed the diplomatic community. The U.S., Japanese, and other embassies expressed concern for the safety of their nationals in Makati, and de Villa finally reconsidered his decision. He would delay an all-out assault and give negotiations a chance.

On the night of December 5, the rebels' executive committee decided to release all foreigners, and soon after midnight the following morning, a Scout Ranger officer telephoned Brigadier General Arturo Enrile, superintendent of the Philippine Military Academy, and asked him to come to the Nikko Garden Hotel for talks. Buses from the Department of Tourism began shuttling between the hotels and condominiums to pick up the foreigners. A branch of the administration responsible for encouraging foreigners to visit the Philippines was now in charge of getting them out. With the release of the foreigners, however, the rebels had played their last card, and it was only a matter of time before they would have to surrender.[20]

Although the danger of a rebel victory was ebbing quickly, the strain of the ordeal on Cory Aquino was growing ever more apparent. Once again, members of the armed forces had risen up against her, this time

20. *Ibid.*, 274–84.

with a fury that nearly swept her away. She had been forced to turn to the United States for help, a humiliating gesture for the leader of a country that was once under American colonial rule. The coup attempt seemed doomed to fail, but it had stripped away the veneer of stability she had so carefully nurtured for her government.

After the foreigners were evacuated from Makati, she declared a state of national emergency, giving the government broader powers over transport and utilities; in an emotional television speech, she appealed to her people not to forsake her. "I am telling you now that I put so much at stake for democracy," she said, speaking in Tagalog to be better understood by the common people. "I have lost my husband. . . . It is very clear that these people want to kill me, to eliminate me so that they can rule our land."

Meanwhile, de Villa's allies in the armed forces were working feverishly to negotiate an end to the rebellion, regardless of the surrender-or-die rhetoric from the palace. On the night of Wednesday, December 6, General Enrile met with Lieutenant Colonel Rafael Galvez, commander of the Scout Rangers in Makati, and other rebel leaders, and they agreed to surrender the Makati buildings and return to barracks. Enrile promised not to prosecute low-ranking enlisted men and to allow the rebels to leave with their weapons as a matter of honor.

That night, the rangers removed the land mines they had placed in the buildings, and the next morning, about 8:30, nearly eight hundred of them began marching through Makati's broad avenues for Fort Bonifacio. It looked like a victory parade. The rangers sang martial songs, raised clinched fists, and made the "time out" sign, implying that their struggle was far from over.

With the Makati siege ended, Cory Aquino and her administration could finally boast of victory. Rebels were still holding out in Cebu, but they surrendered on December 9. On Friday, December 8, the government organized a victory celebration at a Catholic shrine on EDSA, near the site of the 1986 uprising against Marcos. Nearly one hundred thousand people turned out, although most were government employees bused in from nearby provinces.

During the ceremony, Aquino was in a combative mood. Speaking in the earthy Tagalog of a Manila fishmonger, she openly denounced her rivals, Vice-President Laurel and Senator Enrile, as virtual allies of Gringo

Honasan, although no one had yet provided proof of their involvement. "Before coming here, I said to myself, 'Should I even bother to mention Doy Laurel, or should I just flick him away like a fly,'" she said, speaking extemporaneously. The crowd howled with approval at her description of Laurel as a fly.

At Camp Crame, constabulary troops watched the president's performance on television and grew more and more angry at what they saw. Aquino was thanking General Enrile, General Biazon, and virtually everyone else for saving her government except the constabulary troops who had confronted the Scout Rangers and marines. "She's taking us for granted," shouted one enlisted man. "We were solid behind her and this is what we get in return." Montaño knew the situation was still volatile and that the government needed the loyalty of every soldier it could find. He went downstairs in the headquarters building, where a large group of soldiers was gathered, and lied: "The president called to say she forgot to mention us in her excitement," Montaño told them. [21]

As in the other coup attempts, military rebels hoped they could re-create the magic of February, 1986, when a small-scale mutiny attracted massive civilian support. But the "EDSA miracle" was not to be repeated. In 1986, the public had an alternative to Ferdinand Marcos in the person of Cory Aquino; in 1989, there was no clear alternative to Cory. Years of martial law had left the public hesitant to follow the military messiahs, regardless of complaints against her.

By the end of the nine-day drama, 99 persons had been killed and about 570 wounded. [22] The government's image of stability had been shattered. Gone also were the grand dreams of social and economic reforms that heralded her rise to power. Now, the Aquino government's chief concern was its own survival.

Perhaps the only Filipino who could take consolation in the events of December was Jose Alcuaz, the former telecommunications chief. In early November, he had predicted the coup in several newspapers, as well as to one of the authors. After it failed, he said in a radio interview, "In all humility, perhaps I can whisper now, 'I told you so.' The 'fed-up factor' has reached alarming proportions." [23]

21. Montaño interview by Guerrero.
22. Davide Commission *Final Report,* 376.
23. Interview with Jose Alcuaz in Pasig by DZXL Radio, December 9, 1989, monitored by AP.

12 CORY UP CLOSE

IT WAS A SUNDAY night in March, 1989, as the government's radio station, Radyo ng Bayan, broadcast the regular weekly program *Magtanong Sa Pangulo,* or "Ask the President." The program was conceived as a means of putting Cory Aquino back in touch with her people. Ordinary citizens could overcome the bureaucratic hurdles and directly approach the president with their problems or ask her about national policy. Those who wanted to participate were asked to submit their questions to local offices of the Philippine Information Agency, which forwarded the queries to Manila; there they were screened by the president's staff. Those who were selected taped their questions, which the president answered during a taping session on the day before the program was broadcast. Sometimes the questions were submitted in writing and were read by the program's anchorman. That ensured that the president would not be hit by any unexpected queries.

That evening, one of the questioners was a mother, Rosie Tejano, who lived in a barrio on Leyte Island. Mrs. Tejano explained that her village had been a stronghold of the New People's Army and that the armed forces had recently stationed a detachment there to protect residents against the insurgents. "Unfortunately, the abuses of these government troops assigned to us have turned our happiness to fear," the woman said. "I myself was the victim of rape committed by one of the soldiers assigned to the barrio." Mrs. Tejano said she reported the alleged rape to the local military inspector general a month earlier but without satisfaction. "My honor and reputation in the barrio and that of our family is at stake," she said. "May I request for your help?"

Aquino's reply was brief and cold. Before a nationwide audience, she said she had referred the complaint to the commanding general of the Philippine Constabulary who "concluded that your allegation has no basis." The president did not let it go at that. "The four companions [of the alleged assailant] at the time of the alleged incident have stated that you invited [him] and his friends to a drink in your house and that within the time that your guests were in your house, no untoward incident happened." The president then commented crisply that statements of the woman's corroborating witnesses "were highly doubtful."[1]

Rape carries a deep social stigma in the Catholic Philippines, and it seemed unusual that a female head of state would humiliate a woman by mentioning her name and questioning her honor. If the allegation were false, why bother to repeat it? The answer could have been provided discreetly, or Aquino could have stopped after telling the woman, and millions of other Filipinos, that the allegation was baseless.

Cory Aquino had presented herself to the Philippines and to the world as the gentle, caring little mother of the Filipino masses. The image played well politically in a nation where veneration of the Virgin Mary is fanatical, even by Catholic standards. It was an image, however, that masked a complex character: warm and cold, naive and shrewd, solicitous and abrasive.

In the presence of foreigners or well-educated Filipinos, Aquino could be relaxed and disarmingly engaging. Her ability to charm visiting U.S. congressmen, foreign reporters, and international businessmen helped reinforce her modest, unpretentious image, one that was instrumental in winning international support for her campaign against Marcos.

Aquino often spoke of her devotion to the poor, and in May, 1991, in an interview for a Japanese television network, she said she wanted to be remembered as "a president who truly cared for her people and made the people's interest her pioneer interest." But when she was in the company of the "masses," she often appeared ill at ease and out of place. During a visit to Panay Island in 1990, she addressed a group of impoverished

1. Corazon Aquino, "Ask the President," Radyo ng Bayan (Radio of the Nation), March 15, 1989, text in AP files.

fishermen about the government's plans for economic development. As she droned on in English, Cardinal Sin, a native of Panay, gazed at the blank stares of the audience and then gently suggested it would be better if she spoke in a native language such as Tagalog, which the fishermen might understand.

She would often turn up in poor rural areas dressed in outfits more appropriate for an afternoon tea. In 1991, she sprained an ankle stepping from a helicopter, when her high-heeled shoe got caught in the rut of a dried ricefield.

Aquino's lack of a politician's common touch could be seen in the way she addressed problems in her "Ask the President" radio show. The questions came from the common folk, and most of them involved requests for help in finding jobs and in resolving rental, labor, and property disputes. Invariably, the callers said they were turning to the president after failing to get satisfaction from local authorities. They wanted their president to cut the red tape. Usually, however, she referred the problem back to whatever local official or agency had failed to resolve the issue in the first place. Callers who sought help in finding government jobs got standard answers: "Please submit your application to the Department of Labor. If you are qualified and if there are available positions, you will be hired."

In the same radio program during which she berated Mrs. Tejano for her rape complaint, another woman from a poor central island appealed for help against soldiers who were trying to drive her family from their home. Aquino promised to look into the matter but then admonished the woman that she was living on a government game preserve and "we have to protect these endangered animals."[2] Ostensibly, the soldiers were there to keep out poachers and to provide general security against NPA rebels.

Cory brought a unique style to the presidency. Much of her charm during the 1986 election campaign lay in her apparent innocence. Four days before the balloting that year, she appeared before a conference of the Joint Philippine and Foreign Chambers of Commerce, a prestigious business group. "I welcome this opportunity to be able to address this distinguished assemblage of men and women of varied nationalities," she

2. *Ibid.*

said. "I was even thinking of having my fingernails done for the occasion."[3]

As her years in office passed, she could still make the sort of remarks one never expects to hear from a national leader. Once, Manila newspapers reported that the *Oxford Unabridged Dictionary of the English Language* had defined "Filipina" as "domestic" in its latest edition. Aquino waded into the fray, telling reporters she would instruct the Department of Foreign Affairs to file the appropriate protest. It turned out someone had seen the word "Filipina" but had read the definition for the following entry, "fille de chambre." "I was so embarrassed," she later told the author. "I assumed they had checked it."[4]

Aquino was once asked to recall the problems she faced during the first, uncertain hours of the August, 1987, coup attempt. After relating the problems in regaining control, she said, "If I were a male president, all I would have to do is get dressed, comb my hair, and that's all. But if you're a female president, then you have to worry about makeup."[5]

Cory was deeply sensitive to the fact that she was the first female president of a male-dominated society, especially one in which macho colonels and politicians were contesting her power. During the election campaign, Marcos made a crack about a woman's place being in the bedroom; she often said he was not the first man to underestimate her. "I guess because my being a woman has something to do about that," she once said in reference to allegations of weakness. "I don't know how to handle a gun, but spiritually, I am very strong."[6]

Her formula for problem solving was simple, and as much as possible, she never allowed national crises to stand in the way of comfort. After a few weeks on the job, she started suffering from headaches and decided that most problems could wait until the next morning. Like most Filipinos, Cory Aquino was a fatalist. "I reason it out, 'Will it be solved if I stay awake at night?' I would be a wreck the following day if I don't sleep,

3. Corazon Aquino, speech to the Joint Philippine–Foreign Chambers of Commerce, Manila, February 3, 1986.

4. Corazon Aquino, oral communication to Robert Reid, Manila, October 20, 1989.

5. Corazon Aquino to Foreign Correspondents Association of the Philippines, Manila, October 30, 1987.

6. Interview with Corazon Aquino by Maria Shriver, "Sunday Morning," NBC News, October 6, 1987.

and then I hope the next day would be better. So I sleep, and hope that the next day would be better than the previous day."[7]

Aquino often spoke of her reluctance to seek the presidency, with its grave responsibilities, and of her dream of retiring at the end of her term to write or work with social activist organizations. But she loved the perks of office, especially foreign travel. After years in the shadow of husband Ninoy, she enjoyed being the center of attention, with protocol officers, friendly reporters, and world leaders fawning over her. After coup attempts and other crises, the administration would announce a freeze on foreign travel so that everyone could focus on the problems at home. Cory was usually among the first to break it.

President Aquino seldom passed up an opportunity to travel abroad, even turning up in 1989 at the ritual circumcision of the son of the Sultan of Brunei, who was not among her admirers. She was especially fond of French president François Mitterrand, whom she had expected to be aloof until she met him for the first time. "He was so gracious," she gushed to the author during a luncheon in 1989. "He told me, 'Madam President, there are no schools for presidents. We must all learn by experience.'" She found the West German leaders more formidable ("They're so tall," she told one of the authors) but recalled fondly how the Italian chef at the German government guesthouse, the baroque Schloss Gymnich, begged her to let him prepare her an elaborate breakfast. "When I visit other countries, when you are really given the grand treatment, that is something that really makes me happy and proud that I am president of the Philippines."[8]

. Daughter Kris had another explanation for Cory's fondness for state visits. She told Filipino reporters traveling with the president to Canada in 1989 that her mother enjoyed escaping from the constant criticism of the Manila press and visiting faraway places, where she was still the sainted champion of people power.[9]

The public relations staff never seemed able to make up their minds whether the president should be depicted as "presidential" or as a "woman of the people." During her first months in office, Aquino jour-

7. Corazon Aquino to Orlando Mercado, "Dialogue with President Aquino," People's Television, May 7, 1986.

8. Aquino, oral communication to Reid, October 20, 1989.

9. Kristine Aquino to the Manila *Times*, November 7, 1989.

neyed to a barrio to meet with its residents, and, as is customary, she joined them in a meal that she ate with her fingers. The palace press office refused to release a picture to the local media because it was deemed unpresidential.

Paradoxically, Cory could be warm and supportive at a personal level. Her life's experience was primarily that of wife and mother, and she often conducted herself as if she saw her role as "first mother" of the country. Once, in 1991, she devoted her entire, one-hour weekly radio program to a celebration of the values of home, family, and motherhood. Her guests included a bridal-gown maker and the wife of Senator Aquilino Pimentel, whose son had recently scored highest on the national bar exams. After Mrs. Pimentel told the audience that she prepared all the food for her son, Aquino blurted out: "Maybe you can share that diet with us, so future bar examinees can use the secret so they can also get good grades in the bar exam." [10]

In 1987, Aquino attended the annual Christmas party for the palace press corps and brought along her homemade liver pâté, which she had prepared herself. She was very proud of her pâté but considered her specialty to be Peking Duck. A soap opera junkie since the boring days in sleepy Concepcion town, her favorite television program was "Lovingly Yours, Helen," which featured matronly actress Helen Vela solving the personal problems of ordinary Filipinos. "The program is very good," she once explained to reporters. "It's very good that once in a while, you forget the problems of state." [11]

Aquino seemed to see herself in the same role as Helen Vela, and once even mimicked her distinctive, somewhat mannish hair style. Wives of cabinet members would come to her with their personal problems, many of which stemmed from the pressures of public service. When the marital problems of the governor of Ilocos Norte province, Rudolfo Fariñas, and his actress wife hit the Manila tabloids, Aquino told reporters that she considered offering to advise them. "But friends were telling me that it will be difficult to get into that mess," she explained. [12]

10. Corazon Aquino, "Ask the President," May 12, 1991.
11. Corazon Aquino to Filipino reporters, Manila, May 16, 1989, as related to authors by Tita Valderama on June 5, 1989. Valderama was a reporter for the *Journal* and a member of the presidential press corps during the Aquino era.
12. Aquino to reporters, May 16, 1989.

Apart from soap operas, her passions included weekend mah-jongg games with close friends and brandy-filled chocolates, which contributed to a matronly spread in the latter years of her presidency. With her own family, she was extremely protective—a difficult task considering the number of relatives who became high-profile figures after she took office. The press was particularly tough on her younger brother, Peping, for his political and business wheeling and dealing. During a press conference, one Filipino reporter, Vic Augustin, asked why she thought Peping had become "such a lightning rod in his choice of friends, hobbies, or business interests." Cory became visibly agitated with the direction of the question, and no sooner had Augustin gotten the words from his mouth than she jumped into a rambling defense of her family:

> Can I say something about that? There is no organization in the whole country where you can say they are one hundred percent . . . thoroughly desirable or perhaps the best members ever. Even in the Malacañang press, I don't know if one hundred percent of the Malacañang press are among the most distinguished or the best of the lot. Certainly, this is also not casting aspersions on you. As the Bible says, he who is without sin, let him cast the first stone. [13]

Peping had been so visible during the congressional and regional elections that he was perceived as the power behind the throne. Perhaps unconsciously, Aquino contributed to this image of him by making all sorts of excuses for permitting her relatives to ignore the antidynasty provision of the constitution and run for office.

It was said that she could not control Peping, but this was not the case. When she wanted to, she could stand up to both Peping and even her elder brother, Pedro. In early 1991, Peping and Pedro visited Cory at the palace to ask for favors, which she refused to give. The discussion degenerated into a shouting match. Elder siblings are accorded lifelong respect in Filipino families, but his angry sister accused "Don Pedro" of meddling in her affairs. Pedro stormed out of the office, shouting "I promise you, I'll never, never come back as long as you are president." The two reconciled moments later when Cory rushed to her elder brother and apologized. "Kuya [elder brother], I just blew my top." Nevertheless, she

13.   Corazon Aquino, open press conference, Manila, September 7, 1989.

would not budge on their request. "OK, we'll just forget it," Peping said meekly.[14]

Peping created considerable image problems for Aquino throughout her term, and the rumors about Peping clearly bothered her. During a ceremony awarding sports trophies, the presidential protocol staff arranged for her to sit next to the chairman of the national athletic commission—none other than brother Peping. Cory examined the seating chart and frowned. "Why did you put Peping beside me?" she asked. The staff explained that the arrangement was according to protocol because Peping was the sports commissioner and not because he was the president's brother.[15]

Aquino was especially protective of her youngest child, Kristine Bernadette, or "Kris." She spoke of a special bond with Kris, who had grown up largely without a father and was still in her teens when her mother became president. Kris was an infant when her father was arrested during martial law, and Cory called her the "martial law baby." The only time Kris had a full-time father was during the two years the family lived in Massachusetts.

Kris had blossomed into an attractive young woman and was smitten with show business. Her uncle Butz had been a B-grade actor and aunt Lupita was a producer, but Mama was sternly opposed to the idea of a movie career. After months of pleading, however, she finally relented— quite a step for a conservative, Roman Catholic mother. The Philippine popular press fawned over actors and actresses like the Hollywood scandal sheets of bygone decades, and nearly every Filipino seemed to know who in the film community was sleeping with whom in a given week. Philandering was virtually a requirement of the trade. Aquino insisted that Kris stay in school, and she personally screened the scripts to make sure love scenes remained within the bounds of Catholic sensitivities. The presidential executive secretary, Joker Arroyo, took time away from affairs of state to make sure that Kris's contracts were in order.[16]

Kris fell in love with a young actor, Robin Padilla, and rumors circulated in 1992 that the two would marry. It would be hard to imagine

14. Horacio Paredes, Aquino's press secretary, oral communication to Eileen Guerrero, Manila, April 5, 1991.
15. *Ibid.*
16. Interview with Jose Alcuaz by Robert Reid, Manila, March 19, 1991.

anyone Cory would have liked less as a son-in-law. Padilla was a rowdy, inarticulate "bad boy" of Philippine cinema. Worse still, he had fathered a child by another woman. Aquino confronted her daughter about the rumors during a trip to a northern beach resort during Easter holidays in 1992, and urged her to look around for others as potential husbands. Soon, Mother Cory was asking wealthy friends if they knew of any eligible bachelors for Kris. "A mother wants her daughter to marry somebody who thinks like them," she told a television reporter in May, 1992. "I am very conservative because I have always believed that marriage is forever." [17]

Personal conduct was important to Aquino in judging those who worked with her. She tried to reconcile her tourism minister, Antonio Gonzalez, and his estranged wife but gave up after the official refused to part company with his beauty queen girlfriend. He was promptly replaced. She stood by her abrasive but talented transportation secretary, Reinerio Reyes, as the press savaged him for Manila's transport crisis. But Reyes's star fell after he and his wife tongue-lashed presidential bodyguards for lounging on their furniture before a party at the Reyes home Cory was to attend. She never forgave Reyes for verbally abusing her guards, and he resigned in December, 1989, after learning he was to be replaced in a forthcoming cabinet shuffle. [18]

Aquino would have made a great queen. She always seemed to have time for the frivolous aspects of public service, such as convening conferences, cutting ribbons, inaugurating public works projects, and receiving official visitors. But senior government officials used to complain of formidable staff hurdles to get an appointment to talk business with her. "You see, Cory has time for officials when they die, when they get hurt, or when they get shot at," joked former telecommunications chief Jose Alcuaz. [19]

Alcuaz should know. Once, unknown assailants sprayed his home with gunfire, injuring no one but scaring him and his family. Aquino sent for Alcuaz, whose father-in-law held a senior post in the Philippine Constab-

17. Interview with Corazon Aquino by Noli de Castro, ABS-CBN Television, Quezon City, May 9, 1992. In December, 1994, Kris, now twenty-three, announced that she was living with a forty-five-year-old married actor and was three months' pregnant by him. Aquino said she would forgive Kris but not her lover.
18. Alcuaz interview by Reid, March 19, 1991. Alcuaz was Reyes's deputy at the time.
19. *Ibid.*

ulary, and asked, "What is your father-in-law doing about this?" Alcuaz thought the question strange, considering the fact that, as president, she was responsible for enforcing the law, and if extra measures were required, she could simply order them. "To me, that betrayed that Cory looks at government as family," he said. [20]

Aquino rarely missed a funeral or a wake, a good thing considering the large number of soldiers and officials slain during her administration. As a widow, she knew how much public displays of support mean to the bereaved. She once confided to reporters that she was fascinated with morticians' work, and she would look for details such as the position of the eyes, strength of the chin, and other macabre handiwork when she paid her respects to the dead. Filipinos normally hold open-casket wakes and funerals, and she would stand at the bier, silently noting the appearance of the departed. [21]

Image-conscious, the president set high standards for her personal conduct. When she entered politics, she was very aware of her position as a widow plunging into a world largely inhabited by men. Early in the 1986 campaign, she admonished Salvador Laurel not to give her any pecks on the cheek in public, lest the Marcos camp spread rumors that the two were more than running mates. She also confided to friends that she was bothered by rumors linking her romantically to Cesar Buenaventura, a prominent businessman and widower. [22]

Would-be hosts who wanted Aquino to attend their parties had to adhere to one strict rule: no smoking. Asthmatic, she detested cigarette smoke, and aides always sprayed rooms in advance of her arrival to rid the air of any trace of tobacco odors.

She could be stubborn to a fault, reflecting a sense of self-satisfaction at odds with her early image of shyness and uncertainty. "When I am just with a few close friends, I tell them, 'OK, you don't like me? Look at the alternatives,' and that shuts them up," she said in an October, 1987, interview with NBC. "I really didn't promise you that things would happen or changes would happen immediately." [23]

20. *Ibid.*
21. Corazon Aquino, oral communication to Malou Mangahas, reporter for the Manila *Times,* May, 1989, as told to authors by Tita Valderama, Manila, September 20, 1991.
22. Interview with Ernesto Maceda by Robert Reid, Manila, May 15, 1991.
23. Aquino interview by Shriver, October 6, 1987.

Sometimes, her uncompromising stubbornness stood in the way of statecraft. The rifts with Salvador Laurel and Juan Ponce Enrile were never healed, and as a result, opposition leaders were seldom brought in on policy-making, where their input could have helped build a national consensus on important issues. During the Gulf crisis of 1990 and 1991, Laurel recommended convening the National Security Council, of which he and Enrile were members, to discuss ways of protecting the hundreds of thousands of Filipinos stranded in Kuwait, Iraq, and Saudi Arabia. Aquino rejected the proposal and instead decided to organize a "multi-sectoral" conference, excluding the vice-president. "Since Mr. Laurel has consistently opted against supporting this government, it serves no purpose to invite him to this gathering," she said in a statement.[24]

Aquino's attitude toward criticism made clashes with the press inevitable. During the struggle against Marcos, the Aquino camp vigorously courted the press, especially foreign reporters who were exempted from the state's media controls. By and large, the international media fell in line behind her crusaders during the 1986 election; in acknowledgment of that support, the government handed out certificates on the first anniversary of Marcos's flight from power, proclaiming foreign reporters as heroes of the revolution. Earlier, only four months after taking office, she stated at a press conference, "I have always been for a free press and in fact, I owe not only the local press but the international press possibly my election."

In private, however, Aquino loathed the press. She detested criticism and rarely read Manila's most critical dailies. She believed she had won the 1986 election despite the opposition of the state-controlled press.[25] After Ninoy's murder in 1983, Cory was so angry at what she considered pro-Marcos coverage by the Manila press that she banned local reporters from a press conference. She relented only after a Filipino reporter explained to her that individual journalists opposed Marcos but were at the mercy of their pro-Marcos editors regarding what was actually printed.[26]

Successive press secretaries fought an uphill battle to get the president to meet with reporters, and her press conferences became fewer and fewer

24. Written statement to Presidential Press Corps, Manila, September 13, 1990, from OPS.
25. Interview with Teodoro Benigno by Robert Reid, Makati, April 3, 1991.
26. Paredes communication to Guerrero, April 5, 1991.

as the years went by. Toward the end of her administration, Aquino's contacts with the media were limited largely to daily written responses to questions submitted each morning by the Malacañang press corps. The questions often were lengthy with numerous subsections covering all aspects of a complicated issue. For the most part, reporters received one-sentence replies referring them to whatever cabinet department was handling the issue. The answers were drafted by underlings in the press department and were invariably brief, curt, and wholly uninformative. When she did appear before reporters, her answers were replete with the phrase, "as I have said."

Those reporters who did manage to get interviews with the president often came away wondering why they bothered. Her answers were canned recitations of previous statements, which revealed little beyond what was already public record. During an interview in 1989, the author pressed her to reveal her thinking on the future of U.S. military bases. "I've answered enough questions on the bases," she snapped.[27]

It was no wonder that her advisers were not keen on expanding media contact. When caught off guard, Aquino sometimes became flustered and revealed a lack of knowledge about details. After the second assassination attempt on Nemesio Prudente, reporters cornered her outside her office and asked if the suspects, all police, would be tried before military or civilian courts. She turned to an aide, Flerida Ruth Romero, and repeated the question. "It should really be a civilian court," Romero replied. Cory then told the reporters, "If the civilian court is supposed to prosecute it, then so be it."[28]

Since Aquino's image was all-important, shielding her from criticism was a priority of government, even at the expense of hands-on leadership. She herself seemed only too happy to let advisers and cabinet officials take the heat for unpopular programs. As the business community pressured her in 1991 to remove a 9 percent levy on imported goods, the president featured the issue on her weekly radio program. She told her audience that she had invited Finance Secretary Jesus Estanislao to explain "his policy" on the tariff, as if he alone were responsible for something the entire cabinet had accepted.

27. Interview with Corazon Aquino by Robert Reid, Malacañang Palace, September 14, 1989.
28. Corazon Aquino to reporters, Malacañang Palace garden, July 9, 1988.

One palace adviser likened Cory's approach to that of a mother who doesn't want her daughter to go to a party and washes her hands of responsibility by using as an excuse, "Your father doesn't approve." [29] The effect of such a style created the image of a balkanized administration, with each department going off on its own policy path, depending on the whims of its chief. But if the policy failed, it was the department's fault, not the president's.

Except for her relatives, Aquino often was willing to let people twist in the wind, even those who had done the most for her. In 1988, a left-wing West German magazine published what it claimed was a list of Central Intelligence agents in the Philippines, among them the U.S. ambassador, Nicholas Platt. It was Platt who had personally warned Gringo Honasan during the August, 1987, coup attempt that Washington would withdraw all aid from the Philippines if Aquino were ousted. His support of her administration had been unflagging. Instead of defending Platt, Aquino said the Americans should offer an explanation and, if necessary, defend their ambassador's reputation. A few years later, Platt risked his own prestige within the U.S. government by arguing successfully for American military support for Aquino during a coup attempt. "Outrage," Platt once told his staff, "is the cost of doing business in the Philippines." [30]

If there was one constant in Cory Aquino's life, it was her Catholic faith. When the revolt against Marcos broke out in Manila, she retreated to a convent near Cebu before returning to the capital. She often spent time with nuns and even sought their advice when she needed time for reflection. Prayer gave her strength, and she prayed when she arose in the morning and then retired at night. She used to tell friends that she was convinced her victory in the struggle against Marcos had been engineered by the Virgin Mary, who had a special place in her heart for the Philippines.

But Aquino seemed blind at times to the fact that Filipino society also includes Muslim, Protestant, Buddhist, and other faiths. Intellectually, she may have accepted the doctrine of separation of church and state, but the acceptance was superficial. During a 1991 appearance before a group of Catholic educators, the president said that more should be done to enable

29. Paredes communication to Guerrero, April 5, 1991.

30. Stanley Schrager, former U.S. Embassy spokesman, oral communication to Robert Reid, Manila, August 21, 1991.

young Filipinos to enjoy the advantages of Catholic education, seeming to forget that her administration was operating its own secular educational system.

During an Easter celebration, she appealed for reconciliation between Christians and Muslims, overlooking the fact that the latter do not accept the doctrine of Jesus' resurrection. Aquino finally discovered the spirit of ecumenism, however, when the Iglesia Ni Cristo, a homegrown Protestant sect linked to Marcos, threatened to join leftists in a general strike in July, 1991. Iglesia Ni Cristo was a highly disciplined organization capable of mustering out millions of followers. Threatened, Aquino promptly sent emissaries to negotiate with the church's leader, Eraño Manalo. After Manalo called off the strike, she proclaimed a rare ecumenical day of prayer.

Despite her religious character, Aquino could be unpresidentially petty and unforgiving to those who had crossed her. One of those was Ninoy's old friend from his Massachusetts days, Senator Ernesto Maceda. Cory had gone against the advice of some of her confidants and agreed to accept Maceda on the administration's senatorial ticket in 1987, even though he had been fired a few months before as minister of natural resources, following allegations of corruption. In order to change his image, Maceda used his senate seat to launch a public relations crusade against corruption and inefficiency in government; he soon became as vocal a critic of the administration as Enrile was. That enraged Aquino, who considered Maceda an opportunist and a traitor. In 1991, the palace scheduled a ceremony for her to sign legislation establishing the Philippine National Police, a measure Maceda had sponsored. As she scanned the list of those invited to the ceremony, she stopped when she saw Maceda's name. "What's this doing here?" she asked her protocol staff. The staff then withdrew Maceda's invitation.[31]

Leaders of military coups were naturally held in special contempt. Any chance of a reconciliation between Aquino and Gringo Honasan vanished when her son was wounded in the August, 1987, coup attempt. And she never missed an opportunity to belittle the macho colonels who thought they should wield power, such as her reference to Gringo's moustache in July, 1989, during her State of the Nation address (see Chapter 1).

---

31. Paredes communication to Guerrero, April 5, 1991.

Those willing to give Aquino their unquestioning devotion were rewarded with unbending presidential support. One such favorite was the former rebel Bernabe "Dante" Buscayno. At first, it seemed unusual that there would develop such a bond between patrician, Catholic Aquino and a peasant who had spent much of his adult life killing those who defended the system that produced Cory Aquino. But she admired people who devoted their lives to a difficult cause, and although she abhorred Marxism, she respected Buscayno for his commitment to uplifting the poor. In addition, Buscayno's other ace was his personal bond to Ninoy. As the two languished in prison facing the death sentence, Buscayno, the Marxist rebel, and Ninoy Aquino, the establishment politician, had sworn that whoever was released first would take care of the other's family. "Dante, if I die before you, you take care of my family," Ninoy told his friend. "If you die first, I'll take care of your family." Buscayno assumed the mutual pledge was simply another one of Aquino's theatrics, and he soon forgot about it. Buscayno refused offers of freedom from Marcos in exchange for fabricating testimony against Aquino. "I'll do everything I can do to help set you free," Buscayno told Ninoy. "I know you can do a lot more for our countrymen. I'll take all the blame as long as it means you go free." [32]

When Ninoy Aquino was assassinated, Buscayno remembered the vow, but he was still in prison with no prospect of freedom. All that changed when Ninoy's widow became president and freed the political prisoners, including the legendary Ka Dante. On the day of his release, when Buscayno was taken to the Cojuangco building in Makati to be granted his freedom, he thought about the oath he and Ninoy had taken many years before. Buscayno felt it was his duty to fulfill the vow, but how? During his meeting with Aquino, Dante told her: 'I'm a poor man. I can not help your family the way Ninoy could have helped mine.'" She smiled and replied, "Never mind that. I just want you to help me." Cory then summoned her son, Noynoy, and told him of the mutual vow. [33]

Buscayno fulfilled his oath by supporting Aquino, even as many of his old comrades returned to the Communist underground. "That's the way I could help her," Buscayno told one of the authors. "That's the way I

32. Interview with Bernabe Buscayno by Eileen Guerrero, Tarlac province, April 11, 1991.
33. *Ibid.*

could make good my promise to Ninoy to take care of his family." Buscayno left the Communist movement he had helped organize and disavowed armed struggle. Instead, he returned to his home province of Tarlac and established a farmer's cooperative, which Aquino publicly endorsed and lavished with state support. She rarely missed the opportunity to hold up Buscayno as a model for the nation.

She even arranged for Buscayno to have a special radio link with the palace so she could summon him any time. For years, the one-time enemy of the state would slip in through the backdoor of the presidential palace, and Cory would make him sandwiches in the kitchen. For hours, she would talk to "Commander Dante" about her personal problems. For his part, Buscayno would offer homespun advice and a poor man's view of Philippine politics, while a president who detested "unsolicited advice" would sit patiently and listen. [34]

Aquino also liked Buscayno because he never asked for anything. A few months after his release, Buscayno appeared at the palace. Cory received him but expected him to ask for a favor. "What do you really want?" she asked. Buscayno was taken aback. "Nothing," he replied. "I'm just here to offer you my thoughts." In not asking for favors or money, Dante won a special place in her heart. [35]

If Aquino had a warm spot for Buscayno, she had hatred and contempt for Ferdinand Marcos and his family. Marcos was the man she believed had imprisoned and murdered her husband and tormented her loved ones. Removing him from office was the reason she ran for president, and stamping out any vestige of the detested regime was her life's goal. One of her first official acts as president was to abolish formally the Marcos-era national motto, *Isang Bansa, Isang Diwa,* or "One Nation, One Thought." The motto seemed harmless enough and was little different from her own frequent appeals for national unity. But it was Marcos's slogan. It would not be hers. [36]

During the 1986 election campaign, issues such as social reform and the strengthening of democracy were secondary to Aquino's personal goal of getting rid of Marcos. Her spokesmen and advisers might speak of platforms and policies, but she had a singular mission. "I'm obsessed with

34. *Ibid.*
35. *Ibid.*
36. Presidential Memorandum Order No. 34, Manila, September 10, 1986, OPS.

just removing Mr. Marcos first," she told foreign reporters four months before entering the race. "I really see no possible solution to our economic and political problems as long as Mr. Marcos continues to be head of our government." As president, nothing hurt more than allegations that her administration was no better than the previous one. She defined her own administration in terms of Marcos: "I have always said, I am the complete opposite of Marcos." [37]

The Marcos factor colored Aquino's entire view of the world. She could never entirely forgive the United States for supporting Marcos for so many years, even though Washington had played such an important role in her elevation to power. Any chance the Soviet Union had of increasing its own influence in the Philippines went out the window when the Soviets became the first foreign government to congratulate Marcos for his "victory." Soon after taking office, Aquino was asked what she thought of relations with the other superpower. She brushed aside the question. "I haven't even thought about them after they congratulated Mr. Marcos." [38]

The mirror image of her hatred of Marcos was an obsession with the legacy of her husband. His death was the raison d'être of her presidency; when she took office, Benigno Aquino was elevated to the role of a virtual national saint. Statues of the bespectacled Aquino sprouted up throughout the country, and his face appeared on television nearly as often as that of his wife. When the government's fortunes appeared at their darkest, such as during the coup attempts, Cory and her stalwarts would resurrect the image of Ninoy's death as her credential for governing the nation.

Ninoy had dedicated his life to the quest for the presidency, but in supreme irony, it was his widow—who avoided politics as much as possible—who finally achieved that goal. The sense that the presidency should have been Ninoy's seemed to haunt the administration, especially in its early months, and was partly responsible for the inordinate attention paid to his martyrdom. The phrase "when Ninoy was incarcerated" appeared over and over in her speeches. "You might ask, 'When will the president stop invoking Ninoy's name?'" she asked during her final State

37. Interview with Corazon Aquino by Luis Beltran, People's Television, Manila, April 21, 1986.
38. Corazon Aquino, press conference, Manila, March, 1986.

of the Nation address in July, 1991. "My answer is, when a president stands here other than by Ninoy's grace."

As the years in office passed, however, even Cory seemed to emerge from the shadow of Ninoy, for better or worse. During an interview with NBC after two years in office, Aquino reflected on the unusual turn of events in her life. "I never thought of myself as ever becoming president," she said. "I suppose he [Ninoy] himself would be unbelieving at this point that I, his wife, who just said 'amen' to whatever he said and, now, being president of more than fifty million Filipinos."[39]

39. Aquino interview by Shriver, October 6, 1987.

13   Cory Clings to Power

THE COUP ATTEMPT in late autumn, 1989, had exacted an enormous toll. The economic planning secretary, Jesus Estanislao, estimated that it had cost the government more than $13 billion in damage and lost investments and would reduce the gross national product a full percentage point.[1] Fearing another putsch, the military stepped up security in the capital. Manila took on the appearance of a city under siege, with armed soldiers patrolling major streets.

On the day the Makati siege ended, President Aquino summoned congressional leaders to discuss how to restore public confidence. She insisted that those responsible for the coup must be punished, including civilians who provided financial and moral support. Salonga told her the upper chamber was already forming a committee to study the coup attempt and recommend measures, including punishment. He said the committee would include Juan Ponce Enrile as a gesture to the legal opposition.

Aquino flew into a rage. She slammed her fist on the table and fixed steely eyes on the aging senate leader. "Are we fooling each other?" she shouted. "Enrile should be investigated himself."[2] Instead, she appointed

---

1. Estanislao gave reporters this estimate in an "ambush interview"—local parlance for buttonholing an official going to or from a meeting—Malacañang Palace, December 13, 1989.

2. Aquino related her anger at Salonga during a speech at a progovernment rally, Quezon City, December 8, 1989.

her own committee under the chairmanship of former Supreme Court justice Hilario Davide.

The Davide Commission held ten months of exhaustive hearings into the entire cycle of coup attempts. In October, 1990, it released its findings in a six-hundred-page report, much of it critical of Aquino's stewardship. Without exonerating Honasan and his cohorts, the committee concluded that the conspirators believed they were fighting against favoritism, ineffective government, corruption, poor military leadership, "lack of genuine reconciliation," and "failure of civilian government to effectively address economic problems." The report stated: "Despite the installation of the formal structures and the advances in the democratic processes, the EDSA Revolt that installed Corazon C. Aquino as President did not result in the far-reaching revolution many people had hoped for. Most of these expectations were embodied in the Constitution but have largely remained unfulfilled."[3]

The report also laid down an agenda for the remaining months of the Aquino administration: establishing accountability in government; creating a policy-making role for the legal opposition; streamlining the criminal justice system; mobilizing the private sector to assist the government; decentralizing public administration; enacting laws on economic reform; and "democraticizing" the electoral process. Such were the reforms the public had expected Aquino to implement after the people power revolution. "A democracy in a crisis of transition calls for a firmer and more direct hand at the helm," the report concluded.[4]

The extent and strength of the coup attempt also shook the Bush administration into reviewing its approach to the Aquino government. Since the time of Ambassador Stephen Bosworth, who preceded Platt, the U.S. Embassy in Manila had followed a strict policy of never criticizing her or her administration in public. The Aquino administration, however, seemed incapable of action except when under pressure. The subtle approach was often ineffective in dealing with Manila.

The Bush administration decided it was time to deliver a more forceful message to Cory Aquino. A month after the coup attempt was crushed, in January, 1990, Bush dispatched his deputy national security adviser,

3. The Davide Commission, *Final Report of the Fact-Finding Commission* (Makati, 1990), 518.
4. *Ibid.*, 519.

Robert Gates, to Manila ostensibly to demonstrate solidarity with the Aquino government. "President Bush asked me to come here to express his personal support for democracy and the constitutional process in the Philippines," Gates told reporters in Manila. Privately, however, Gates brought another message to Aquino: get your house in order if you expect U.S. support to continue.[5]

Ambassador Platt knew that Aquino would not take kindly to such treatment by a foreign envoy, and he had urged that Gates's visit be given no advance publicity. Gates was a Soviet specialist with little background in Philippine affairs, and he had a reputation for high-handed behavior. Not only did the White House announce the Gates mission in advance, but officials leaked the general outlines of the message to several leading U.S. newspapers. In a few days, the story was splashed all over Manila dailies too.

Aquino was outraged. She and her advisers were still deeply suspicious of the U.S. for its longtime support of Marcos and suspected it might turn against her as it had her predecessor.[6]

Cory got her chance for revenge a month later, when Defense Secretary Richard Cheney was to visit Manila to discuss upcoming talks on the future of U.S. military bases. A week before Cheney's arrival, Aquino announced on her weekly radio program that she would not be meeting with the U.S. defense secretary, and he would confer with Ramos instead. Lest anyone doubt that the move was a snub, she added, "I've been thinking that we talk of one thing and afterward, something else is published in American newspapers. . . . Because of our sad experience . . . I think it is best that Secretary Ramos meet with his counterpart and [Cheney] does not need me at the moment."[7]

The decision was vintage Cory—personal, emotional, and proud, even vindictive. But the snub had a devastating effect on her standing within the Bush administration and the U.S. Congress. "I think she should see him," fumed President Bush in an interview with *Newsday*. "Every time I talk to Dick Cheney, I come away smarter and I know a little bit more than when I sat down with him."

5. Stanley Schrager, former U.S. Embassy spokesman, oral communication to Robert Reid, Manila, August 21, 1991. This was also reported before Gates left by the Washington *Post* and the Los Angeles *Times*.
6. Interview with Teodoro Benigno by Robert Reid, Makati, April 3, 1991.
7. Corazon Aquino, "Ask the President," February 11, 1990.

Never again would the Bush administration be as accommodating to the Philippines or to Corazon Aquino as before the Cheney snub. U.S. diplomats in Manila began telling reporters the best thing for the country would be for Aquino to end her term and transfer the presidency to an elected successor.[8]

After revamping her cabinet following the coup attempt, the president turned her attention to her enemies. On February 27, 1990, a special prosecutor indicted seven civilians for their alleged roles in the coup attempt, including Aquino's old nemesis, Senator Juan Ponce Enrile. The state claimed that on the first day of the coup attempt, Enrile had entertained Gringo Honasan at his Makati home and that the two had discussed future plans in the event the putsch succeeded.

Enrile denied any such meeting, and the evidence against him seemed thin. The charge was based mostly on the testimony of three waiters who catered a party at Enrile's home on December 1. The waiters claimed to have seen Honasan and about one hundred rebels at Enrile's residence. Later, investigators acknowledged that the names of the "waiters" did not correspond with those on the caterer's list. Nonetheless, Cory Aquino had had enough of Johnny Enrile.

To make sure that Enrile could not pull any legal tricks to stay out of jail, the government leaked reports that the charges would be filed in the Makati Regional Trial Court. Enrile's lawyers were on hand with a list of legal challenges. The only charge filed in Makati, however, was harboring a fugitive; the more serious charges were filed discreetly in Quezon City. Immediately, the case was referred to a judge who issued an arrest warrant for the senator. The warrant charged him with "murder complexed with rebellion," an offense for which there was no bail. In 1954, the Philippine Supreme Court ruled that the "complexed" charge was unconstitutional, but Marcos revived it during martial law. It was among numerous presidential decrees that Ninoy Aquino and the opposition had branded as dictatorial.

A few days after his arrest, the supreme court ordered Enrile freed on bail, and the government eventually reduced the charge to simple rebellion, a bailable offense. He was never brought to trial, however, and was elected to the house of representatives in 1992.

8. Schrager to Reid, August 21, 1991.

Nature compounded the nation's woes. On July 16, 1990, Luzon Island was struck by an earthquake measuring 7.7 on the Richter scale. The quake caused little damage in Manila, but it was devastating to central and northern Luzon. In Cabanatuan, sixty miles north, a school collapsed, trapping more than three hundred pupils inside. In Baguio, 130 miles north, eight luxury hotels collapsed. Across the affected area, nearly seventeen hundred people perished.

The Aquino government was unprepared for such a catastrophe. Mayors were required to develop disaster plans, but few had fully complied. Years of neglect of national telecommunications had left the country without a reliable system for provincial communities to report damage and casualties. Local officials wound up telephoning radio stations to broadcast appeals for help, hoping authorities in Manila would hear them.

On the day after the quake, the president journeyed to Cabanatuan to inspect the damage and to be seen by her people as taking charge in a time of crisis. When she arrived, she immediately asked, "Who's in charge?" then scolded officials for their ineffective rescue efforts, although her government had given them few resources for the task.

Next she toured the hospital where the surviving schoolchildren had been taken. It could have been a perfect opportunity for a grandmother to be seen consoling injured children, especially a "woman of the people." Instead, she wandered through the ward with her military aide, occasionally pointing to an injured child and asking, "Is that a victim?"[9]

As the days passed, people in the devastated areas grew more and more angry over the government's clumsy rehabilitation efforts. Press Secretary Tomas Gomez insisted that the relief effort was proceeding without a hitch and that reports to the contrary were simply lies spread by Aquino's enemies. That was far from reality. Government rescuers did not even reach Nueva Vizcaya province until four days after the quake, and they arrived without enough food, medicine, and supplies for the tens of thousands of victims.

The Aquino government was also slow to ask for international assistance, especially from the United States. U.S. officials suspected that the government was afraid that asking for American help might somehow influence future talks on the military bases. American diplomats offered

9. Corazon Aquino, remarks overheard by Eileen Guerrero, Cabanatuan, July 17, 1990. Guerrero and other reporters followed the president through the hospital.

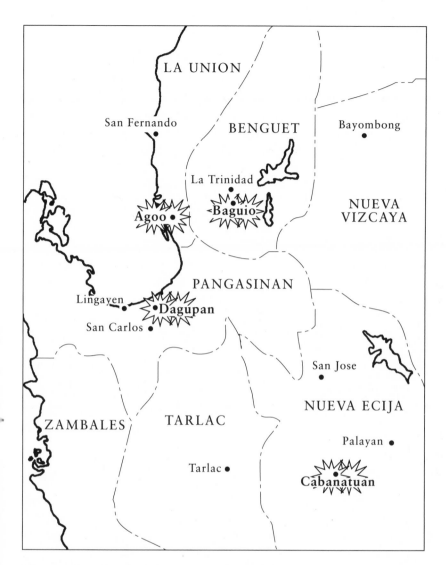

Map 7.   Central and northern Luzon, showing the area of greatest devastation during the 1990 earthquake.

help, but after failing to get a response, they simply asked a U.S. team to get on the first available plane and go to the Philippines.[10]

Instead of making it easy for foreign donors to help, the presidential staff drafted a cumbersome set of regulations that discouraged all but the most determined. The guidelines stated:

> Interested overseas donors or their local representatives are to submit written offers to the Presidential Management Staff. Once notified of the government's acceptance, the donors are to accept a bill of lading or airway bill for clearance by the Presidential Management Staff, which in turn transmits all necessary documents to the Bureau of Customs. The Bureau of Customs initiates the processing of import documents and releases the donation to the Office of the President. Finally, the Office of the President turns over the donations to the designated recipient, agency or organization.[11]

Nevertheless, Aquino's government had survived four years of such ineptitude, and the end of her administration was in sight. As the economy slowly began to rebound, the flight of capital that followed the December, 1989, coup attempt eased. Furthermore, Aquino's chief armed opponents—military dissidents and Communist rebels—were on the wane. Honasan remained at large, but it would take months to organize a new coup attempt on the scale of the last one. By that time, she would be on her way out of office, and the pressure to remove her by force would be ended.

Military successes on the battlefield had turned the tide against the New People's Army, and the arrests of key Central Committee figures presented the party with a crisis of leadership. A power struggle between Sison in the Netherlands and party leaders back home sapped much of the movement's vigor, while a series of purges prompted many young cadres to drop out in disillusionment.

Both groups, however, remained dangerous, and eight months after the latest failed coup, Honasan's forces struck again with a rash of bombings in Manila. Most were directed at businesses owned by key financiers and industrialists closely identified with Aquino. Rumors of an impending coup, this time centered outside Manila, again swept the capital.

---

10. Schrager to Reid, August 21, 1991.
11. "Implementing Guidelines," Office of the President, July 19, 1990, authors' files, Manila.

On October 4, 1990, a renegade colonel, Alexander Noble, led a ragtag band of 350 Higaonon tribesmen from the jungles of Agusan del Sur province to Cagayan de Oro, a major port on the northern coast of Mindanao Island. There, they seized the headquarters of the army's Fourth Division without firing a shot.

Noble, a tall, colorful figure with an elaborate goatee and shaggy black hair, had once served as chief of staff of the Presidential Security Group and was personally decorated by President Aquino for gallantry in action against the Communists. He was later transferred to Mindanao to command a battalion that seized Mactan Island during the 1989 coup attempt. Noble escaped arrest and fled into the jungles of Mindanao Island, where he joined the Higaonon tribe and became something of a cult figure.

Having failed repeatedly to seize power by launching a coup in Manila, the military dissidents decided instead to try a mutiny outside the capital. They were aware of the widespread dissatisfaction in the provinces— especially on Mindanao Island—with rule from Manila. Mindanao, the second largest of the seventy-one hundred Philippine Islands, had always felt discriminated against in favor of Luzon, which produced most of the nation's leaders. That dissatisfaction had led to the Muslim revolt of the 1970s and to an abortive attempt to declare the island's independence by a Christian politician, Reuben Canoy, in 1986.

Noble's attack in Cagayan de Oro was to have set off a series of provincial mutinies. Canoy and some of his civilian followers joined Noble. The strategy of triggering revolts among provincial military garrisons, however, failed. With the government now jailing and prosecuting mutineers, fewer and fewer soldiers were willing to risk their careers and freedom in a political adventure, especially with the Aquino administration drawing to a close.

In Davao, the island's largest metropolis, local business leaders heard of the plot and approached the garrison there to try to convince them to remain loyal to the government. As an incentive, the businessmen agreed to provide the soldiers with free rice and other food, since they complained that the military's per diem allowance was too low. As a result, the Davao garrison refused to join the mutiny.[12]

12. Syvelyn Tan, oral communication to Robert Reid, Davao, September 28, 1994. At that time, Tan was regional chief of the Department of Trade and Industry in Davao.

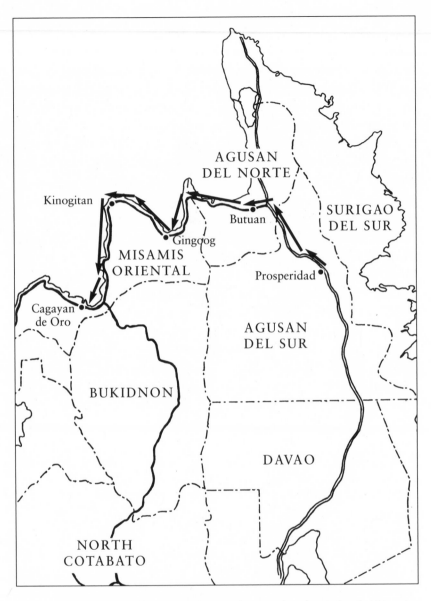

Map 8. Route through northeastern Mindanao taken by Colonel Alexander Noble in the final coup attempt against President Aquino in October, 1990.

For nearly three days, Noble and his band occupied the Cagayan de Oro garrison. Elsewhere in Mindanao, Negros, and northern Luzon, a few sympathetic soldiers staged protest actions, including rallies and sit-down strikes, but the planned general uprising never materialized. Noble surrendered on October 6 and was flown to a stockade in Manila, where he was held until his release in 1993, after Aquino had left office. He was granted amnesty and ran unsuccessfully for governor of Agusan del Sur in 1995.

It was a farcical ending to the military dissident movement, which began under Marcos, helped propel Corazon Aquino to the presidency, and later appeared poised to drive her from power. After so many failures, the steam was gone from the movement, and she would not face a rebellion from the ranks again.

14   POLICY BY PINATUBO

OSCAR ORBOS WAS a man in a hurry. In 1987, "Oca" was an obscure member of the house of representatives. Less than four years later, he had risen to the position of presidential executive secretary, succeeding Catalino Macaraig after he was replaced in late 1990. The appointment of the forty-year-old whiz kid brought an entirely new style to the presidential staff, as Cory Aquino began her last full year in office.

Orbos, dubbed by the press as the "Action Man," seemed to personify a new generation of Philippine politician. With his rolled-up shirtsleeves and unruly shock of thick, black hair, Orbos looked like a Bobby Kennedy clone. He brought both vigor and a keen sense of public relations to the staid, often inert administration. Orbos pushed through a plan to streamline operations by reducing the number of cabinet-level officials from thirty-two to twenty. He also abolished a series of coordinating committees that had simply added a new layer of bureaucracy.

There was plenty of work to be done, and no task more difficult or divisive as negotiating the future of the American military bases. The agreement allowing the U.S. military to remain in the Philippines would expire on September 16, 1991, and talks on a new arrangement had stalled. Orbos decided he was just the man to break the deadlock. In doing so, Oca Orbos would be able to count on Washington's support in the next presidential election.

The issue of Clark Air Base and the naval base at Subic Bay was a political powder keg. The United States considered the bases part of its commitment to defend the Philippines from aggression. Compensation for use of the bases amounted to nothing more than paying a foreign government for the "privilege" of defending it. Filipinos, however, perceived no external threat, and to them it was a business deal, requiring payment.

The presence of the bases was the foundation of a "special relationship" between the United States and its only former colony, which it had ruled from 1898 until independence in 1946. To protect its military interests, the U.S. had lavished the Philippines with billions of dollars in foreign aid and at times meddled deeply in domestic political affairs, such as during the Huk rebellion and the Marcos era. As long as the bases were in the Philippines, the Americans would continue to support their former colony. Most Filipinos approved of the arrangement, but a small yet influential segment of the population—including academics, professionals, and intellectuals—saw the bases as a residual symbol of colonialism that contributed to prostitution, drug addiction, and other social ills.

Antipathy to the bases increased during the Marcos administration because of U.S. support for his regime. To the Philippine intelligentsia, Washington had abandoned its democratic principles for the expedience of maintaining its military bases. Hatred of Marcos became intrinsically linked with opposition to the bases.

In 1984, Corazon Aquino signed an opposition manifesto that called, among other things, for the removal of U.S. forces from the Philippines.[1] Her lack of enthusiasm for the American presence was rooted less in geopolitical or nationalist considerations than in her hatred of Marcos. During a radio address on August 25, 1991, Aquino said it was "very painful for us that the military bases were being used to prop up a dictator. It was clear to us then that since the Americans needed these military bases, they supported this dictator," meaning Ferdinand Marcos.[2] As president, however, her perspective changed. She needed U.S. support. She promised Washington the bases could remain until at least 1991, and after that she would "keep my options open."

As the 1991 deadline approached, Aquino asked Foreign Secretary Raul Manglapus to handle negotiations for an extension. Manglapus, a

1. Declaration of Unity, Manila, December 26, 1984.
2. Corazon Aquino, "Ask the President," August 25, 1991.

small, courtly man, had been a leading politician until martial law ended his career. He fled to the United States, returning only after Marcos was overthrown. He had never forgiven Washington for its longtime support of Marcos and was determined that if the bases were to remain, the Americans would have to pay dearly for them. During a review of the agreement in 1988, Manglapus insisted on raising the annual bases-related assistance from $180 million to a staggering $2 billion. Ultimately, he settled for $460 million. But the acrimonious tone of the 1988 review showed Washington that winning an extension would be difficult.

Ambassador Platt wanted talks on a new bases agreement to begin as early as 1989. Aquino, however, was in no hurry. She named a committee to draw up plans for alternative uses for Clark and Subic if no agreement could be reached, naming as chairman Jose Abueva, president of the University of the Philippines and a strident bases opponent. But Abueva found that his committee was operating virtually in the dark because members did not know whether they were planning for some or all of the bases. Aquino was indeed keeping her options open and providing little guidance.

Filipinos were not the only ones having second thoughts about the desirability of the bases. The Berlin Wall had fallen in November, 1989, and the Soviet Union was nearing collapse. The Cold War was ending and with it, the necessity of holding onto Clark and Subic at all costs. The Filipinos, however, failed to grasp that fact. From the halls of Malacañang to the average man in the street, Filipinos remained convinced that the bases were so important to the United States that they would never be abandoned. The only challenge would be to hold out for the best price possible for their use.

Negotiations were to begin on Monday, May 14, 1990. On the eve of the opening session, Communist rebels assassinated two young American airmen as they waited to catch a ride in Angeles City, located outside Clark Air Base. Leftists in Manila announced plans for demonstrations against the talks.

The chairman of the U.S. delegation was forty-five-year-old Richard Armitage. Although he was a skilled, experienced negotiator and a veteran of Washington politics, it was hard to imagine anyone whose personality was culturally less suited to deal with Filipinos. Bald and barrel-chested, Armitage had played linebacker at the naval academy and went on to serve two tours in Vietnam, where he was decorated for valor. He was frank where Filipinos are obtuse, outspoken where they are reserved.

Manglapus began the negotiations by complaining that the U.S. Congress had reduced the amount of aid promised in 1988, and that by his calculations, the Americans owed more than $220 million in back rent. "I don't stand next to a cash register when conducting foreign relations," Armitage snapped.[3] The next day, Manglapus presented the U.S. delegation with a "notice of termination," which stated that the bases must close by September 16, 1991, unless a new agreement could be forged and ratified by two-thirds of the Philippine senate.

U.S. negotiators believed that Manglapus wanted an agreement, but they were not so sure about the panel's vice-chairman, Alfredo "Alran" Bengzon. Bengzon, who was secretary of health, was a member of the Catholic church-oriented clique instrumental in forming the Convenors group, Aquino's springboard to the presidency four years earlier. It was Bengzon who had urged her to sign the manifesto against the U.S. bases.

After five days of exploratory talks, the two panels adjourned on May 18. Manglapus told reporters that the Bush administration had agreed to seek more aid for the Philippines and that the promise was enough "to enter into discussions on future relations." He also said the talks would not be aimed solely at a new bases agreement but a broader treaty to cover the entire range of Philippine-American relations, including trade, scientific and educational cooperation, and other areas.

Armitage tried to signal the Filipinos that it was risky to tie all aspects of their relationship to the bases, which he described as a "declining asset." He reminded the Filipinos that money alone "cannot cement friendships or confirm friendships of alliances." No one seemed to be listening, however. Manglapus declared that Manila wanted control of Clark Air Base as soon as possible but was willing to talk about the future of the Subic Bay naval base. Panel spokesman Rafael Alunan spoke of a U.S. reduction as a "terminal phaseout" and said if there were no progress by January, the Philippines might abandon the talks.

The Americans were furious. They saw the hand of Bengzon behind Alunan's hard-line statements, which went beyond anything Manglapus

3. Richard Armitage, opening statement at R.P.-U.S. talks on the future of U.S. bases, Manila, May 14, 1990, USIS Library, Makati. Copies of official texts of the talks can be obtained from the library.

had said during the closed-door sessions. After hearing about "terminal phaseout," Armitage confronted Manglapus. "I must protest the words of your spokesman," Armitage said. Manglapus, taken aback, turned to Bengzon and asked, "What comments?"[4] More than seventy years old, Manglapus had trouble focusing on the issues or remembering what had been discussed already. From the U.S. point of view, he was clearly a problem.

The talks settled into a pattern. Armitage would fly to Manila for four or five days of talks, then they would adjourn for weeks or months before resuming. In the interim, the two sides were supposedly conferring at the "experts' level" and exchanging discussion papers by facsimile. In fact, U.S. officials say that little or nothing was accomplished during the breaks. "We would send papers to Manglapus, and we'd never get an answer," one diplomat complained.[5]

Armitage was growing more irritated with the delays. He sent a message to Ambassador Platt asking him to tell the president that if she wanted an agreement, she should fire her entire panel, starting with Manglapus. Platt knew that delivering such a message was the best way to make sure Aquino would do exactly the opposite. Instead, he informed her that the United States was impatient with the speed of the talks.[6]

Platt and his staff believed Cory Aquino was the key to breaking the logjam. If only she would take a more active role in providing guidance to the panel, she could overcome the rivalry between Manglapus and Bengzon and finalize the agreement.

Enter the Action Man—Oscar Orbos. The new executive secretary approached Ambassador Platt and assured him that he could deliver an agreement; there was no formal deal struck and no American quid pro quo. Orbos, however, had ambitions for the presidency. He was already the darling of the media and several key figures in the Catholic hierarchy; U.S. support would make him the obvious front-runner. After talking with Orbos, Platt told his staff that he had a new and secret conduit to Cory Aquino, one who just might deliver a new military bases agreement.[7] But

4. Stanley Schrager, oral communication to Robert Reid, August 21, 1991. Schrager was a member of the U.S. negotiating panel and was privy to all aspects of the talks.
5. Ibid.
6. Ibid.
7. Ibid.

the Action Man had begun making enemies among those at the palace jealous of his popularity. He would soon become a victim of his own ambition.

In late April, 1991, Orbos tipped reporters that Aquino was about to ask for Ramos's resignation as defense secretary because he was clearly preparing to run for president, and the administration wanted to appear neutral. Orbos, meanwhile, was already working on his own campaign. His "action staff" had drafted an "Integrated Communications Plan" designed to promote the executive secretary as the best choice to succeed Aquino. Ramos aides obtained a copy of the draft plan and leaked it to the press; it was published on April 30. Orbos denied the story, but the storm surrounding the report was so great that he was forced to lie low.

Politically, Orbos was doomed. His high-profile style had already alienated Aquino's influential daughter Maria Elena Cruz, who was her mother's appointments secretary and who was enraged by the appearance that Orbos, not Aquino, ran the government. In addition, the draft plan revealing Orbos's presidential ambitions destroyed the ties with House Speaker Mitra, his patron, who himself planned to run for president in 1992. Rumors of personal misconduct by Orbos began circulating throughout Manila, and on July 4, the Action Man submitted his resignation to Aquino. He was replaced by Secretary of Justice Franklin Drilon. Petty politics had again undermined a crucial policy matter. [8] In light of the events that followed his leaving, however, it is problematical whether Orbos's negotiating skills would have changed the final bases agreement.

Armitage returned to Manila soon after the Orbos story broke. Instead of finding the Philippine panel ready to strike a deal, he found that Manglapus was still sticking to his original demand: $825 million a year in compensation for a five- to seven-year agreement. After five days of fruitless talks, Armitage again left without a final arrangement, even though— a year after negotiations had begun—the two sides were close to a deal. What they did not count on, however, was Mother Nature and an obscure peak in the Zambales Mountains few had ever heard of.

From the military housing area at Clark, Mount Pinatubo was barely discernible from the dozens of other peaks in the Zambales range. Mount

8. *Ibid.*

Pinatubo was known to be a volcano, but it had not erupted since the fourteenth century. In April, 1991, residents of the Zambales reported steam rising from cracks on the western slope of 5,874-foot Mount Pinatubo. A few weeks later, the chief of the government's volcanology institute, Raymundo Punongbayan, concluded that the volcano was about to erupt. He warned the cabinet, including Manglapus, of the dangers to Clark and Subic. Manglapus and his colleagues, however, made jokes about the warnings and took no steps to change either the government's negotiating position or to revise the conversion plans for Clark.[9]

On June 3, Mount Pinatubo spewed ash from its vents for the first time in six hundred years. The volcanology institute warned of a major eruption within days. The U.S. Air Force flew its planes to Guam and Okinawa and told personnel to be prepared to evacuate at a moment's notice. Pinatubo spewed ash again on Sunday, June 9, and the next day, the air force ordered troops and their families to evacuate by car to Subic, thirty miles to the southwest.

At 8:51 A.M. on Wednesday, June 12, 1991, Pinatubo erupted with a fury. A huge, dark column of ash and steam rose fifty thousand feet into the sky, billowing into a mushroom shape that resembled a nuclear explosion. Scientists warned the worst was yet to come.

Two days later, Mount Pinatubo exploded in one of the century's most tremendous eruptions. It was a day that millions of people who lived through it will never forget. Repeated explosions hurled tons of ash and stones—six billion tons by some estimates—into the sky, where the swirling winds churned up by a tropical storm spread debris as far as Palawan Island, 375 miles south of the volcano. Thick rainclouds laden with volcanic ash covered the skies, and by mid-afternoon Manila and central Luzon were as dark as night. The ash shower was so intense that it collapsed the roofs of thousands of houses, toppled trees, and piled up along the highways. The earth rolled in repeated tremors.

When the sun rose the next morning, Filipinos awoke to a scene of incomparable devastation. Gray, sandlike ash blanketed the landscape like dirty snow. Hundreds had died. The Clark and Subic bases were not spared. More than 150 buildings at Subic had been damaged, and the navy's largest warehouse outside the United States had been destroyed.

9. Raymundo Punongbayan related to reporters several times during October, 1991, that officials had laughed off his warnings.

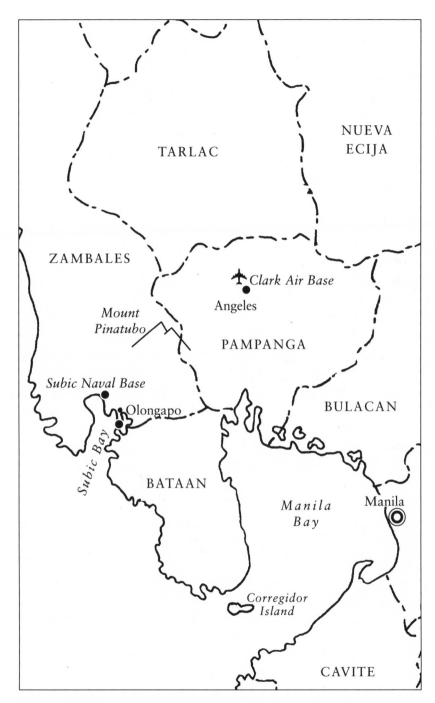

Map 9. Mount Pinatubo, in Central Luzon.

The runway at Clark was blanketed in a half foot of volcanic ash. Avalanches of mud roared through the base, destroying parked cars and buildings in their path.

Manglapus pretended that nothing had changed and kept insisting the Philippines would not accept a lower compensation figure. He visited Clark on June 23 and told reporters he might even ask for more money "because the suffering of the Philippine economy is much, much more compared to the destruction at Clark." He even suggested that if the U.S. decided to abandon Clark, they should clean up the damage left by Pinatubo first.

The devastation of Pinatubo, much of it in Aquino's political strongholds, erased whatever misgivings she had about extending the American presence. Hundreds of thousands of Filipinos depended on the bases, directly or indirectly, for their livelihood. The bases could hardly be closed at a time when the surrounding provinces were facing ruin.

Armitage returned to Manila on July 15, and the two panels announced an agreement. The United States would abandon Clark Air Base, which was unusable, by September 16, 1992, but would retain its naval facilities at Subic Bay for at least ten more years, with the possibility of an extension. The Americans agreed to pay the promised $230 million annually, subject to congressional approval. On the evening of July 17, Armitage was greeted with applause as he appeared at a U.S. Embassy reception. "Do you think you muscled them?" Ambassador Platt asked. Armitage smiled. "We did muscle them," he replied.[10]

Signing the agreement signaled the end of Aquino's "open options" policy. She would now fight for its ratification in the senate, where two-thirds' approval was required. All but two of the twenty-three senators had run on her ticket in the 1987 election, and many of them had been political lightweights who would never have been elected without her support. That should have guaranteed ratification.

But times had changed since 1986, and Aquino no longer had the same stature among Filipinos. Too much infighting and too many disappointments had eroded her position as her term drew to a close. Opposing Cory no longer carried the same political risks as before. Six senators—Pimentel, Tañada, Mercado, Saguisag, Guingona, and Salonga—were

---

10. Bob Drogin, Los Angeles *Times* correspondent, oral communication to Robert Reid, September 28, 1991.

stalwarts of the Marcos opposition and fundamentally opposed to extending the U.S. bases agreement. They were not prepared to compromise, despite their ties to Aquino.

In late July, the senate president, Jovito Salonga, called an informal caucus to discuss the treaty. He convinced his colleagues to take an informal straw vote to judge the sense of the chamber. The others went along, and the results showed sixteen opposed. Several senators were not firm in their opposition; a few of them believed that the Americans might raise the compensation figure again if it appeared the agreement was headed for defeat. Salonga, however, told reporters the results of his straw vote and identified the opponents by name. His disclosure put the "soft nos" on the line. If they switched sides, they would be denounced in the antibases press for selling out to the United States.

The Philippine ambassador to the U.S., Emmanuel Pelaez, returned from Washington to lobby for the agreement. He warned that rejecting the agreement would mean "turbulent times ahead" for the Philippines and its relations with the United States.

The issue divided the president's own family as well. Soon after the straw vote, Aquino summoned most of the senators to her office to lobby personally for the treaty. Among them was her brother-in-law, Butz Aquino. She argued about economic advantages and the need to protect ties with Washington. Butz was not convinced. "You're hardheaded," Aquino snapped at him after one call. Finally, she asked Butz that if he would not change his vote, would he at least not campaign openly against it? Butz agreed, but two weeks later, he announced publicly that he would oppose ratification. Aquino was so angry that she telephoned Butz at his office, and when he came on the line, she hung up on him without speaking.[11]

As the senate began public hearings September 2, it became clear that the Aquino administration had failed miserably in its political strategy on behalf of the agreement. Richard "Dick" Gordon, the forty-five-year-old mayor of Olongapo City, adjacent to the Subic installation, argued forcefully for ratification. "It's all right for you to say 'Yankee Go Home,' because you have jobs and your personal security to turn to," Gordon told the senators during a public session. "Your family won't starve

---

11. Agapito Aquino, oral communication to Eileen Guerrero, Manila, September 12, 1991. Guerrero covered the hearings.

whether the base stays or goes." But to the ardent nationalists, all from well-heeled families, bread-and-butter arguments meant little. "I think it is time for our people to suffer a certain shock in the rejection of this treaty because we might reform ourselves," testified former senator and Marcos's vice-presidential running mate, Arturo Tolentino. During a break in the sessions, Rene Saguisag observed, "I fought for democracy [against Marcos], not for the right to eat." [12]

As the treaty appeared doomed, Cory Aquino decided to play her last card: the people. She would lead a mass rally and march on the senate building on Tuesday, September 10, to show that the people were behind a new base agreement. Foolishly, the palace predicted up to one million people would turn out for this revival of people power.

No effort was spared to muster a huge crowd. Millions of pesos were directed away from government programs to finance the rally and bring people to Rizal Park near Manila Bay for the festivities. Mayors of towns and cities throughout central Luzon were given quotas that had to be met. The government's Commission on Urban Poor, which cared for squatters in the capital, was directed to make sure at least fifty thousand appeared at the rally. Pupils were excused from classes with the promise of a day off, free food, and transport to and from the rally.

Cory Aquino got her crowd, but it was not people power; rather, it resembled the government-sponsored rallies organized by Ferdinand Marcos. The turnout was respectable, somewhere between fifty thousand and one hundred thousand, but far smaller than the one million predicted. Many of them were simply there on an outing. A Muslim woman standing in front of the senate building with a pro-bases banner admitted she had no idea what the sign said but explained that her mayor had offered a free lunch if she participated. One woman pointed to a sign that proclaimed "Yes to U.S. Bases," then turned to a reporter and asked, "What's that?"

Aquino herself drew only perfunctory applause. Thousands were already leaving because a thunderstorm was approaching. Those who stayed heard the president ramble on in Tagalog about how the antibases senators had betrayed the trust she had placed in them in 1987. She won-

---

12. Rene Saguisag, oral communication to Eileen Guerrero, Manila, September 14, 1991.

dered aloud whether the opponents would no longer travel to the United States for medical treatment or send their children to school there.

Why did she go to such efforts on behalf of an agreement for which she had shown so little enthusiasm for so many years? The answer lies in the character of Cory Aquino. She was stubborn and a fighter. Winning the fight became more important than the issue at stake. "She was hurt," Butz Aquino told one of the authors. "To her it became a personal issue." [13]

The senate began formal debate the following day, September 11. Tañada stood at the speaker's rostrum and introduced his resolution of non-concurrence, urging rejection "because we refuse to bind this nation and its people in an unequal contract." The most gripping speech that day, however, was delivered by Senator Juan Ponce Enrile. It was Enrile's chance to strike back at all the injustices he felt he had received under the Aquino government. "The U.S. Phantom jets that darkened our skies at the height of the December, 1989, coup attempt are but the most uninhibited demonstration of how poorly the United States regards our sovereignty and independence," Enrile thundered.

On the opening day of the debate, Butz Aquino received a telephone call at the senate. It was his sister-in-law, the president. Butz was nervous about accepting her invitation to see her but had no choice. He knew that Cory was capable of putting great pressure on him, both as a politician and as a family member. Knowing he could not refuse, he asked Saguisag to accompany him for moral support.

They found the former housewife in such a businesslike, no-nonsense mood that she did not even offer the customary coffee. Both senators made it clear to her that their decision to vote against the treaty was final. Saguisag, however, offered a face-saving way out. Since the U.S. was not prepared to leave immediately after the senate had voted, why not offer a three-year withdrawal period during which the Philippines would accept no compensation? That would give the government time to begin programs to convert both Subic and Clark to civilian use and perhaps save some jobs. In the meantime, the Americans would still employ thousands of base workers, spend thousands of dollars on the local economy, and have time to relocate their forces elsewhere in the Pacific. Aquino promised to consider the idea. [14]

13. Agapito Aquino to Guerrero, September 12, 1991.
14. Rene Saguisag, oral communication to authors, Manila, September 14, 1991.

Pelaez and Finance Secretary Jesus Estanislao discussed the idea with the new U.S. ambassador, Frank Wisner, who had replaced Platt in August. He seemed receptive although perplexed by the offer to reject compensation. Wisner made no firm commitments but agreed to refer the matter to Washington.

The senate convened at 10:00 A.M. on Monday, September 16, the date the government had always maintained marked the expiration of the 1947 R.P.–U.S. Military Bases Agreement. The visitors' gallery was jammed with people, most of them antibases advocates who came to savor an expected victory. Millions of other Filipinos, including Cory Aquino, tuned in to the proceedings on television, which broadcast the session live nationwide. The vote was by a show of hands: eleven supported ratification, eleven rejected it.

Senate President Salonga broke the tie and cast the twelfth vote against the treaty. Eight "no" votes were all that had been required to defeat it. Ninety-three years of U.S. military presence in the Philippines had come to an end. Cheers broke out in the gallery from visitors, reporters, and senate staff members, most of whom opposed the agreement.

After the show of hands, each senator was allowed to take the floor to explain his vote. Outside the senate building, tens of thousands danced in a monsoon rain, chanted "No to the U.S. bases," sang protest songs along with a rock band, and greeted one another with "Happy Independence."

Salonga took the rostrum for the final speech. More than any other opponent, Jovito Salonga had outmaneuvered the United States and Cory Aquino. "Today, we have summoned the political will to stand up and end 470 years of foreign military presence here in the Philippines," Salonga declared in deep, resonant tones. "September 16, 1991, may well be the day when we in this Senate found the soul, the true spirit of this nation, because we mustered the courage and the will to declare the end of foreign military presence in the Philippines."[15]

Instead of trying to work out a compromise with the senate on a time-table for the U.S. withdrawal, Aquino's advisers scrambled to arrange appearances for her on early morning U.S. television shows. "I would like to assure the American people that the great majority of the Filipino peo-

15. Jovito Salonga, September 16, 1991, Records of the Philippine Senate, Executive House, Manila.

ple would like the Americans to stay on at Subic Bay," she told NBC-TV's "Today Show." She told ABC-TV's "Good Morning America" that she would seek a people power referendum to overturn the senate decision. The referendum proposal never got off the ground, however—another "brushfire" idea. Most of the legal establishment, including framers of the constitution, told her the move would be unconstitutional.

Aquino offered the U.S. a three-year withdrawal schedule, but her new executive secretary, Franklin Drilon, insisted on adherence to the anti-nuclear provisions of the constitution and on a firm withdrawal schedule. Clark Air Base was handed over to the Philippines in November, 1991, and Subic a year later. The last troops sailed away on November 23, 1992, aboard the USS *Belleau Wood,* as the ship's speakers blared Lee Green-wood's country song "I'm Proud to Be an American." More than forty thousand Filipino base workers lost their jobs.

The special relationship was over. Ambassador Frank Wisner tried to be upbeat publicly. "It is now time to start thinking of a new relationship," he told the Manila media. Privately, however, he told U.S. correspondents: "The Philippines will now have to deal realistically with its problems. Unfortunately, it has not had much experience in doing so." [16]

16. Frank Wisner, U.S. ambassador, oral communication to American journalists at a dinner party, Makati, February 27, 1992, Reid notes.

15 GHOSTS OF MARCOS PAST

THE PROMISE OF people power was the promise of justice to the nation for the abuses of the Marcos era. During the first months of her government, Corazon Aquino began steps along two fronts to fulfill that promise. Seven months after she took office, the Philippine Supreme Court overturned the acquittals in the Ninoy Aquino assassination trial. The government indicted forty people, including sixteen of the original defendants, and began a second trial. In addition, on February 25, 1986, in her first executive order the president established the Presidential Commission on Good Government (PCGG) to recover the fortune that Marcos and his associates allegedly pillaged during his twenty years in power.

The commission was given broad powers. It could seize or sequester properties believed illegally acquired and bring to court those who had abused the public trust. The commission was also made exempt from civil suits in order to prevent Marcos cronies from using the law to subvert and tie up its operations. The Marcoses' "hidden wealth" would be regained through the legal system. Factories, real estate, and other assets could be seized on suspicion that they had been illegally acquired, but the administration would have to prove its allegations in court. At the time, Aquino's choice of Jovito Salonga as the first commission chairman was widely applauded because of his reputation for integrity and long political career in the Marcos opposition.

The task facing the commission was enormous. It had no idea how much money and property had possibly been illegally obtained. During a press conference, reporters pressed Salonga to provide some kind of estimate on the extent of the so-called hidden wealth, and for want of a better figure, he threw out $10 billion, nearly 29 percent of the entire Philippine gross national product for 1986. Salonga knew at the time that the amount could well have been inflated; he later acknowledged that it was indeed too high. When asked by reporters for the source of his estimate, Salonga referred them to a series of articles in the San Jose *Mercury-News,* which won a Pulitzer prize in 1986 for its exposé on the Marcos fortune.[1] Much of the series' material came from U.S.-based Filipino exiles—in particular, Heherson Alvarez—and the figures are suspect, to say the least. Nonetheless, the $10-billion figure became the yardstick for measuring the success or failure of recovery efforts.

The second problem facing the commission was that most of the Marcos fortune was believed to be abroad, hidden in a network of dummy corporations, numbered Swiss bank accounts, real estate registered under false names, foundations, and under the names of Marcos associates.

The commission had its strengths too, not the least of which was an overwhelming reserve of goodwill, not only from the Filipino people but from the world community. Allegations of the extent of Marcos's greed had shocked the world, and the events of February, 1986, had given Cory Aquino and her followers an international image approaching political sainthood. Offers from assistance from ordinary Filipinos, prominent lawyers, and former Marcos associates poured in to the commission offices. In an unprecedented move, the Swiss government slapped a precautionary freeze on all bank accounts linked to the Marcos family and offered legal assistance in recovering the money.

The Swiss move was a historic breakthrough. Switzerland's economy rests on the integrity of the country's secretive banking system. The Swiss had even refused to freeze accounts held by the Shah of Iran after the 1979 Islamic revolution drove him into exile. "The PCGG enjoyed a lot of goodwill and we were receiving information left and right," said Caesar Parlade, a young accountant who left a lucrative job with a private firm to join the commission in 1986. "People were offering their services without any compensation."[2]

1. The series on "Marcos's Hidden Wealth" appeared in 1985 in the San Jose (Calif.) *Mercury-News.*

2. Interview with Caesar Parlade by Eileen Guerrero, Makati, July 24, 1991.

The commission also received early, valuable leads from documents Marcos had left behind at Malacañang Palace. Other documents were seized by U.S. customs officials when the deposed first family arrived in Hawaii. At the palace, investigators found scraps of paper on which Marcos practiced signatures of "William Saunders," one of the pseudonyms used on foreign accounts. Customs agents in Hawaii also uncovered papers linking Marcos and his family to real estate in Manhattan. Salonga rushed to the United States and convinced authorities to prevent Marcos from unloading the Manhattan properties or transferring them to dummy corporations before a claim could be lodged.

As investigators studied the documents, they realized the mammoth task facing them. Marcos maintained shadow corporations, property, and bank accounts as far away as Brazil, Liechtenstein, and Luxor, Egypt. And these did not include the separate network maintained by some three hundred "cronies," including Aquino's cousin Eduardo "Danding" Cojuangco; the former ambassador to Japan, Roberto Benedicto; and Imelda's brother, Benjamin "Kokoy" Romualdez. As a start, the commission established three broad guidelines for the search. It would concentrate efforts on Marcos assets in Switzerland and the United States, where local authorities and the courts were sympathetic, and it would also consider out-of-court settlements with certain cronies but not with the Marcos family.[3]

That strategy, which has been confirmed by former commission officials, seemed to be at odds with public statements from Aquino. From time to time, she would indicate her willingness to cut a deal with Marcos in return for most, if not all, of the hidden wealth. She hinted to reporters in April, 1986, that if Marcos wanted to come home, he should first consider returning the allegedly embezzled funds. A few days later, she even raised the possibility of amnesty. "At least part, or a greater part, of the whole is better than nothing at all," she said in a television interview. "And we feel that maybe we can get this back faster if we will be able to offer them amnesty."[4]

As the Marcos loyalists stepped up their challenge to the Aquino government, the word amnesty disappeared from the administration's lexi-

3. *Ibid.*
4. Interview with Corazon Aquino by Luis Beltran, People's Television, Manila, April 21, 1986.

con. It became clear that "national reconciliation" did not apply to the Marcos family. All offers by Marcos for returning money carried one condition that Aquino would not accept: the right to return to the Philippines. "Marcos wanted to come home in exchange [for money]," said David Castro, who later served as chairman of the commission. "He wanted to go again into politics in this country."[5]

The freeze orders and other early developments encouraged a sense of unfounded optimism that recovery efforts might soon pay off. Salonga traveled to the United States in April and returned with assurances that Manila would soon receive title to hundreds of millions of dollars in real estate that the Marcoses had purchased in the New York area.

Optimism increased when a Filipino businessman and Marcos associate living in British Columbia, Jose Y. Campos, offered to cooperate. Campos surrendered land titles covering nearly nineteen thousand acres of prime Philippine real estate, which he admitted holding for the former president. Campos also identified six offshore companies and more than two dozen Philippine corporations that he admitted organizing as fronts for Marcos.

Commission lawyers traveled to Honolulu in late September, 1986, to take depositions from Ferdinand and Imelda Marcos regarding allegations of hidden wealth. They interviewed the Marcoses for two days in the couple's Makiki Heights home. Marcos, still proud and stubborn in defeat, was so uncooperative during the lengthy deposition that his own lawyers urged him to be patient. He invoked the Fifth Amendment a total of 197 times. Imelda was no more cooperative. She broke into tears during six hours of questioning and took the Fifth Amendment more than two hundred times.[6]

While stonewalling in public, Marcos and his Honolulu entourage were sending private signals to Manila that they were prepared to deal: a portion of the hidden wealth in return for dropping all legal actions and allowing them to return to the Philippines. But Arroyo and others in the palace adamantly refused the overtures because they did not want to give Marcos any opportunity to come home and mount a challenge against them.

5.   Interview with David Castro by Robert Reid, Pasig, August 12, 1991.
6.   Text of depositions taken on September 30 (Marcos) and October 1 (Imelda), 1986, as released by the Philippine government. The depositions were for the U.S. District Court, Central District of California; copies obtained by authors.

With millions, if not billions, of dollars at stake, there were plenty of others willing to deal with Marcos. One of them was a Filipino financier, Michael de Guzman, who was living in Vienna. De Guzman conceived a plan he claimed would have returned billions of dollars to the Philippines in return for a 25 percent "finder's fee." The plan, which he dubbed "Operation Big Bird," called for embezzling the embezzler—tricking Marcos into signing away his fortune to the Aquino government.

A few weeks after Marcos fled to Hawaii, de Guzman traveled to Beirut to meet with Lebanese financiers whom Marcos had allegedly used to transfer money secretly from the Philippines to safe havens abroad. De Guzman and his Beirut contacts devised a plan in which de Guzman would volunteer his services to the Marcos family to move funds from Switzerland to his own bank, Exportfinanzierungs Bank (Export Financing Bank), in Vienna. De Guzman claimed he would in turn sign over the money to the Philippine government.

De Guzman arranged a meeting with members of the Marcos family in Honolulu, and on March 20, 1986, received letters of authorization from Marcos's son, Ferdinand, Jr., to transfer funds from secret Swiss accounts. Before de Guzman could reach Switzerland, the accounts were frozen. Undaunted, he flew to Manila and presented his plan to Peping Cojuangco, as well as to officials of the PCGG. De Guzman argued that despite Swiss offers of help, it would take years to recover the funds through Switzerland's decentralized legal system.

Filipino officials showed interest in the plan, and in July, 1986, de Guzman returned to Switzerland along with Solicitor General Sedfrey Ordoñez and retired brigadier general Jose Almonte, who at the time served as director of the government's Economic Intelligence Bureau. On July 4, the delegation met with Peter Hess, director of the Swiss federal police; his deputy, Pierre Schmid; and Lionel Frei, chief of the Section for International Judicial Assistance for the federal police.

During the meeting, de Guzman presented his authorization documents as well as other details on numbered accounts and the amount of money held in each of them. De Guzman said the Swiss officials agreed to "unfreeze" accounts worth at least $200 million and promised to ask the cantonal court in Zurich to authorize transfer of the funds to the Philippine government account at de Guzman's bank.

Ordoñez, however, feared de Guzman might be working for Marcos and that he could possibly find a way to transfer the funds to a country that would refuse to turn them over to the Philippine government. He rushed back to Manila before a final meeting and discussed his misgivings with Arroyo and Salonga. In the meantime, the government in Manila had done some checking into de Guzman's background and found that his bank was nearly insolvent. That raised fears of a double cross.

Instead of accepting de Guzman's bank as the recipient, the government instructed the Swiss to deposit the money in a Manila account at Credit Suisse Bank in Zurich—an arrangement different from the one the Swiss had reached with de Guzman. Angry with the confusion in Manila, the Swiss broke off the deal in September, 1986. The money stayed where it was.

De Guzman and Almonte claimed the government had missed a "historic" opportunity to get its hands on the Marcos wealth. Arroyo maintained that he had blocked a "monumental scam" that would have cost the government any chance to recover the Marcos fortune. In December, 1986, Almonte and de Guzman sought a meeting with Aquino to present their version of the events. Almonte said they arrived at the president's office, only to be intercepted by Arroyo. When her appointments secretary told them the president was ready for the meeting, Joker snapped, "This is too complicated a matter for the president. Tell the president she won't understand it." Operation Big Bird was dead.[7]

The effort, however, did succeed in identifying secret numbered accounts of the Marcos family in Switzerland. That information formed the basis of the government's legal claim on the Swiss fortune.

With the demise of Operation Big Bird, the Philippines focused its efforts on the Swiss offer of legal assistance. Establishing the existence of Marcos accounts was not enough for the Swiss. The Aquino administration had to prove, by Swiss legal standards, that the money was illegally obtained and illegally transferred. That meant Cory Aquino would have to place her predecessor on trial and win a conviction in court.

Lawyers at the Presidential Commission on Good Government were aware from the start that they could never recover substantial amounts

7. The material here on Operation Big Bird came primarily from Reid's interview with General Jose Almonte, Camp Aguinaldo, Manila, April 3, 1991. Details can also be found in the records of the Philippine House of Representatives, Committee on Public Accountability, which held hearings on the operation on July 10, 1989.

of the Swiss accounts unless they brought the former president to trial. Civil suits alone would not suffice. On April 3, 1986, Salonga told reporters that criminal charges, including embezzlement and "malversation of public funds" would be filed against Marcos within thirty to sixty days. Otherwise, Commissioner Pedro Yap explained to Filipino reporters, Swiss authorities would lift the freeze order.

Cory Aquino, however, was caught in a trap. Her government desperately needed the money. The Swiss were insisting on a criminal trial as a precondition for releasing the money, but such a trial would force her to allow Ferdinand Marcos to come home. The new constitution banned criminal trials in absentia, and Philippine legal tradition provided for the defendant to be present during the arraignment.

At the same time, however, Marcos loyalists in the Philippines were staging large, weekly demonstrations demanding that their leader be allowed to return to his homeland. The presence of the former president on Philippine soil, even under detention, could have unleashed forces no one could control. Aquino decided to defer filing charges; instead, her government convinced the Swiss to continue the freeze.

Aquino's concerns were well founded. From his Hawaiian exile, Marcos was working furiously to engineer his own, triumphant return. After the failure of the Manila Hotel putsch in July, Marcos contacted Saudi arms dealer Mohammed al-Fassi to help finance the purchase of $25 million in weapons—enough to outfit ten thousand men—for an "invasion" of the Philippines. Al-Fassi set up a meeting between Marcos and two U.S. businessmen, Richard Hirschfeld and Robert Chastain, to arrange for the purchases and the export licenses necessary to ship the arms through a third country, possibly Thailand.[8]

During a meeting in early 1987 at his Makiki Heights residence, Marcos told the two Americans that he wanted antitank weapons, antiaircraft missiles, mortars, recoilless rifles, and small arms to be shipped secretly to the Philippines in time for a coup by July 10, 1987.

But Hirschfeld and Chastain were carrying recording devices during the meeting, and copies were furnished to U.S. and Filipino authorities. Luis Villareal, the director of the Philippine Intelligence Service, said the

---

8. Testimony of Robert Chastain and Richard Hirschfeld, July 7, 1987, U.S. House, Subcommittee on Asian and Pacific Affairs, 100th Cong., 1st sess. (Washington, 1987).

plan called for Marcos loyalists to seize Aquino and, if necessary, kill her.[9] Predictably, Marcos disavowed any knowledge of the operations and claimed the cases had been fabricated by the Aquino government to humiliate him. But the evidence was strong enough for the State Department to confine Marcos to Oahu Island.

On March 9, 1987, Salonga resigned as chairman of PCGG in order to run for the senate and was succeeded by fellow commissioner Ramon Diaz. Diaz built a reputation as a capable and thorough administrator, but despite his talents, the commission began to lose its aura. Critics complained it was quick to sequester properties without sufficient evidence that they had been obtained illegally. Corporations worth millions of dollars were seized and placed at the mercy of fiscal agents earning about $5 a day. Allegations of favoritism and corruption surfaced in the Manila press.

With no authority to file criminal charges, commission lawyers instead brought thirty-five civil suits against Marcos and dozens of former associates, hoping that would satisfy Swiss requirements. But the Swiss remained firm. On July 1, 1987, the Swiss Federal Court ruled that funds could not be repatriated unless Marcos were tried and convicted in a criminal proceeding. One month later, the government's lawyer in Switzerland, Sergio Salvioni, traveled to Manila to explain the requirements to Aquino personally. "Your authorities must make a choice," Salvioni told reporters. "They have two main alternatives: they summon Marcos to come here and they judge him here, or they can ask for a trial, maybe in Hawaii."[10]

The prospect of trying Ferdinand Marcos anywhere except in the Philippines intrigued Aquino and her legal advisers. She signed an order extending the authority of the *Sandiganbayan,* or antigraft court, beyond Philippine territory, and Solicitor General Francisco Chavez asked U.S. diplomats about the possibility of convening the tribunal in Hawaii. The Americans were not interested, and the idea was eventually abandoned.

Aquino was left with one option: the United States. Grand juries in Virginia and New York were already investigating Marcos and his family about possible violations of U.S. law. If a court within the United States tried and convicted Marcos, it would spare the Philippines the wrenching

9. *Ibid.*
10. Sergio Salvioni to reporters, Manila, August 19, 1987.

experience of its own trial. In addition, a conviction in an American court might satisfy Swiss demands and free the bank accounts. Plans to bring Marcos back for trial were quietly shelved, and instead, the PCGG and other agencies of the administration began cooperating with U.S. prosecutors.[11]

In Manila, however, the search for Marcos's money was making little headway. Newly elected congressmen, including Cory's cousin Emigdio Tanjuatco, were urging that the commission be abolished because of alleged corruption. Some of the criticism was self-serving because several prominent congressmen—some elected under the Aquino standard—had business links with leading Marcos cronies who were anxious to regain control of their assets. Critics claimed that the commission had sequestered property unfairly and was simply raking off millions by retaining control of alleged illegal assets.

The commission's mandate was so broad that it soon became embroiled in bureaucratic infighting with other agencies responsible for various aspects of law enforcement, including the solicitor general's office. The commission was responsible for collecting evidence against Marcos associates, and the solicitor general tried the cases in court; however, the boundaries of responsibility often were vague.

The commission had seized a garment factory purportedly owned by Marcos's daughter, Imee. But Solicitor General Chavez, a publicity-minded figure with political ambitions, asked the supreme court to lift the seizure order, claiming Chairman Diaz had overstepped his authority. A public campaign of name-calling and denunciations soon followed.

The president summoned the two for a reconciliation meeting, but when that failed, she ordered both of them to take indefinite vacations to cool off. Eventually, Chavez returned to his job, but Diaz was shunted off to Canada as the ambassador. He was replaced by Mateo Caparas, an elderly lawyer and the commission's third chairman in three years. The shake-up further tarnished the reputation of the PCGG, which was increasingly seen as an ineffective instrument of a partisan, vindictive government.

Aquino's own actions on behalf of a relative played into the hands of those seeking to discredit the commission. In August, 1988, Manila news-

---

11. Parlade interview by Guerrero, July 24, 1991.

papers reported that her brother-in-law, Ricardo "Baby" Lopa, had been able to buy thirty-nine companies from Imelda's brother shortly before the PCGG began its operations two years before. Commissioner Jose Laureta went to Malacañang and personally informed the president that, in his opinion, the sale could not be consummated because the shares in question should have been sequestered, even though they were transferred before the commission was formed.

In a lengthy reply, Lopa said the companies were originally owned by Cory Aquino's late father and his other partners and were purchased legally by Imelda's brother in 1974. Lopa insisted the sale was legal at the time, and he was simply buying back the assets. Nevertheless, Senator Juan Ponce Enrile quickly pounced on the story as an example of presidential favoritism of her relatives. Enrile argued that the courts should decide whether the transfer of ownership was legal.

Aquino disregarded the legal questions. She considered Enrile's statement as an attack on her family. No sooner had Lopa issued his statement than Cory announced she was satisfied with the explanation. "I am really the one whom my enemies want to destroy," she said during a radio address. Although her suspicion was not entirely without foundation, her position made it appear there was one set of rules for presidential kin and another for everyone else. "Her moral posture was eroded by her own instant statements on a matter which has yet to be resolved," wrote left-wing historian Renato Constantino. "Unfortunately, it seems that familial ties were too strong. She acted not as a president but as a sister-in-law." [12]

As the commission's efforts foundered, the U.S. case against Ferdinand Marcos was proceeding toward a resolution. Federal authorities were so confident of the evidence against Marcos that the U.S. attorney for New York, Rudolph Giuliani, informed the State Department that he could guarantee a conviction.

The case was politically charged. A former head of state of a friendly government would face criminal charges before an American court. The U.S. legal system could be seen as acting as a prosecutorial agent for a government made up of people who had spent years denouncing the United States for propping up a "dictator." Regardless of the past, the U.S. government had cast its lot with Cory Aquino and had worked hard to ensure her success.

12. Renato Constantino, *Demystifying Aquino* (Quezon City, 1989), 175.

The White House preferred a plea bargain to a full-blown trial. On Tuesday, October 18, 1988, President Reagan personally approved a final offer to his old friend. Marcos's lawyers, Richard Hibey and John Bartko, were summoned to the Justice Department in Washington, where U.S. Attorney General Richard Thornburg outlined the terms: plead guilty and surrender millions in real estate, art, and jewelry in return for a guarantee of no prison sentence. Thornburg wanted an answer from Marcos within three days. [13]

Marcos refused, and on October 21, 1988, Ferdinand and Imelda Marcos were indicted by a federal grand jury in New York on racketeering charges. The indictment accused them of looting $100 million from the Philippine treasury to purchase real estate and art in New York; they were also charged with defrauding three lending institutions of more than $165 million. Saudi financier Adnan Khashoggi and five others were also charged. The charges carried a possible prison sentence of 120 years and millions of dollars in potential fines.

In Manila, a confident Cory Aquino hailed the indictment, saying it would speed the return of the hidden wealth. She added that the New York trial would have "no effect whatsoever" on future prosecution of Marcos in the Philippines. In fact, however, the indictment all but precluded ever bringing Marcos to trial in his homeland.

But Marcos's health was failing. Once a vigorous and athletic man, he had been suffering for years from the degenerative disease lupus, which slowly attacks and destroys the body's internal organs. He had undergone a secret kidney transplant nearly a decade before his downfall, and by the time of his exile, the disease had spread. Imelda was summoned to New York for arraignment, but Ferdinand Marcos was excused for reasons of health. The former first lady entered her not-guilty plea and was released on a bond of $5 million, put up by her old friend, tobacco heiress Doris Duke.

On January 15, 1989, Marcos was rushed to St. Francis Hospital in Honolulu, suffering from heart, kidney, and respiratory problems. Doctors were able to arrest his decline, but the prognosis was grim. With Marcos apparently dying, Vice-President Laurel rushed to Honolulu in early February for what was to be his final visit with the former president.

13. Richard Hibey, October 19, 1989, records of the U.S. District Court for southern Manhattan.

Laurel spent thirty-five minutes at his bedside and emerged shaken. Once-robust, Marcos now weighed less than one hundred pounds and was running a high fever. He slipped in and out of consciousness and did not recognize visitors.

Imelda appeared desperate. She urged Laurel to use what influence he still had with Aquino to convince her to let Marcos die in his homeland. She hinted about a possible deal to much of the Marcos fortune if the administration would relent on its ban.

Laurel flew back to Manila on February 4 and told reporters at an airport press conference that he had an important message to deliver personally to Aquino. He refused to reveal any details but said he would seek a meeting with the president as soon as possible. But she would not see him. Instead, she suggested that Laurel should first "share it with the Filipino people."

For the next several months, doctors managed to keep the former president alive, although he slipped repeatedly in and out of comas. When his condition worsened, negotiations would accelerate, then he would improve slightly and the urgency would ebb. Regardless, Laurel was unable to arrange a deal.

Imelda then turned to billionaire businessman Enrique Zobel and suggested a formula under which about $5 billion could be returned through a foundation administered jointly with a Vatican representative. All that was needed was Marcos's signature on the authorizing documents. Although Aquino was still reluctant to reach any accommodation with the man she so deeply hated, Zobel pushed ahead with the plan and flew to Honolulu in early September with the necessary legal papers. By the time he arrived, however, Marcos was too weak to sign them.[14]

Marcos fell into a coma and died at 12:40 A.M. Hawaiian time on September 28, 1989. It was already early evening in Manila, and Aquino was attending a reception. She issued a statement that barely concealed the contempt she held for the former president: "I personally condole deeply with the family he leaves behind with all sincerity. For I and my children know the pain of a loss." That was a clear reference to the murder of her husband, for which she held Marcos responsible. The body of her

14. Enrique Zobel, oral communication to Robert Reid, Makati, June 12, 1992. The conversation took place at the ENZO Building, which Zobel owns.

predecessor would be barred from returning to the Philippines "for the tranquillity of the state and the order of society."

Giuiliani resigned as U.S. attorney in January, 1990, and ran unsuccessfully for mayor of New York. The case was turned over to his assistant, Charles Labella. Imelda hired Gerald Spence, a flamboyant Wyoming lawyer who boasted he had never lost a case. Meanwhile, Imelda sent desperate signals to Manila, often through the media, that she was prepared to return vast sums of money if the case were dropped.

Imelda would be arraigned in New York City on March 20, 1990. On that day she released excerpts from a letter to President Bush,[15] in which she offered to cooperate in finding funds allegedly taken from the Philippines, on condition that the money be used for charity in the Philippines. The funds would be turned over to a five-member international commission that would make sure they would be received by the Filipino people. Whatever communication took place between Washington and Malacañang, the Aquino administration—confident of a conviction—was not interested in making a deal.

Later that day, Imelda Marcos stood before Judge John Keenan for arraignment and pleaded innocent. A jury of three postal workers, two transit and utility employees, a retired secretary, a teacher's aide, an engineer, a computer operator, and an estate manager would decide the guilt or innocence of a person once described as among the world's richest and most powerful women.

The trial dragged on for more than three months. The prosecution produced numerous witnesses who testified to illegal money transactions, lavish purchases, and a lifestyle the Marcoses could never have afforded on their legal, acknowledged sources of income. None of the witnesses could link Imelda to a crime. Spence painted the picture of a wife who was willing to spend vast sums of money without asking her husband about the source. He called not a single witness on Imelda's behalf, confidently telling the court there was no need to do so because the prosecution had failed to prove its case.

On July 2, on the fifth day of deliberations, the jury returned its verdict: not guilty on all counts. "Just because she was married to him doesn't

---

15. White House spokesman Marlin Fitzwater told reporters that the president had received Imelda's letter but would not elaborate, except to say that no reply had been sent to her as of March 20.

mean she was guilty," forewoman Catherine Balton said. Juror Thomas O'Rourke offered another opinion, one shared by many Filipinos: "We are not big brothers to the people overseas."[16]

A principal reason for the collapse of the Justice Department's case was the refusal of a witness, Philippine congressman Ronnie Zamora, to testify. He had given testimony before the grand jury, and investigators expected him to be able to link Imelda to wrongdoing. But Zamora refused to testify in open court, citing attorney-client privilege. Without him, prosecutors could not tie Imelda to any crime.[17]

It was well after midnight in Manila when the verdict was announced. Press Secretary Tomas Gomez rushed to his office, discussed the verdict by telephone with Aquino, and issued a statement in her name: "I am sorry to hear that the courageous efforts made by the American prosecution have not succeeded. The acquittal does not alter the national interest and security grounds on which we have premised our decision not to allow the return of Mrs. Marcos at this time."

Aquino put up a brave front, but the outcome of the New York trial was devastating. The entire strategy of deferring to the United States in the prosecution of Marcos and his family had come crashing down. So had all the grand dreams about quick recovery of vast amounts of hidden wealth. Without a conviction, the Swiss would not order the secret accounts transferred.

Two months later, the Aquino assassination trial, then in its fourth year, dragged to a close. In a nationally televised proceeding, the Sandiganbayan announced the verdict: sixteen defendants, all former soldiers, were convicted and sentenced to life imprisonment. The rest of the defendants were acquitted.

On the day of the ruling, Cory Aquino cloistered herself at her residence on Arlegui Street and watched the proceedings on television. A press aide, Lourdes Siytangco, drafted a statement in her name, in which the president accepted the decision of the court. Nothing else could be said.[18] The trial, however, failed to answer the question Cory and the nation wanted to hear: who ordered the slaying? The court admitted that

16. Catherine Balton and Thomas O'Rourke, jurors, press conference following the verdict, New York, July 2, 1990, AP.

17. Parlade interview by Guerrero, July 24, 1991. Zamora has never confirmed this.

18. Interview with Lourdes Siytangco by Eileen Guerrero, Manila, April, 1991.

it could not provide the answer. As with the search for hidden wealth, the outcome of the Aquino assassination trial remained incomplete.

With Imelda's acquittal in New York, the search for the Marcos fortune through legal avenues had hit a stone wall. Since 1986, the PCGG had recovered only about $400 million in assets, virtually all in the Philippines. The search had cost the commission $8 million in legal fees, most of it paid to foreign lawyers, and another $14 million in operating costs.

Nevertheless, David Castro, who had served on the PCGG for several years and who became its new chairman on September 1, 1990, believed he was on the verge of a spectacular success that would redeem the commission's reputation. Thanks to Operation Big Bird and the cooperation of the Swiss, the PCGG had identified accounts established by Marcos in Switzerland that were worth about $350 million. Castro, however, was convinced this was only a small percentage of an enormous fortune in gold—at least 320 tons according to his estimate—that he and others in the government believed had been smuggled out of the country by Marcos between 1983 and 1985.[19] Castro also suspected that not all the gold had been sent abroad and that a great deal of it was buried throughout the country. Castro's conviction was based on the claims of an Australian citizen of Swiss origin, Reiner Jacobi, who had contacted him in December, 1988; during a meeting at the Cafe Roma in the Manila Hotel, Jacobi had offered his services to track down the gold supposedly smuggled out of the country to Switzerland.

Castro was fascinated by the forty-six-year-old Jacobi, who said he had been an informant for the Drug Enforcement Administration and hinted of links to various intelligence agencies. Castro agreed to pay Jacobi 10 percent of any gold recovered.

Jacobi stayed for months in the five-star Philippine Plaza Hotel playing the role of an international gold buyer looking for business. Eventually, he was approached by Adoracion Edralin-Lopez, a distant cousin of Marcos and his former cook. According to Jacobi, she claimed to be a trustee of a secret Marcos account and to have documents pertaining to a gold supply stored at the Zurich branch of the Union Bank of Switzerland.[20]

For years, rumors had circulated through the Philippines that Marcos

19. Castro cited this figure at a press conference at PCGG headquarters, Pasig, August 14, 1991, and said it was based on Jacobi's information.
20. Castro interview by Reid, August 12, 1991.

had found a fortune in gold left behind by Japanese troops at the end of World War II. Imelda claimed the story was true and that Japanese gold, not embezzlement, was the source of her husband's fortune. The Aquino government had sanctioned several gold excavations, including one in 1987 at the sixteenth-century Fort Santiago on the banks of the Pasig River. No gold cache was ever reported found, however.

True or not, the rumors of fabulous caches of Japanese gold were so strong that they created a subculture of "Indiana Jones" figures who scoured the countryside in Luzon, Mindanao, Mindoro, and other islands searching for instant wealth. Using sonars and other state-of-the-art equipment, they displayed all the enthusiasm of the conquistadores who sought cities of gold across Latin America centuries ago.

Castro always suspected that reports of Marcos's secret gold hoards were true. In the early 1980s, he had served as the lawyer for Orlando Dulay, a former military colonel and provincial governor who had been close to Ferdinand Marcos. But Dulay had been sentenced to life imprisonment for the deaths of several Aquino campaign workers in the 1986 election. Even before Jacobi came forward, Dulay had contacted Castro from prison in 1988 and offered a deal. According to Castro, Dulay claimed he had personally taken part in a secret excavation in the Antipolo hills outside metropolitan Manila in the mid-1970s, in which Marcos's agents had unearthed Japanese gold. Dulay said he knew of other caches, some still buried, and offered to tell the government what he knew in return for a presidential pardon.[21]

Castro met with Imelda in the United States in the spring of 1991, and the two agreed that Dulay could serve as an intermediary in negotiations. The Aquino administration, however, did not trust Dulay and refused any deal.

Based on tips from Dulay and other informants, Castro revived gold searches in the Philippines. Crews had excavated on the Marcos property on Leyte Island in 1989, even exhuming the bodies of Imelda's parents, but no gold was found. Although digging was suspended there, Castro resumed it after he became chairman, and it continued for more than a year.

In January, 1991, Jacobi reported that his talks with Mrs. Edralin-

21. *Ibid.*

Lopez were going well and that he had contacted another trustee, Maria Gosilater, who supposedly had served as a courier for Marcos. Jacobi said he had found a buyer if the gold could be released by Union Bank of Switzerland.

Castro rushed to Switzerland to meet with Edralin-Lopez and, by his account, convinced her to sign over the accounts to him. Castro agreed that the government and the Marcos family would share in profits from the gold sale; otherwise, the accounts would remain frozen and benefit no one.

A PCGG lawyer in Zurich drew up necessary papers to transfer the account to Castro, as chairman of the PCGG. He and Jacobi then visited the bank, but bank officials said that since 1989, the account had been listed under the name of a Swiss attorney. Castro suspected that Marcos had secretly signed over the account to someone else to prevent anyone from tracing it.[22]

Castro returned to Manila empty-handed, but Jacobi stayed behind. Several months later, Peter Cosandey, the Zurich district attorney, discovered that a computer hacker had tried to break into the computer system of the Credit Suisse Bank of Switzerland, apparently to get information about alleged Marcos accounts. Cosandey traced the alleged break-in to one of Jacobi's informants. Furious, Cosandey ordered Jacobi's arrest.

On July 11, 1991, German police, at the request of Cosandey, arrested Jacobi at a Munich hotel on charges of economic espionage. Jacobi maintained that his activities were on behalf of the Philippine government, of which he was a deputized agent. Because German law requires a special procedure when an agent of a foreign government is arrested, the judge ruled that the warrant was improperly drawn and Jacobi was released on a technicality.

In Zurich, Cosandey said he was suspending cooperation with the Philippines until he received a satisfactory explanation of Jacobi's activities. Cosandey eventually agreed to cooperate with Solicitor General Francisco Chavez, the longtime PCGG critic. Chavez flew to Switzerland, made some unflattering statements about Castro, and returned to Manila with enough material to indict Imelda on several charges of illegally transferring foreign currency abroad. Nevertheless, the Jacobi affair nearly

22. *Ibid.*

wrecked whatever chances remained of recovering substantial Marcos funds.[23]

The many questions about the so-called Marcos gold were never answered to anyone's satisfaction during the Aquino years. Swiss officials continued to deny the existence of a secret gold horde, but many Filipino officials and journalists privately suspected the Swiss were concealing information to keep a fortune securely in Switzerland. It became clear to the Aquino administration, however, that the only hope of resolving the issue was to play by the rules—to accept the Swiss legal conditions and allow Imelda Marcos to return to the Philippines and stand trial.

On July 31, 1991, the Aquino government finally lifted its five-year ban on Imelda and her three children. A cabinet official announced that Mrs. Marcos and the others were free to come back, but the ban on bringing the former president's body remained in force.

Imelda was anxious to return home. As long as she stayed in the United States, she was simply another rich widow: in the Philippines, however, she was "Queen Imelda," still revered by the Marcos faithful. In addition, she had her eye on the presidency in the May, 1992, elections. The date was set for her triumphant return—Monday, November 4, 1991.

Imelda left New York City and arrived in Honolulu on Halloween for a final visit at her husband's crypt and to finalize arrangements. After three days in Hawaii, she and her entourage of reporters, television crews, aides, and sycophants lifted off before dawn from Honolulu International Airport, bound for Manila and her "war of the widows" with Cory Aquino.[24]

At first, the journey was almost somber. Reporters expected a nonstop press conference as the plane sped over the Pacific.[25] Instead, the normally effervescent Imelda paced nervously down the aisles, fingering rosary beads, seemingly oblivious to those around her. She did not know what to expect upon returning to the capital that had angrily expelled her nearly six years earlier. Too excited to sleep, she gushed to reporters that

23. *Ibid.*
24. The press coined the term, although Aquino herself issued few public statements concerning Imelda's return; she seemed withdrawn, as if purposely avoiding any action that might draw attention to her longtime rival.
25. Eileen Guerrero flew to Hawaii and accompanied the Marcos entourage back to Manila on the same plane. The description of the flight and subsequent events are from her notes.

she was "bursting with emotion, both with sadness and joy. . . . I'm just trying to keep my balance at the moment."

About forty-five minutes out of Manila, the crew announced the plane was approaching Philippine air space. As the aircraft shook in a thunderstorm, Imelda and her party prayed and sang the "Ave Maria." Her mood suddenly brightened. Imelda and her closest aides moved to the upstairs compartment, where the crew had uncorked a bottle of Le Domaine champagne. Imelda took a few sips from a long-stemmed glass, then took a second glass and announced: "This means double luck. One for me and one for President Marcos." She dipped her fingers into the glass and dabbed champagne, like perfume, behind her ears and those of her party for good luck. The group wept for joy, lifted their glasses in toasts, and posed for pictures. It was like a victory party.[26]

Shortly before 8:00 A.M. on November 4, the wheels of the Boeing 747 touched down at Manila's Ninoy Aquino International Airport. Imelda stared from the window, clutched the hand of her seatmate and aide, Soledad "Sol" Vanzi, and whispered, "We're home." She then wept. Almost six years after fleeing into exile, Imelda Marcos had returned.[27]

The government had prepared an elaborate security plan for the arrival of the former first lady and had briefed Imelda's staff on its details weeks before she returned. As a precaution, she was to leave the plane by a staircase and walk directly to the tarmac rather than through the arrival hall. Laurel was on hand at the airport with a limousine, specially equipped with a licence plate bearing her initials, "IRM."

After arriving in Manila, however, the mercurial Imelda refused to follow arrangements. She appeared nervous and insisted on leaving the plane through the normal sleeve into the arrival hall. Once she was inside the terminal, officials pleaded with her to follow the prescribed arrangements, but she adamantly refused. The ashen-faced Imelda fidgeted and was visibly nervous and agitated. "I'm afraid, I'm afraid," she stammered to her aides during the lengthy standoff.[28]

26.   Soledad "Sol" Vanzi, Imelda Marcos spokeswoman, oral communication to Eileen Guerrero, Manila, November 4, 1991. Although reporters were barred from Imelda's private compartment, Vanzi, her longtime aide, was not. She briefed Guerrero as the plane taxied down the Manila airport runway.

27.   *Ibid.*

28.   Major Manuel Gaerlan, oral communication to Eileen Guerrero, Manila, November 6, 1991. Gaerlan was part of Imelda's security detail at the Manila Hotel.

Imelda had apparently been struck by the similarities to Ninoy Aquino's homecoming, which ended with his murder. What brought back those scenes was the unexpected presence of a *Time* magazine correspondent, Sandra Burton, on the plane to Manila. Burton was a friend of Cory Aquino and had accompanied Ninoy on his last trip home nine years before.

To the superstitious Imelda, Burton's presence was a bad omen. Imelda's aides had given strict instructions in Honolulu that under no circumstances should Sandra Burton be allowed on the plane. In the confusion, however, Burton went to the Makiki Heights residence, plunked down her $1,000 airfare, and was promptly added to the manifest. Imelda was angry when she learned what had happened, but by then it was too late to bump her off the plane.[29]

After nearly two hours of haggling, the authorities finally relented and allowed Imelda to walk through the arrival hall. As crowds cheered, Imelda ignored Laurel and climbed instead into the front seat of a van driven by the vice-governor of Ilocos Norte province, Rolando Abadilla.

What followed was a spectacle that would have been unthinkable only a few years before. About ten thousand Marcos loyalists turned out to greet the former first lady. Although Imelda Marcos may have been reviled around the world as an extravagant dilettante with twelve hundred pairs of shoes, millions of poor Filipinos remembered the Marcos administration for its public works programs and job-creating projects, which channeled state funds to the barrio level. The poor and the ignorant were Imelda's constituency, and she was their glittering queen. They welcomed her with genuine enthusiasm.

As Abadilla's vehicle moved slowly through the streets of the capital, the cheering crowd ran alongside, creating the illusion on television screens around the world of an even bigger turnout. "My countrymen, I came home not to fight," Imelda told exuberant followers in the Westin Philippine Plaza hotel parking lot. "I came home so we can unite in the Philippines."

Imelda was facing dozens of civil and criminal charges involving alleged corruption during her husband's administration. Her legal problems, however, barely slowed her down. She journeyed through Pam-

29. Vanzi to Guerrero, November 4, 1991.

panga province, an Aquino stronghold, smiling and waving to crowds of curiosity seekers who turned out to catch a glimpse of her. "This is Aquino country for you," Imelda gloated to her entourage. [30]

Imelda was eventually indicted on more than eighty criminal charges, including illegal currency transfers to the secret Swiss bank accounts. She had not been convicted of any of them by the end of Aquino's administration. The Marcos fortune remained intact in Switzerland, totaling at least $350 million.

Efforts to recover the fortune had bogged down. Frequent leadership changes at the PCGG produced confusion in policy and direction, while ineptness, corruption, and a lack of resources stymied the work of dedicated staff members. "The PCGG was conceived in grace and delivered in sin," observed Solicitor General Francisco Chavez. [31]

More important, Aquino's own decision not to allow Marcos to return, even to stand trial, wrecked the chances of recovering substantial funds during her administration. The decision was based not only on security concerns but also her singular hatred of the man she blamed for killing her husband. Unfortunately, her adamancy deprived the country of more than Marcos's money. It also denied the nation the opportunity for a full and impartial judgment of Ferdinand Marcos and, with it, justice for all those who suffered during his regime.

30. Imelda Marcos, remarks overheard by Eileen Guerrero, November 7, 1991.
31. Interview with Francisco Chavez by Eileen Guerrero, Manila, July 24, 1991.

16 HOMESTRETCH

IN JANUARY, 1992, Imelda Marcos announced she would run for president, a move she hoped would draw Cory into the contest. Aquino had already ruled out a second term, however, and Deputy Press Secretary Horacio Paredes said Cory would not change her mind even if "Satan himself" were running. [1]

The 1987 constitution limited presidents to a single, six-year term. The charter also stated that the first "regular election" under its mandate would take place in May, 1992, which most legal experts interpreted as a loophole that could have enabled Cory to run again. However, in her State of the Nation address to congress on July 22, 1991, Aquino promised that she would become the first Philippine president not to seek a second term. She would set an example for future leaders by handing over power at noon on June 30, 1992, to a successor chosen in free and fair elections. Her place in history and future generations' judgment of her accomplishments would depend on the election and its outcome. Most of her other promises of social reform and economic advancement, which had been part of the people power dream, remained unfulfilled.

As the last decade of the twentieth century began, East Asia was enjoying the world's most vibrant economy. The Philippines was among the

1. Horacio Paredes, oral communication to Eileen Guerrero, Manila, March 15, 1991. Both authors covered the 1992 election campaign extensively; this chapter is based primarily on their personal observations and reportage.

area's few exceptions. In 1991, the economy grew by less than 1 percent. Nearly 60 percent of the population lived in abject poverty, eking out an existence in clapboard urban shacks or palm-leaf huts in the countryside, often without proper sanitation, clean water, and other amenities. In addition, the decisions back in 1986 to abolish the Ministry of Energy and to mothball the nuclear power plant had left the country with a critical electricity shortage. Manila's eight million residents were without electricity for up to twelve hours every day. Losses in productivity were staggering.

Population was growing at Malthusian rates—2.8 percent a year— and the government was unwilling to risk the Catholic church's anger by implementing a vigorous birth control program. The devastation of the nation's forests, urban overcrowding, and the absence of air and water pollution controls added to the bleak outlook.

The closing of the U.S. military bases had weakened the Philippines' relationship with the United States—which, as its former colony, had included substantial financial aid—just as the Cold War was ending. As a result of that international shift, many former U.S. adversaries such as Russia, Vietnam, and the Eastern European states were now competing with the Philippines for Washington's favor.

Nevertheless, the situation was not altogether dismal. The Communist insurgency was waning. With the collapse of Marxist states in Europe, the Communist Party of the Philippines could no longer count on the financial support of front organizations in Western Europe. A vicious, internal power struggle had sapped the movement of much of its vitality. Military gains on the battlefield had routed rebels from traditional strongholds, and most of the key leaders had been arrested. Party chairman Sison and peace negotiator Zumel had taken refuge at the party's office in the Netherlands, where they could do little to influence events in the Philippines.

The armed forces no longer seemed a threat. Honasan and his chief lieutenants were disillusioned by their lack of public support and worn out by years on the run. Gringo himself remained in hiding after the December, 1989, coup attempt until December 23, 1992, when he and six other RAM officers resurfaced and signed an agreement with Defense Secretary Renato de Villa to begin peace talks and immediately halt all operations against the government.[2] Those civilians who had secretly funded and sheltered the mutineers were more interested in financing election campaigns than in overthrowing a government that would soon be out of power.

The future, therefore, would be charted by Aquino's successor. Filipinos were looking for someone to provide strong leadership and stability after six turbulent years.

Imelda had hoped to unite the opposition much as Cory had done six years before; her return, however, served only to divide it. Aquino did not consider Imelda a significant electoral threat. The real adversary was her estranged first cousin, Eduardo "Danding" Cojuangco, who had been reorganizing the old Marcos political network since his return in 1989. By the middle of 1991, he had decided to run for president. Danding lacked charisma, but as one of the nation's wealthiest tycoons, he had little trouble winning the allegiance of most of the Marcos political lieutenants.

A quiet, pleasant man, Danding was popular, especially among those who worked for his many companies. He was a skilled practitioner of patron-style politics. He boasted that his proven record as a successful manager and businessman made him the obvious choice to rebuild the nation's economy.

Aquino's tenure was coming to an end, and to preserve something of the dream of 1986, she needed a candidate strong enough to stop Danding. Clearly, her favorite was Fidel Ramos, who had helped instigate the revolution against Marcos and then had stood beside her through all the attempts to oust her from power. Ramos had become a national figure as a result of crushing the coup attempts, and he had used his position as defense secretary to travel around the country aboard military planes to forge alliances and build regional support.

Others considering a bid for the presidency were Vice-President Laurel, who was sure to run and this time would not be dissuaded as he had been in 1985, and Ramon Mitra, Aquino's first agriculture minister. As speaker of the house, Mitra had served the administration faithfully, often working for Aquino's programs at the expense of his own image. He personified

2. The talks have dragged on since January, 1993, with no real resolution. Meanwhile, Honasan and other associates operate a Toyota dealership in a Manila suburb, and he was elected to the Philippine senate in May, 1995.

the old style of patronage politics, however, and was generous in funneling pork barrel funds to his congressional allies, which won him their loyalty. That often translated into legislative votes for Aquino, as well. Nevertheless, his style reinforced his image as a traditional politician at a time when the press and much of the urban public was looking for a new approach to politics.

Aquino had other reasons to distrust "Monching" Mitra. He was a personal friend of Danding Cojuangco for starters. A striking figure with silver hair and a full beard, Mitra also had an eye for women, and rumors of his philandering and flirtatious behavior abounded. Although other major figures in the administration were linked to women other than their wives, the president was a close friend of Mitra's wife, Cecile, and considered Mitra's conduct a personal insult.[3]

Ramos had his own image problems. Although married, he was linked to a prominent socialite, Rose Marie "Baby" Arenas. Many of Aquino's closest allies resented his role as the national police commander during martial law, and Cardinal Sin was distressed at the idea of a Protestant president.[4] Although Ramos was widely known, he had never run for public office. In addition, he was widely disliked in the armed forces because of perceived favoritism, which he himself had condemned during Ver's tenure.

But Mitra controlled the Struggle of the Democratic Filipino Party (Laban ng Demokratikong Pilipino, or LDP), the largest and best organized political machine. He was certain of winning the nomination and, with it, the support of the political establishment.

For months, Aquino had kept the public and the political establishment guessing over her favorite. Before any public endorsement, she said Ramos must first establish himself as a viable candidate and win the LDP nomination, which Mitra appeared to have locked up. Although the LDP had been organized as an avowedly proadministration party, she had refused to join its ranks, claiming she wanted to remain above politics. Despite this image of nonpartisanship, however, she worked feverishly behind the scenes to influence the leadership on Ramos's behalf.

Her brother Peping sought to engineer rule changes in the party that

3. Paredes to Guerrero, March 15, 1991.
4. Cardinal Sin issued numerous statements questioning Ramos's credentials, although never mentioning him by name but only by inference to Ramos's role during martial law.

would have boosted Ramos's chances for the nomination, but he failed. Peping even suggested that Mitra could step aside, win reelection to the house, and then be named prime minister after a future constitutional review restored a parliamentary system. Mitra angrily refused, and at the LDP nominating convention on November 30, 1991, he beat Ramos handily.

Nevertheless, Aquino owed Ramos an enormous debt for saving her in the coup attempts. On her fifty-ninth birthday—Saturday, January 25, 1992—she announced her choice. "Secretary Eddie Ramos, I am confident, will fearlessly pursue the vision of this democratic society that our people have fought hard to reestablish," she stated.[5]

An hour later, the LDP formally proclaimed Monching Mitra as its candidate for president. Laurel joined the race for the presidency, along with Danding Cojuangco, Imelda Marcos, Senator Joseph Estrada, Senator Jovito Salonga, and Miriam Defensor Santiago, a bombastic, former agrarian reform secretary who waged a single-issue campaign against corruption.

The long campaign generated little public enthusiasm, certainly nothing approaching the tension and excitement of the 1986 race. Few issues divided the candidates. All promised economic revival, good government, attention to the poor, and increased foreign investments. Victory would depend on the right chemistry of political machinery and personality, the ability to project an image of competence and trust.

Despite his formidable political machinery, Mitra did not catch fire, seeming unable to shuck off his image as another "wheeler-dealer" politician. But Mitra's stalwarts remained convinced that their network of regional bosses could deliver the votes, even if the administration was backing their rival.

Imelda certainly had the personality required for the campaign; she was especially effective when campaigning among the poor, who were dazzled by the residual glamour of the Marcos regime. But her assets were frozen by foreign courts, and her campaign suffered from financial problems. Her political lieutenants expected to be paid for their support, and when the money did not flow their way, many of them drifted to Danding Cojuangco.

5.   Aquino's endorsement was made in a nationally televised address, with Ramos beside her; text on file with AP.

Danding's campaign was slick and well funded. Estrada dropped out of the presidential race and joined Danding as his vice-presidential running mate. Estrada's show business friends came to Danding's rallies, drawing large turnouts. As a former actor, Estrada knew how to work crowds, and his appeal to lower-class Filipinos was enormous. Although Filipinos can split their votes for president and vice-president, Danding's camp was sure that Estrada's presence on the ticket would boost their candidate's chances.

The Cojuangco campaign received another boost when the Philippine religious denomination Iglesia Ni Cristo endorsed his candidacy. It was a political coup. The Protestant group required members to vote according to the dictates of the church leadership, and its leadership was all too happy to help organize large turnouts at campaign rallies. With Iglesia Ni Cristo mustering out its members in force, Danding appeared to be gaining momentum.

Ramos's campaign, meanwhile, seemed to be stumbling. Aquino campaigned for him but not heavily, his staff was disorganized, and the turnouts at rallies were unspectacular. Although she insisted that Ramos represented a new style of nontraditional politics and that he would carry on the people power spirit, behind the scenes she was using all the traditional political measures to get him elected. The president of the Philippine National Bank, Edgardo Espiritu, refused administration orders to disburse funds to regional governments because he suspected the money was secretly going to Ramos's campaign. [6]

Several of Ramos's senior staffers were dragooned into the campaign by the president herself. The governor of Pampanga, Bren Guiao, admitted that he was working for Ramos only because Aquino had asked him to do so. The trade secretary, Peter Garrucho, was sent to manage the Ramos national campaign. He and Drilon, who remained presidential executive secretary, coordinated strategy from Malacañang Palace. Even though Aquino and the anti-Marcos forces had long berated the practice of using state funds and the machinery of government on behalf of Marcos and his supporters, now she and her allies were using similar tactics. For his part, Ramos made the obligatory references to Aquino and people power during his campaign; his message, however, was that as a former

---

6. Espiritu's refusal was widely reported in the media.

military man, he could provide the stability the nation so desperately needed.

The only candidate who seemed to generate broad enthusiasm was the outsider, Miriam Santiago. "Colorful" could not do justice to the stylish former judge, who used to boast of having the sexiest legs in politics. As immigration commissioner, she gloried in eccentric statements, once calling a congressional critic a "fungus face" and suggesting he place his finger in "a wall socket." Her agency was traditionally one of the most corrupt, and she once threatened to chop up her wayward employees and feed them to the sharks in Manila Bay, averring that the sharks would probably not eat them, however, out of a "sense of professional courtesy."[7]

Santiago had become a Cory favorite earlier in her administration and was promoted to secretary of agrarian reform after the Garchitorena scandal in 1989. She fell out of favor after suggesting that Aquino should step aside as chairman of the agrarian reform committee in deliberations involving her family's Hacienda Luisita. When Santiago's name appeared on a list of proposed junta members during the December, 1989, coup attempt, that was all Aquino needed to fire her.

Undaunted, the forty-six-year-old Santiago traveled extensively for speaking engagements, preaching her anticorruption theme. With little money and a handful of student volunteers, she became a serious political force. Her most enthusiastic supporters were idealistic university students longing for political change, but she also struck a responsive chord among housewives, professionals, shopkeepers, and others, especially among the more politically aware Manila voters. Her style and agenda harked back to the reformist people power spirit of 1986. Nevertheless, Miriam's eccentricities were too much for Aquino, and she never seriously considered endorsing her.

As the campaign drew to a close, polls showed a three-member race: Ramos, Cojuangco, and Santiago. Ramos and Santiago were virtually neck and neck, with Danding gaining. A few days before the balloting, Cojuangco staged his final rally in Manila, drawing a huge crowd at Rizal Park. The turnout alarmed the anti-Marcos establishment. Commentators spoke of a Danding ground swell, and several uncommitted colum-

7. Santiago's quotes are from *The Miriam Defensor Santiago Dictionary* (Manila, 1991), a handbook published by her campaign vehicle, the Movement for Responsible Public Service.

nists warned that only Ramos could prevent a return of Marcos-style politics.

Such fears were exaggerated. Reporters, including both the authors, who canvassed the crowd that day found that the vast majority were members of Iglesia Ni Cristo and had been ordered by church leaders to attend. Although the denomination votes as a bloc, its voting-age membership was only about 700,000 in an electorate of more than thirty million. Danding succeeded in creating an illusion of strength, thus alarming many of the undecided voters who feared a return of Marcos-style government.

Voting was surprisingly smooth, and after the polls closed at 3:00 P.M. on May 11, the first returns were reported: Miriam Santiago was leading, followed closely by Ramos and Cojuangco. All three had presented themselves to the electorate as nontraditional politicians, newcomers who could bring a breath of fresh air to the national leadership.

As the laborious count proceeded, Santiago lost her lead and charged fraud. Others joined in. Santiago's claim of fraud was largely based on her insistence that she had led in all the surveys and therefore could not lose an honest count. The most reliable surveys, however, had shown her virtually tied with Ramos by the end of the campaign, with nearly a third of the voters undecided. What seems more likely is that Danding's rallies backfired by scaring undecided voters into supporting Ramos as the only candidate who could prevent a Marcos-camp comeback.

Nevertheless, it was clear that the election was not entirely clean. Wholesale vote buying occurred, especially in local contests. In Leyte, hundreds of voters swarmed around the precincts as balloting drew to a close, hoping that candidates would pay more for last-minute ballots. But the fraud appeared tame compared to the excesses of 1986.

As the count dragged on for weeks, the public appeared anxious to put aside the election and get on with a new government. A full-blown investigation of fraud would probably have found faults within all camps, which would have discredited the entire election and raised questions the public was in no mood to answer. The nation was relieved that the vote had gone as well as it had. It was now time to move on.

Congress convened on Tuesday, May 26, 1992, to canvass the returns and declare a new president and vice-president. When the votes were finally tabulated, Ramos had won, but with less than 25 percent of the votes—the weakest mandate of any president in Philippine history. Estrada, who had been fired as mayor of San Juan six years earlier, won the vice-presidency, nearly doubling Ramos's vote totals.

Ramos's lead over Santiago was only 800,000 votes out of twenty-three million cast. Her amazing showing—without party machinery, massive funding, and presidential support—showed clearly that Filipinos still longed for a new style of politics, which Cory Aquino had promised but failed to provide.

Danding Cojuangco finished a close third. Had Imelda Marcos not entered the race, Cojuangco could possibly have won; the two pro-Marcos candidates combined won more votes than Ramos. Although Imelda had lost the election, she received nearly three million votes—a personal vindication of sorts. Her son, Ferdinand, Jr., was elected to the house of representatives from Ilocos Norte. The Marcos family had managed to regain a foothold in Philippine politics.[8]

For Doy Laurel, defeat was the final grade of a slide to obscurity that began when he accepted Aquino's offer to run with her years before. The defeat also ended the long and distinguished career of Jovito Salonga. Now seventy-one, Salonga had been touted as presidential timber for more than twenty years, but when his chance came, age was his most formidable opponent.

For Fidel Ramos, the presidency capped a spectacular rise to power. More than any other figure, Fidel Ramos was responsible for Cory Aquino finishing her term. With the exception of the president herself, no other person had been so instrumental in defining and redirecting the course of the nation's experiment with democracy. The mantle of people power once taken up by Ninoy Aquino's widow was now in the hands of the one-time commander of the national police during martial law.

8. Figures from the final tally are available from the Commission on Elections, Intramuros, Manila.

EPILOGUE

AFTER NEARLY A year and a half in office, Fidel Ramos made his first visit to the United States as president in November, 1993. He visited eight cities, preaching a message that "the Philippines is back in business in the heart of Asia." He wooed American investors with promises that his government was friendly to business and anxious to open its doors to international investment. It was a message quite different from the early years of the Aquino administration, when slogans advocating freeing the economy from the shackles of foreign domination were the rage.

In the United States, the visit attracted little media attention, certainly far less than the tumultuous reception Cory Aquino received in September, 1986. With the closing of the military bases and the end of the Cold War, Washington's attention in Asia was focused on its relations with the strong economies of Japan, China, and the newly emerging industrialized states. The Philippines, for better or worse, would have to chart its own path in the world.

Ramos was quietly steering the nation along a different course. With the U.S. military gone, his foreign policy focused on building commercial and political ties with the rest of Southeast Asia. Domestically, he restored capital punishment, which had been abolished under the 1987 constitution. Agrarian reform took a backseat to industrial development. He sent peace overtures to the Communist, Muslim, and military rebels, all of which were largely spent forces.

Moves to decentralize public administration away from Manila, begun under President Aquino and continued by President Ramos, put more authority in the hands of local governments, some of which displayed admirable skills in improving the lives of their people. The Philippines began to describe itself if not as a "tiger of Asia," at least as a "tiger cub." U.S. and Taiwanese businesses set up operations at the old naval base at Subic Bay. Ramos traveled the world, taking trips in 1992, 1993, and 1994 to Asia, Europe, North America, and the Middle East, always re-iterating that the Philippines sought the world's business. Slowly, the na-tion's economy began to show promising signs of improvement, growing at between 5 and 7 percent annually after years of stagnation.

The long years of misrule and turmoil, however, had taken a heavy toll. Exports in 1993 amounted to about $12.2 billion (U.S.), compared with $88.7 billion for Taiwan, $48.4 billion for Malaysia, and $41.2 billion for Thailand. The foreign debt had grown to $35.3 billion (U.S.).[1] At current rates of population growth, the Philippines will need years of economic progress and sustained good government to reach the standard of living of its more prosperous Southeast Asian neighbors.

In an attempt to put contentious issues to rest, Ramos permitted Imelda to bring home the body of her husband from Hawaii. Marcos was interred in a glass coffin on September 10, 1993—the day before his seventy-sixth birthday—in a refrigerated crypt next to his family home in Batac, Ilocos Norte province. Another chapter in the Philippines' turbulent history was closed.

Two weeks later, on September 24, Imelda was convicted for the first time of a crime—misappropriating funds—and sentenced to eighteen to twenty-four years' imprisonment. She remains free on appeal. So confi-dent was she that she would ultimately escape prison, Imelda ran for a house of representatives seat in the May, 1995, elections. She won by a landslide.

Did the Philippines change significantly during the six years of Cory Aquino's presidency? The country was certainly a quieter place. The Com-munist Party of the Philippines, wracked by internal dissension, had lost its direction and no longer posed a serious threat to the government. With the Marxist insurgency receding, human rights abuses by the military and police declined.

1. *Asiaweek*, October 12, 1994, p. 59.

Yet in many ways, the Philippines remained what it had been for generations: a turbulent land, poorly governed at the national level, encumbered by poverty and corruption. As an example, while Ramos was traveling through the United States, gunmen from a Muslim extremist group kidnapped an American linguist, Charles Walton, in the remote Sulu Islands. He was freed three weeks later, after the government quietly paid the kidnappers nearly $11,000.

Elsewhere, gangs linked by credible evidence to the police and the military launched a wave of ransom kidnappings.[2] Most of the victims were Filipinos of Chinese origin. The inability to curb the kidnappings prompted many Chinese-Filipino families to shift their businesses outside the country at a time when the government was promoting investment. A highly publicized campaign to collect illegal firearms failed largely because many of the weapons were held by politicians whose support Ramos needed.

Despite people power rhetoric, the odious pattern of vote buying, patronage, parochialism, and domination by political power brokers persisted. In the Senate campaign of 1995, for example, Ramos forged an alliance between his Lakas Party and what was left of Mitra and Peping Cojuangco's Laban ng Demokratikong Pilipino (LDP) and produced a common ticket. Three of the twelve coalition Senate candidates were either children or grandchildren of former presidents. Marcos's son, Ferdinand "Bongbong" Marcos, Jr., ran on an opposition ticket. Ramos's Senate ticket also included his former nemesis Juan Ponce Enrile as well as three others—Ramon Mitra, Marcelo Fernan, and Aquilino Pimentel—who had run unsuccessfully in 1992 for either president (Mitra) or vice-president (Fernan and Pimentel). In order to convince Laban to join the coalition, Ramos agreed to support the party's incumbent governors, town mayors, and House members, many of whom belonged to established political clans. That was hardly the spirit of "new politics" that the uprising of 1986 had promised to usher in. Lakas showed no hesitation in delaying disbursement of Countrywide Development Funds, a pork-

---

2. Numerous police and military personnel, including the chief of the narcotics command and the former chief of the antikidnapping task force from the National Police, went on trial in 1993 and 1994 for kidnapping charges. To date, the two chiefs have not been convicted. Reid was told personally in January, 1993, by the former chief of the National Police, Raul Imperial, that he suspected his own men were involved in kidnappings.

barrel fund, to areas governed by the opposition. Political loyalty remained dependent on access to the administration's patronage rather than on ideals.

Aquino returned to her family's comfortable home on Times Street in Quezon City. She had come full circle. She traveled abroad, where she still commanded a degree of attention because of the romance of the people power revolution, but at home among her own people—who understood all too well the failures of that "revolution"—Cory Aquino drifted into obscurity.

As an opposition symbol, Corazon Aquino had been a success. She galvanized the Marcos opposition as no other available leader could have done. Others played significant roles in the people power revolution, but without her, it is unlikely that the events of February, 1986, would have unfolded as they did. The Filipino "revolution" would never have won broad acceptance without her. By ousting Marcos, she ensured her place in history.

The tragedy of Cory Aquino, and of the nation she led, was that she brought little else to the presidency. Her goal in the 1986 election was the ouster of Ferdinand Marcos. So deep was her hatred of Marcos that she and many of her stalwarts deluded themselves into thinking that his removal would thus remove the root cause of the nation's ills.

That was hardly the case. At the heart of the Philippine crisis was an inequitable distribution of wealth, which in turn produced a people saddled with poverty, poor education, lack of economic opportunity, corruption, and social injustice. Marcos did not create the system. Indeed, the system had created Marcos. After six years of Aquino's leadership, all those problems remained.

The story of the Aquino presidency demonstrates that restoring democratic institutions alone does not guarantee political stability. Peoples emerging from years of authoritarianism are impatient to see material progress in their daily lives. Political forces left over from previous regimes are quick to exploit public disappointment. Without a clear vision and without a solid political base, new democratic governments can be tempted, as was Aquino's, to compromise ideals in the interest of political survival, which leads to shifts in policy that can worsen the sense of drift and create further instability. This phenomenon emerged not only in the Philippines but in the newly restored democracies of Eastern Europe as well. "Seven years after EDSA, we have come to realize that it is much easier to set up the external trappings of democracy than it is to make it work to the satisfaction of our people," wrote Father Bernas, one of the members of the Convenors group and later an architect of Aquino's 1986 campaign.[3]

The great expectations that accompanied Corazon Aquino's rise to power were in large measure the result of a flawed international view of the nature of her people power revolution. Television cameras and superficial reporting painted a picture of a nation rising against tyranny. They failed to convey the truth of a complex interplay of forces—the Catholic church, the armed forces, the business community, and the economic elite—that were the real arbiters of power. With neither a broad agenda nor the skills to implement one, the Aquino coalition soon broke apart amid jealousies and intrigue.

Furthermore, the choice of a U.S.-style presidential system, with its extensive checks and balances, diffused power to the extent that even a capable chief executive would have found it difficult to govern. The system may have prevented a return to totalitarian rule, but it also enabled entrenched special interests—landlords, industrialists, and regional politicians—to block reform efforts.

At a time when more authoritarian governments in Singapore, Malaysia, South Korea, Thailand, and Taiwan were outpacing the Philippines economically, the Filipino experience provides a warning for other emerging democracies about the need to balance free expression with the urgency of extensive and painful socioeconomic change. "The tragedy of Cory Aquino is incompetence and the lack of preparation for statecraft and governance," said Representative Bonifacio Gillego, a former army colonel and a political exile during the Marcos era. "You cannot thrust people into leadership without experience in the fundamentals of politics."[4]

With Aquino at the helm, the people power revolution proved to be no revolution at all. It was a restoration of the political and social order that existed before Marcos imposed martial law in 1972. Whether that social order will collapse again, as it did in 1972, will depend on the

3. The Reverend Joaquin Bernas, in the Manila *Chronicle*, February 23, 1992, p. 5.
4. Interview with Representative Bonifacio Gillego by Eileen Guerrero, Quezon City, June, 1992.

personalities and skills of future Filipino leaders, rather than on the strengths of the institutions that Aquino left behind.

Cory Aquino did, however, buy her nation time. She survived. By doing so, she gave the Philippines time to begin healing the wounds of the Marcos era, time to ponder the future, time to experiment with new formulas and ideas.

But she also squandered a unique, historic opportunity to correct the injustices of Philippine society and to set the country on a positive course for the next century. The Aquino "revolution," which glowed so brightly in 1986, burned out as quickly as a brushfire on a grassy plain.

BIBLIOGRAPHY

PRIMARY SOURCES USED in this book consist mainly of interviews conducted by the authors and their first-hand reportage of events. All notes and transcripts are in their personal files and those of the Associated Press, Manila. Secondary sources include communications from various persons in government and the media, as well as accounts in numerous newspapers and transcripts of radio and television broadcasts. Institutions where such information can be obtained are the Office of the Press Secretary and the Philippine Information Agency; the Philippine National Library; the Manila Press Club and the Press Foundation of the Philippines; the U.S. Information Service Library; archives of newspapers that operated during the Aquino era; and records of the Philippine Senate and House of Representatives, Executive House, Manila. Other sources are listed below.

Aruiza, Arturo. *Malacañang to Makiki.* Quezon City, 1991.
Bonner, Raymond. *Waltzing with a Dictator: The Marcoses and the Making of American Policy.* New York, 1987.
Constantino, Renato. *Demystifying Aquino.* Quezon City, 1989.
———. *The Philippines: A Past Revisited.* Quezon City, 1975.
Coronel, Antonio. *Libel and the Journalist.* Quezon City, 1991.
Davide, Hilario G., *et al. The Final Report of the Fact-Finding Commission.* Makati, 1990.

Joaquin, Nick. *Jaime Ongpin: The Enigma.* Makati, 1990.

Jones, Gregg R. *Red Revolution: Inside the Philippine Guerrilla Movement.* Boulder, Colo., 1989.

Karnow, Stanley. *In Our Image: America's Empire in the Philippines.* New York, 1989.

Kerkvliet, Benedict J., and Resil Mojares. *From Marcos to Aquino.* Quezon City, 1989.

Kessler, Richard J. *Rebellion and Repression in the Philippines.* New Haven, 1989.

Komisar, Lucy. *Corazon Aquino: The Story of a Revolution.* New York, 1987.

Landsdale, Edwin. *In the Midst of Wars: An American's Mission to Southeast Asia.* New York, 1991.

Lawyers Committee for Human Rights. *Vigilantes in the Philippines: A Threat to Democratic Rule.* New York, 1988.

Mata, Nestor. *Cory of a Thousand Days.* Manila, 1989.

Movement for Responsible Public Service. *The Miriam Defensor Santiago Dictionary.* Manila, 1991.

Pedrosa, Carmen N. *The Rise and Fall of Imelda Marcos.* Makati, 1987.

Putzel, James. *A Captive Land: The Politics of Agrarian Reform in the Philippines.* Quezon City, 1992.

Schrimer, Daniel B., and Stephen R. Shalom. *The Philippines Reader: A History of Colonialism, Neocolonialism, Dictatorship and Resistance.* Quezon City, 1987.

Sison, Jose Maria. *Project Liberation: Resistance in the Philippines.* Cologne, 1988.

Smith, Joseph B. *Portrait of a Cold Warrior: Second Thoughts of a CIA Agent.* New York, 1976.

Vreeland, Nena, *et al. Area Handbook for the Philippines.* 2nd ed. Washington, D.C., 1976.

Wurfel, David. *Filipino Politics: Development and Decay.* Quezon City, 1988.

Index